Modern Scottish P

Modern Scottish Poetry

Christopher Whyte

EDINBURGH UNIVERSITY PRESS

© Christopher Whyte, 2004

Edinburgh University Press Ltd
22 George Square, Edinburgh

Typeset in Sabon and Caslon Open Face
by Pioneer Associates, Perthshire, and
printed and bound in Great Britain by
Antony Rowe Ltd, Chippenham, Wilts

A CIP record for this book is available from the British Library

ISBN 0 7486 1600 4 (paperback)

The right of Christopher Whyte
to be identified as author of this work
has been asserted in accordance with
the Copyright, Designs and Patents Act 1988.

Contents

Foreword

The experience of teaching for more than twelve years in the world's only Department of Scottish Literature has been a lively and impassioned one. I owe a considerable debt to my colleagues during this time for their patience, good humour, and forbearance, but also for their profound convictions, the stubbornness with which they hold these, and for their willingness to argue. Something of the intensity of those debates has spilled onto these pages. Thanks are also due to my editors at Edinburgh University Press, and to the friends and colleagues who were kind enough to look at sections of the typescript at different stages in its elaboration, offering advice and comments, most especially Ken Cockburn, David Kinloch, Ronald Jack, Alan Riach and Carla Sassi. I appreciated Helen Lloyd's help with putting the finishing touches to the typescript. The responsibility for what got past them is of course entirely mine. Staff at the National Library of Scotland and in the Scottish section of Edinburgh's Central Library were invariably helpful, and the Scottish Poetry Library once more demonstrated its value as an unmatched source of texts and background information.

It was not always easy to set time aside from creative work in order to concentrate on a critical text of this kind. And one who is himself a writer cannot fail to be conscious of the temptation to arrogate to oneself a position above and beyond what others have written, especially when those others are alive and productive, not just names but known faces not to be walked past in the street without a greeting. What kept me going was the hope that the ideas given expression here, if erroneous at times, could nonetheless be useful, as a spur to argument, debate and eventual correction. And that brings me to my final debt of gratitude, to the students who have hearkened to these ideas across more than a decade and a half, and most especially to those who had the good grace to shake off their lethargy or awe, and disagree.

Forge no false links of man
To land or creed, the true are good enough. Our lives
Crave codes of courtesy, ways of describing love.
DOUGLAS DUNN 'The Apple Tree'

Eine Tasse heißen, giftstarken Kaffee täte mir in dieser
Kälte gut. Man schenkt aber überhaupt nur café national
aus. National *bedeutet in Wirklichkeit nur, daß es sich*
um Ersatz handlet. Das Beiwort 'national' bedeutet
neuerdings überall, daß irgend etwas nicht in Ordnung
ist, es is nicht mehr das, was es sein sollte.
SÁNDOR MÁRAI *Geist im Exil: Tagebücher 1945–57*
(Paris 1946)

Introduction

For a while it was fashionable for composers of serious contemporary music to include passages in their works which offered performers a range of options for their execution. No one could know in advance precisely how these passages would sound, and it was understood that they would not be realised in exactly the same way on any two occasions. Performers had to be in agreement about when such passages would begin and end, and there were strict limits placed on the degree of freedom to be exercised within them. Nevertheless, they formed no less essential a part of the works in question than does the cadenza in a traditional concerto for a solo instrument or instruments.

That is what is meant by 'aleatoric' music, and it is in this sense that the structure of the present study can be described as 'aleatoric'.[1] After two chapters which argue that issues of national identity and canon-building have exerted an excessive influence on readings of Scottish poetry, and of Scottish literature generally, and seek to open up alternative approaches which can complement these, a revisionist reading of the interwar period is offered. After that, an entire chapter is dedicated to each of the six decades of the historical period covered.

Because the development of poetry is marked less by the births and deaths of poets, by significant dates in their lives, or in the history of the states where they reside, than by the publication of collections, books to be bought or borrowed, and read at home or in public libraries, three have been chosen for each of the decades from 1940 to 1980, plus four for each of the last two decades of the twentieth century, making a total of twenty in all. The list of selected volumes is as follows:

the 1940s

Sorley MacLean / Somhairle MacGill-Eain *Dàin do Eimhir agus Dàin eile* (*Poems to Eimhir and Other Poems*) 1943
George Campbell Hay *Fuaran Slèibh* (*Hillside Springs*) 1948
Edwin Muir *The Labyrinth* 1949

the 1950s

Hugh MacDiarmid *In Memoriam James Joyce* 1955
Norman MacCaig *Riding Lights* 1955
Sydney Goodsir Smith *Under the Eildon Tree* (revised edition) 1954

the 1960s

Robert Garioch *Selected Poems* 1966
Tom Leonard *Six Glasgow Poems* 1969
Edwin Morgan *The Second Life* 1968

the 1970s

W. S. Graham *Malcolm Mooney's Land* 1970
Derick Thomson *An Rathad Cian* (*The Far Road*) 1970 (Gaelic),
1971 (English)
George Mackay Brown *Fishermen with Ploughs* 1971

the 1980s

Douglas Dunn *Elegies* 1985
Kenneth White *The Bird Path* 1989
Liz Lochhead *Dreaming Frankenstein and Collected Poems* 1984
Iain Crichton Smith *A Life* 1982

the 1990s

Robert Crawford *A Scottish Assembly* 1990
Kathleen Jamie *The Queen of Sheba* 1996
Carol Ann Duffy *Mean Time* 1993
Aonghas MacNeacail *Oideachadh Ceart* (*A Proper Schooling*) 1996

These 'cameo' portraits form the backbone of the book and, though there is a significant degree of cross-reference, the format has been chosen with readers in mind who want to be informed or stimulated about one single figure, without having to pick their way through the mass of a more explicitly interwoven treatment.

The 'aleatoric' structure offers a backbone for the book. But discussion of each poet's work is rarely confined to a single collection, fanning out to offer an impression of a career and hopefully pinpoint issues relevant to the whole extent of it. Each chosen collection is a point where the individual poet is inserted into the larger picture and also the point of entry, for both reader and critic, to the full range of the poet's work.

Given this backbone, the book could have been actualised in a range of different ways. Another critic might come up with a markedly different combination, though there would surely be substantial overlap in the poets chosen for coverage. Why, for example, represent Iain Crichton Smith by a collection from the 1980s, rather than by one of his earlier books from the 1960s? Why choose Norman MacCaig's first acknowledged collection, from the 1950s, rather than the one that marked the culmination of his poetic career in the late 1980s? And does MacDiarmid's *In Memoriam James Joyce* really belong in the 1950s, when it was published, rather than in the 1930s, when most of it was put together, not to say 'composed'?

The case for each of these choices could be closely argued, but that would not be the point. The point is that the profile offered here does not aim to be inevitable or definitive. A 'transparent' structure of this kind can hopefully abdicate a degree of the power a critic arrogates to him or herself by the mere decision to attempt a study of Scottish poetry in the last six decades of the twentieth century. The omission of a poet should not be taken as a judgement on the value of his or her work. One advantage of the 'aleatoric' structure was to avoid making this the kind of book where inclusion or exclusion, mention or the failure to mention, amounted to an accolade or an offence. Who could possibly maintain that no more than twenty poets from the period chosen merit our attention? On the other hand if, in the Gaelic anthology I edited more than a decade ago, equal space was deliberately allocated to men and women, such an approach would have been inappropriate here. Of the twenty poets studied, only three are women.

Given the richness of the available online bibliographical sources, an extended bibliographical apparatus has not been supplied. The National Library of Scotland is a copyright library. Through its website at nls.ac.uk not only the main catalogue, but two further online resources of particular interest to readers of this book can be accessed. These are the Bibliography of Scotland, which offers an impressively wide-ranging if not exhaustive listing of secondary material on Scottish writers, and the Bibliography of Scottish Literature in Translation. The latter will be of interest to those studying the reception of contemporary Scottish poetry on the European and world stage, and will tell anyone eager to translate what has already been done and where. The website of the Scottish Poetry Library at www.spl.org.uk offers access to an impressively detailed listing of primary and secondary items pertaining to the authors covered here. Bibliographical information has therefore been restricted to a footnote at the beginning of the section on each poet. This indicates the edition or editions used in preparing the section, and gives information about monographs and collections of critical essays where these are available, as well as indications of secondary literature intended for purposes of orientation only. The notes concern poetry specifically. Where the poet was also a novelist or a dramatist, this has not been taken account of in the information offered.

Page numbers are supplied for quotations when the book used as a source lacks a contents page, or an index of titles, or when they are from extended poems. With Scots quotations, words specific to the language are glossed, but not those where readers can arrive at the English equivalent thanks to a simple change of vowel.

The constructional principles of the book are, as has been said, 'transparent'. Individual readers are invited to amuse themselves by speculating how, given these principles, they might have chosen to realise them. Who would they leave out? Who would fill the slot or slots left vacant? No single realisation can claim primacy over all the others. And if the effect of this 'aleatoric' structure, with its transparent and arbitrary character, is to engage the reader in debate from the moment he or she opens the book, then the writer's aims in choosing it will have been fully satisfied.

Note

1. Of the two meanings offered by the *Concise Oxford Dictionary*, the second ('involving random choice by performer') is more helpful than the first ('depending on the throw of a die or on chance') in this context.

1
Scottishness and Scottish Poetry

Aucene esprit juste ne contestera qu'on fait perdre sa valeur universelle à une oeuvre en la dénationalisant . . . Mais n'est-ce pas une vérité de même ordre, qu'on ôte sa valeur générale et même national à une oeuvre en cherchant à la nationaliser?

MARCEL PROUST

. . . jeder glaubt um die Nation ein Letztes zu wissen, wie er glaubt um sich selber ein Letztes zu wissen. Würde man ihn aber fragen, was dieses sei, so würde er antworten wie Augustinus auf die Frage nach dem Wesen der Zeit: Wenn man mich nicht fragt, so weiß ich es; fragt man mich aber, so weiß ich es nicht.

HUGO VON HOFMANNSTHAL

Marcel Proust and Daniel Halévy became close friends after meeting in the playground of the Lycée Condorcet in Paris in Autumn 1887. They had thus known each other for more than thirty years when, in a letter of July 1919, Proust reproached Halévy for putting his name to a manifesto which had appeared in *Le Figaro* on the 19th of that month.[1] The fact that it was intended as a rejoinder to an earlier one, published by the Communist Party in *L'Internationale* on 1 June, did nothing to excuse the manifesto's contents in Proust's eyes. It claimed that any literature can attain universal significance only in so far as it assumes a specific national character. Works lacking such a character can make no contribution to broader European culture, from whose standpoint the works which matter most have to be those representing their country of origin with the greatest fidelity. While not utterly rejecting this position, Proust asked if it were not equally true that, in attempting forcibly to adapt a work of literature to some kind of national paradigm, one risked depriving it, not only of its general value, but of its value to the nation as well. The emergence of aesthetic, as of scientific truths, he argued, was subject to mysterious laws, on which no alien or secondary considerations can be superimposed. The honour a work of art, or a scientific discovery may bring its nation, according to Proust, can only be a secondary consideration for those directly involved, and never a primary objective.

The *Figaro* manifesto contained further claims which much more obviously demanded rectification, such as the insistence that, having emerged victorious from the First World War, France must now place itself at the head of Europe and the world as far as intellectual activities were concerned, acting as the very guardian of civilisation. Proust commented wryly on the role assigned by the manifesto, in the mission it expected France to undertake, to Catholic intellectual life and to the Catholic tradition. Even unbelievers who associated themselves with the Catholic party, he commented, had proved remarkably ineffectual when it came to fighting for justice in the notorious Dreyfus affair.

Like Halévy a Jew, but furthermore a homosexual, and a novelist who may have had a pretty shrewd idea of the importance he would eventually assume within the larger panorama of French literature, Proust showed himself to be peculiarly sensitive to the shadings of different nationalist ideologies, as well as to the implications these can have for writing and for writers. With the benefit of nearly a century's hindsight, it is an easy enough matter to label the *Figaro* manifesto's marshalling together of national religion, national character and national literature as reactionary rather than progressive in tendency, as right-wing rather than left-wing. Proust was clearly aware that by applying national paradigms to a text in a forced and undiscriminating fashion, by privileging above all other aspects the degree to which it expresses a supposed national character and the place to be assigned to it within a national canon, we may distort our perceptions of it, while at the same time blinding ourselves to different yet crucial elements in the work itself. And nonetheless, in discussing the role of national character in our reading and assessment of literary works, his concern was to balance rather than to refute existing positions.

This study of modern Scottish poetry takes as its point of departure a conviction that the balance of the Scottish critical tradition needs redressing, along lines not dissimilar to those suggested by Proust in his letter to Halévy. Rather than rejecting existing readings whose primary concern is with nationalist ideology, or with what will be termed the 'question about Scottishness', this study seeks to adopt an impartial viewpoint, one which will hopefully prove capable of filling out and complementing such readings.

Can it be validly argued that the Scottishness, presumed or otherwise, of Scottish poetry should take precedence over any other feature in our readings? Possibly yes, and possibly no. After an interregnum lasting for close on three centuries, a national parliament was finally convened in Edinburgh in 1999, thanks at least in part to a campaign for political autonomy dating back to the 1920s and beyond. Should we assume that the poetry written during the same period will automatically fall into a coherent narrative pattern echoing that process? That individual poems will act like iron filings, leaping into place when the appropriate magnet (the appropriate historical or political narrative) is applied beneath the paper they are scattered across? How realistic is it to expect that, if we were to bring together the most significant works of Scottish poetry from the last sixty years, they would dutifully reflect a growing desire for and progress towards national autonomy? Or might the preoccupations that emerge be of a different, even an unrelated nature? It is not possible for the present to offer definitive answers to these questions, and it may never be so. But there can be little doubt that, however dominant it has been so far in readings of Scottish poetry, Scottishness and the drive for institutional autonomy are only two among many possible filters through which such poetic material can be viewed. Or that, as critical instruments, both are in urgent need of balancing and contextualisation.

This book sets out to reclaim a degree of autonomy for the creative (in this case, specifically literary) faculty, in homage to the mysterious laws referred to by Proust in his letter to Halévy. There is nothing inevitable about the profile it sketches, of poetry written within or beyond Scotland, by men and women having a strong identification with the country, across a specific historical period. The underlying structure of the book, as argued in the 'Introduction', is 'aleatoric'. Poetic texts are not selected and marshalled in accordance with theories, pre-existing or otherwise, pertaining to a different field of study. Literary production is not treated as if it were subject to, or the expression of, a narrative of a different kind, whether historical or political.

This does not mean that the importance of historical events for writers' lives can be discounted. Many poets in Scotland responded to the perceived débâcle of the 1979 referendum, but not all, and not in predictable ways. The outbreak of the Second World War had profound effects on the lives of most of the individuals who were writing or planning to write poetry at that time. Yet their work can usefully be looked on as a form of resistance to such pressures, a determination not to be dictated to by them, rather than a servile mirroring. Biographical details are not overlooked in the chapters which follow. Attention is paid to these wherever due, not primarily as a means of interpreting the work of single poets, but because they offer us a sense of the time and the location in which that work was produced. The place in which a poet was born, his or her interactions with institutions such as schools or universities and with the mechanics of publication, not to mention movements in and out of the geographical space defined as Scottish, are likely to have left their trace upon the work, while not necessarily determining its nature. In particular, given the limited number of inhabitants of that space, it is still less likely than elsewhere that poets who were writing and publishing during the same period could remain mere names to one another. More often than not, they became known faces and personalities, with the ensuing crop of friendships and hostilities.

Reclaiming such autonomy means that both history and politics must renounce any privileged status as tools for the interpretation of Scottish literature. Surely it is best that those whose prime concern is history should study history, and those whose prime concern is politics, politics. The position the present study takes up regarding nationalist ideology and, more particularly, the 'question about Scottishness', might best be defined as 'agnostic'. Hopefully it can be acceptable to set aside, for the moment, issues of national identity, searching for it, constructing it, reinforcing it, along with the illusion that the primary function of poetic texts lies in identity building, and that they are capable of resolving identity issues. There is an urgent need to approach Scottish texts from a range of different and complementary perspectives. As with the study of both history or politics, the becoming of a nation is only one among many considerations which compete for our attention.

There is clear evidence that, at the beginning of the twenty-first century, both critics and writers continue to be subject to pressures which would have them view literary activity first and foremost in relation to national self-affirmation. A study of the modern Scottish novel published within the last decade begins by claiming that 'the development of the novel is profoundly linked to the development of the modern nation', and argues that 'people would act and would sacrifice themselves for the *national* good in ways that they would never act or sacrifice themselves for purely personal ends'. As the novel develops through the nineteenth century, 'the life of the individual becomes a model in miniature of the life of the society, a synecdoche of the national totality that can never be known except in its fragmentary constituents'.[2] Individual lives, individual stories, are fragments of a larger story, one to which they offer the key and of which they are small-scale reproductions. Yet it would be perfectly feasible to place history and story in opposition to one another, arguing that national belonging and nationalist perspectives restrict as much as they enable individual self-realisation. E. M. Forster's celebrated assertion that 'if I had to choose between betraying my country and betraying my friend, I hope I should have the guts to betray my country' even if 'such a choice may scandalize the modern reader',[3] indicates that the balance between individual and nation need not always be tipped so drastically in favour of the latter. The national is not the only, or necessarily the primary totality, within which the lives of individuals, real or fictive, can be placed, in order to become endowed with meaning.

Poets as well as novelists are subject to these pressures. In a piece about her reaction to the opening of the new Scottish parliament, Kathleen Jamie writes that:

> To speak personally, the movement from the last referendum in 1979, and this year's, coincides with my adult life. I was seventeen in '79, too young to vote, just leaving school, cautiously writing my first poems. I voted Yes Yes this year at 35 years old, a mother, a graduate and what they call an 'established poet'. *The politics are indistinguishable from my life.*[4]

Unmistakable here is the implication that, where a writer's life and personal development succeed in mirroring that of her nation, this can imbue her work with a relevance and significance it might not otherwise have had. Jamie's critic comments approvingly that 'it is incidental but appropriate that the key personal events of Kathleen Jamie's adult life have meshed coterminously with Scotland's drive towards independence',[5] thus highlighting (perhaps unconsciously) how very smoothly such an assumption blends with dominant approaches to Scottish writing. The outstanding poets, those with the greatest claim on our attention as both readers and analysts of literature, will be those whose work is ripe for reading in such terms, who offer us a key to understanding their nation's history and its political development. On this question, yet again, the present study's position is agnostic.

Such pressures indicate how heavily the heritage of the crucial period in the development of nationalist awareness and ideology in Europe, the nineteenth century, continues to influence present day thinking on these topics where Scotland is concerned. It may be worth restating, in slightly caricaturised form, some major assumptions from that period so that, if these do happen to jog the reader's or the critic's arm, this will not happen unawares.[6]

The destiny of all nations, and of small nations in particular, would be (according to such views) to make their own distinctive and inimitable contribution to a larger whole, to a kind of symphony bringing together all the voices of humanity. The latter would, in its turn, be impoverished were any single voice to be left out. Each nation has, as it were, a place marked out for it in advance, and it is the duty of the members of that nation, but most especially of its politicians, military men and artists, to struggle with all the means at their disposal to ensure the gap is filled. The process, then, has a fated quality about it, an inevitability. Two hundred years ago, people might have claimed that God had willed it so, and that any nation which failed to play its part, allowing itself to be submerged or overwhelmed by a more powerful neighbour, was setting its face against a preordained divine plan. A twentieth-century and secular equivalent for this belief would be a narrative of 'normative' national development, one against which the performance of 'failed' or 'anomalous' nations can be tested.

'Scottishness', 'Frenchness', or 'Germanness', are seen as subliminal entities, beyond geography and history, immanent yet compelling, demanding realisation in concrete political and cultural terms. Musicians and artists, but especially writers, carry out their function adequately in so far as they manage to give expression to that entity. A test of their success would be that their work should be free of noticeable foreign influences, or should at least bear witness to a struggle to break free of them. Any link to balladry, or more generally to popular, oral tradition, however bogus or inaccurately conceived, brings crucial validation. 'Native' forms and modes of expression are privileged. The history of national schools in nineteenth-century music has, indeed, often been posited in terms of progressive liberation from foreign influence, and from any suspicion of undiscriminating cosmopolitanism. Nor was Marxism–Leninism, despite its emphasis on international solidarity, alien to such attitudes, which are common to a wide range of right-wing nationalist ideologies. Throughout the Stalinist period, accusations of cosmopolitanism were among the most feared weapons in the armoury of those charged with the responsibility of policing artistic production.

Closeness to 'folk culture' was a valued element in nineteenth-century nationalist thinking, and offered an easy test of the 'Russianness' or 'Hungarianness' of a work, despite the fact that the folk culture in question not infrequently revealed itself to be an after the fact, city-based construction or idealisation. The narrative posited for the history of a small nation such as

Scotland would involve heroic resistance to the pressures of threatened conquest, domination and assimilation, both economic and cultural. A core of 'Scottishness', identified in turn with a stage in the distant past, with the national church, with oral, anonymous literature untainted by the conditionings of the marketplace, with specific habits of speech or of the mind, and with specific writers who are able to put us in touch with it (though they might never succeed in rendering 'Scottishness' tangible, in making it fully available for examination or discussion) would be miraculously preserved down the centuries, until it could be deposited, unharmed, on the altar of national independence finally achieved.

One purpose of writing the history of literature on a national basis would therefore be to demonstrate how this immanent entity had achieved embodiment in the work of writers, composers and visual artists, thereby becoming, thanks to compulsory education and the emergence of a national academy, a touchstone and a guide for future generations. A 'national academy' means, in this context, a body of intellectuals capable of interpreting, teaching and disseminating the national cultural heritage, and of creating a critical tradition suitable for its interpretation.

Agendas of this kind crop up repeatedly in writing about Scottish literature since the Second World War, and continue to be active, often in subtle or disguised forms. The step from writing histories of literature along these lines to attempting to define a Scottish tradition in literature is a very small one. Scottish literature as at present conceived, embracing work in at least three languages, English, Scots, and Gaelic, is a comparatively recent appearance on the critical and academic scene, and what may be termed the 'question about Scottishness' has occupied a central role in deciding precisely what Scottish literature might be. Kurt Wittig, in his 1958 study *The Scottish Tradition in Literature*, argues, not without a degree of tautology, that:

> for as long as even a few Scottish writers are conscious of having inherited a Scottish tradition we shall not do justice to their work unless we study it in relation to that Scottish tradition which they themselves are conscious of having inherited.

He makes no attempt to disguise the extent to which a preoccupation with that tradition, and with the 'Scottishness' it embodies, dictates the nature of his study. He describes it as:

an attempt to expound some of the moral, aesthetic and intellectual values inherent in the Scottish literary tradition. In expounding these values I have picked out the ones which to me seem to be specifically Scottish, and have largely ignored the rest.

Not the texts, then, but the values behind them. And not all the values, but only those which are specifically Scottish. The 'question about Scottishness' is therefore assigned a central role. It will determine not only the choice of authors to be covered, but also which aspects of their work are to be investigated.

Yet the 'question about Scottishness', and the traits which allow us to identify it, is something more than a literary litmus test. It itself contains a series of questions which are remarkably difficult to resolve. What is 'Scottishness'? Of what is it composed? Where does it come from? How can it be defined? Who can be described as 'having' it? Wittig is understandably reluctant to postulate 'inherited racial characteristics'. He nonetheless suspects that some of the defining traits of Scottishness *may* be a racial inheritance', while admitting that a multiplicity of factors, 'geography, climate, history, social conditions, education, religious beliefs, and various conventional attitudes, opinions, and prejudices' have contributed to the national character of which these traits are the 'spontaneous expression'.[7]

That traits or touchstones of Scottishness can prove alarmingly fickle is a fact Wittig makes no attempt to deny. What is perceived as quintessentially national will upset us by suddenly revealing its origins in a quite different setting. The Burns stanza (three successive tetrameters plus an isolated one, all sharing the same end rhyme, alternating with two single dimeters which rhyme separately) was known in the early eighteenth century as Standard Habbie, from Robert Sempill's elegy on the last town piper of Kilbarchan in Renfrewshire. Though a modest achievement in itself, the elegy stands at the head of the eighteenth-century Vernacular Revival, a movement which championed the use of Scots, advertising its debt to seventeenth- and sixteenth-century poetry while also, though less clamorously, drawing in a significant fashion on English Augustanism. David Daiches has spoken of 'Habbie Simson' as 'perhaps the most influential single poem in the whole of Scots literature'.[8] Peter Zenzinger, for his part, argues that the stanza's derivation from medieval mystery plays (he specifically cites the York cycle), with the associated ecclesiastical echoes, was evident to contemporary audiences, and crucial to the poem's effect as then perceived. This same stanza can be traced still further back to a Provençal original, composed by Guillaume of Aquitaine, which is itself likely to be a calque of a medieval Latin hymn.[9] In other words, the form had crossed no fewer than three language divides, as well as the religious and ideological barrier of the Reformation, before Burns could make use of it.

For the poets of the Vernacular Revival, using Scots was tantamount to an aggressive affirmation of their Scottishness. However indebted they might be to writing in English, poems in Scots would, it was assumed, prove more resistant to assimilation by the neighbouring tradition which, under a banner of 'Britishness', threatened to engulf them. Such attitudes continued to be relevant to writing in Scots throughout the twentieth century. And yet, in the concluding section of his allegorical poem 'The Goldyn Targe', the early Renaissance poet William Dunbar had cited Chaucer, Gower and Lydgate as his models, defining the language he used as English ('O reuerend Chaucere, rose of rethoris all . . . Was thou nocht of pure Inglisch all the lycht'[10]), presumably because the term 'Scots' was too ambiguous, and could be taken to mean a Celtic rather than a German tongue.

Scots, then, had at an earlier stage been perceived as a literary medium shared with England, and only later came to offer itself as a potential means of cultural resistance. The transformation is eloquent of the extent to which the 'foreign' can be taken in and successfully 'naturalised', so that it becomes a mark of identity, even a shibboleth. Alongside this process, and almost in symmetrical opposition to it, one can speak of a 'foreignising' of what had at one stage been core elements in national self-definition. The relationship, from the sixteenth century onwards, of writing in Gaelic to writing in the other languages of Scotland can usefully be viewed in terms of such 'foreignising'. What was once the Scottish language *par excellence* is turned into something alien and suspect, becomes 'Erse', with the inevitable unflattering anatomical associations.[11] Indeed, a consequence of giving the Reformation and the introduction of Calvinism a pivotal role in attempts to define 'Scottishness' has been to 'foreignise' the centuries preceding 1560, rendering them opaque, impenetrable to the dominant analytical tools and discourses.

Within the last two decades, anthologists of Scottish poetry have not resisted the temptation to outline characteristic traits of the texts which they have chosen. For Roderick Watson, the 'demotic' and the 'metaphysical' strains, and their interrelations, are fundamental:

> Scottish literature shows a long-standing and unique intercourse between 'scholars' and 'people' . . . our 'high art' has seldom lost touch with the expressive vigour of the vernacular and folk

tradition . . . Scotland has had a long history of belief in its own democratic and egalitarian values, not least in education, and even if such beliefs are no more than 'mythology', they have still been active in how we think of ourselves, and hence in making us what we are in what is still, after all, a small country.[12]

Writing some twenty years after Wittig, Watson is understandably tentative in his drive to outline the factors involved in 'making us what we are'. And as with Wittig, caution leads him into a degree of tautology. What matters is not whether Scottish society is indeed democratic and egalitarian, but rather that a sufficient number of Scottish people should, even delusively, have believed this was the case, for a sufficient length of time. Five years later, in the introduction to their anthology, Robert Crawford and Mick Imlah are more telegraphic and light-hearted. The 'common characteristics of Scottish poetry' are 'its weather', a relatively close degree of contact with Europe, a lively interest in translation, and helping Scotland to 'express a sense of nationhood'. One suspects a degree of tautology here again, even though the editors hurry to add that the overweening characteristic of Scottish poetry is 'its prejudice in Scotland's favour'.[13]

The strategy of foregrounding Scottishness in reading the work of Scottish writers is double-edged. The attempt to define what Scottish men and women have in common, the characteristics and experiences they share, can appear, at first glance, both generous-spirited and inclusive. Yet the process of selecting characteristics in order to 'count in' brings with it, almost inevitably, a parallel 'counting out'. Whether the defining factor be an engagement with Calvinism, in all its hetero-geneous manifestations, indebtedness to the ballads and popular culture, access to a demotic voice which can nonetheless be married with erudition or (as Edwin Muir would have it, in an essay published in 1924)[14] lower middle- or working-class origins, there is a danger of erecting boundaries between those who fit and those who don't. Not just writers, who are often remarkably sensitive to the pressures informing the reception of their work, but critics, too, may be tempted to keep quiet about those aspects of texts which fail to match the pro-posed 'identikit'. If belonging, being 'counted in', is a primary objective, the strategies adopted to achieve it can include silence and self-suppres-sion. And so an approach initially flagged as being inclusive and even celebratory will lead, in the end, to marginalisation and ostracisation.

The choice of yardsticks for national belonging is hardly ever innocent. How could it be? The debate about what it means to be Scottish, and what makes a text Scottish, is also a field of conflict between political and cultural interests, a battle between competing claims to interpretive power. One of the more regrettable consequences of the pragmatic alliance forced upon cultural and social forces in Scotland in the course of the Thatcher years is a residual difficulty in conceiving the Scottish cultural space as an interaction between distinct, often hostile, yet not ultimately irreconcilable agencies, of which class has perhaps been neglected to a greater extent than any other.

To attribute to Calvinism (taking just one example) a privileged status as a means of interpreting cultural and social realities in Scotland, is also potentially to empower those capable of telling us what Calvinism 'means' and how it is to be understood. Fascinating as the undertaking promises to be, it has rarely been approached with the necessary degree of methodological complexity. In the case of Scottish literature, one would want to start by setting up a theoretical model of how religious belief and practice can interact with the creation of fictional and imaginative texts, a model, moreover, which is capable of more general application. One would also have to steer clear of any reification of Calvinism, any suggestion that those phenomena to which the term has been applied across a period of more than four centuries can be assumed, without discussion, to be identical with one another. In a word, one would restore to Calvinism its procreative, amoeba-like nature, splitting repeatedly into new formations, certain of which, as happened with the Scottish churches, could then reunite to form a different kind of whole. And lastly, it would be essential to set the Scottish evidence alongside parallel experiences from the European mainland, in countries such as the Netherlands, Switzerland or historic Hungary (and, beyond these, South Africa) where an entity referred to as Calvinism played a significant cultural and social role. The erection of Calvinism to a mark of 'Scottishness', a core element in both national identity and national literature, mirrors the importance ascribed to French Catholicism in the manifesto Proust was so unhappy with. The search for national character traits or a definable national tradition is repeatedly associated with an urge to denote one form of religious belief as also being specifically national. It is advisable to scrutinise line-ups of this kind closely and with a due measure of distrust.

Introducing the study of the modern Scottish novel already quoted from, and which is subtitled 'Narrative and the National Imagination', Cairns Craig shows himself painfully aware of the dangers involved in 'nationalising' the creative faculty:

The nature of a national imagination, like a language, is an unend-ing series of interactions between different strands of tradition, between influences from within and without, between the impact of new experiences and the reinterpretation of past experiences: the nation is a series of ongoing debates, founded in institutions and patterns of life, whose elements are continually changing but which constitute, by the nature of the issues which they foreground, and by their reiteration of elements of the past, a dialogue which is unique to that particular place.[15]

The danger here is that, in the light of so many provisos, the concept will become so poorly and vaguely defined as to lose its cutting edge. And when Craig describes his study as 'an attempt to identify a national tradition of the novel in Scotland', in which he seeks 'to focus on the underlying features which constitute the distinctiveness of a Scottish tradition', given that the existence of 'a tradition of the Scottish novel' can be taken as 'an index of the continuity of the nation and the national imagining to which it contributes',[16] readers would be justified in asking how different, in the last analysis, Craig's aims are from Wittig's. The 'question about Scottishness' has once more become paramount.

Notes

1. See Marcel Proust *Correspondance avec Daniel Halévy* ed. Anne Borrel and Jean-Pierre Halévy (Paris, Éditions de Fallois 1992), pp. 138–40 for the letter, and pp. 233–4 for commentary, with extracts from the manifesto in *Le Figaro*. A full English version can be found in Marcel Proust *Selected Letters* vol. 4 1918–22 ed. Philip Kolb, translated with an introduction by Joanna Kilmartin (London, Harper Collins 2000) pp. 86–7.
2. Cairns Craig *The Modern Scottish Novel: Narrative and the National Imagination* (Edinburgh, Edinburgh University Press 1999) pp. 9, 10, 12.
3. 'What I Believe' in E. M. Forster *Two Cheers for Democracy* (Harmondsworth, Penguin 1965) pp. 75–84, here p. 76. The essay dates from 1939.
4. 'Dream State: Kathleen Jamie on the New Scottish Parliament' in *Poetry Review* 87: 4 (1997–8) p. 36 (my italics).
5. Kaye Kossick 'Roaring Girls, Bogie Wives, and the Queen of Sheba: Dissidence, Desire and Dreamwork in the Poetry of Kathleen Jamie' in *Studies in Scottish Literature* XXXII (2001) pp. 195–212, here p. 195.
6. The literature on modern nationalism and its historical background is extensive. Three texts may be cited here by way of orientation: John Hutchison and Anthony D. Smith eds *Nationalism* (Oxford and New York, Oxford University Press 1994); John Hutchison *Modern Nationalism* (London, Fontana 1994); and Anthony D. Smith *Myths and Memories of the Nation* (Oxford, Oxford University Press 1999).
7. Kurt Wittig *The Scottish Tradition in Literature* (Edinburgh, Mercat Press 1978, facsimile of the original 1958 edition) pp. 4–5.
8. David Daiches *Robert Burns* (London, Bell & Sons 1952) p. 13.

9. See Peter Zenzinger '"Habbie Simson" and the Early Elegy Tradition' in Dietrich Strauss and Horst W. Drescher eds. *Scottish Language and Literature. Medieval and Renaissance* (Frankfurt am Main, Peter Lang 1986) pp. 481–96, and Frank M. Chambers *Old Provençal Versification* (Philadelphia, PA, American Philosophical Society 1985) pp. 24ff.

10. Priscilla Bawcutt ed. *The Poems of William Dunbar* (Glasgow, Association for Scottish Literary Studies 1998) I, p. 192. The editor comments in a note (II p. 421) that 'Most Lowlanders called their own tongue "Inglis" or "Inglisch" until the end of the sixteenth century.'

11. See Malcolm Chapman *The Gaelic Vision of Scottish Culture* (London, Croom Helm and Montreal, McGill-Queen's University Press 1978).

12. Roderick Watson ed. and introd. *The Poetry of Scotland: Gaelic, Scots and English* (Edinburgh, Edinburgh University Press 1995) p. xxxii.

13. Robert Crawford and Mick Imlah eds *The New Penguin Book of Scottish Verse* (London, Allen Lane, The Penguin Press 2000) pp. xxvi–xxviii.

14. See Edwin Muir 'A Note on the Scottish Ballads' in *Latitudes* (New York, Huebsch 1924) pp. 12–30, here p. 12.

15. Cairns Craig, p. 31.

16. Ibid., pp. 35, 33.

2

Alternative Approaches

Codesto solo oggi possiamo dirti,
ciò che non siamo, ciò che non vogliamo
EUGENIO MONTALE

What then are the alternatives? It is interesting to set alongside the declaration by Kathleen Jamie, excerpted in the previous chapter, the views of another woman, not from Scotland, writing at an earlier stage in the twentieth century. The Russian poets Boris Pasternak, based in Moscow, and Marina Tsvetayeva, then living in French exile, engaged during the summer of 1926 in a fascinating three-way correspondence with the Prague-born, German-language poet Rainer Maria Rilke. Having received a copy of Rilke's volume *Vergers*, containing poems he had written in French rather than German, Tsvetayeva observed that:

> Goethe says somewhere that one cannot achieve anything of significance in a foreign language – and that has always rung false to me . . .
> Writing poetry is in itself translating, from the mother tongue into another, whether French or German should make no difference. No language is the mother tongue. Writing poetry is rewriting it. That's why I am puzzled when people talk of French or Russian, etc., poets. A poet may write in French: he cannot be a French poet. That's ludicrous.
> I am not a Russian poet and am always astonished to be taken for one and looked upon in this light. The reason one becomes a poet (if it were even possible to *become* one, if one *were* not one before all else!) is to avoid being French, Russian, etc., in order to be everything. Or: one is a poet because one is not French. Nationality – segregation and enclosure. Orpheus bursts nationality, or he extends it to such breadth and width that everyone (bygone and being) is included.[1]

In a letter to the critic Yury Ivask, written nearly eight years later, Tsvetayeva confesses:

> And – this last would seem to be the truest of all – in the world I love not what is deepest, but what is highest, and therefore I prefer Goethe's joy to Russian suffering, *that* solitude to Russian convulsion. In general, make no mistake, there is little in me that is Russian (NB! everyone gets this wrong at the start), even my blood is – excessively – mixed . .). Spiritually, too, I am a half-breed.[2]

Her views are characteristically vehement. They reveal a love for the outrageous and the paradoxical that contrasts powerfully with Proust's cautious tones in the letter to Halévy. And yet, if one were to adopt her standpoint, unexplored perspectives could open up on a much wider range of Scottish poetry than that written between the outbreak of the Second World War and the close of the twentieth century. Aspects of these texts could emerge which preoccupation with the question of 'Scottishness' and with the cultural politics of national identity has kept hidden until now. Though they cannot be limited in this sense, Tsvetayeva's remarks raise the question of what role comparative readings ought to play in our understanding of Scottish texts, readings that would cross the boundaries not just between literatures, but between languages. And of course reading across languages, or the attempt to do so, must be a major feature in any study of Scottish literature.

In the same letter, Tsvetayeva speaks of how different Rilke sounds to her in French and in German, of the varying qualities languages exhibit:

> German is deeper than French, fuller, more drawn out, *darker*. French: clock without resonance; German – more resonance than clock (chime). German verse is reworked by the reader, once more, always, and infinitely, in the poet's wake; French is there. German *becomes*, French *is*. Ungrateful language for poets – that's of course why you wrote in it. Almost impossible language!

Tsvetayeva's example (if one includes her prose), like that of Rilke, is of special relevance to Scottish literature, where instances of poetic bilingualism abound. For a considerable time there has been general agreement among scholars and critics that surveys of Scottish literature have to take account of writing in the Gaelic language – that, in spite of the difference in medium, the latter forms an integral part of Scottish literature. Wittig deals with the issue in a less than satisfactory manner. He cites the influence, both lexical and phonetic, that Gaelic has had on

Scots. But he makes no attempt to explain why the influence, in the opposite direction, of both Scots and Scottish English on Gaelic should have been so much more powerful. The exchange has taken place on a basis that is anything but equal. He merely, and somewhat lamely, asserts that 'Though he is largely unaware of it, the staunch Lowlander carries on his back a Gaelic biological and linguistic heritage.' One is tempted to answer that the extent to which literary features, or any element in the cultural superstructure, can be transmitted 'biologically', beneath the level of consciousness, remains open to discussion. Wherever such discussion might lead, the fact remains that, in a Scottish context, what was lost once a language boundary had been crossed irrevocably, as community upon community abandoned Gaelic for a form of English with no hope of turning back, has had an infinitely more determining role than anything that was retained. The issue is not the putative continuity posited by Wittig, but a very real discontinuity, a rupture.

Wittig then evokes, rather than any 'literary "source"', an ill-defined oral culture as a theatre of exchange. Although he finds it impossible 'to point to chapter and verse', it is 'through such devious channels' that 'Gaelic conceptions of poetry must subtly but powerfully have influenced Lowland Scots literary taste'.[3] Though the desired evidence is not to hand, he maintains that a Gaelic to Scottish continuity must have existed. The claim is in line with his project of unearthing a unitary 'Scottishness', a coherent tradition which can link together the series of texts he has elected to the canon. And he has not been alone in calling on a poorly-defined oral culture to substantiate his argument, one that would require radically different tools, not deployed in his own study, for its examination.

If one were to attempt an outline survey of Gaelic language poetry and song written in Scotland over the past four centuries, there are real grounds for arguing that the significant intertext, rather than writing elsewhere in Scotland, would be writing in the Irish language of the same period. Where indeed does Gaelic poetry belong? And to what extent has the 'question about Scottishness' blinded us to the enormous complexities of the very notion of a Scottish literature? Where the modern period is concerned, despite Sorley MacLean's friendship with and admiration for Hugh MacDiarmid, and despite his having frequented Robert Garioch, George Campbell Hay and Sydney Goodsir Smith, the crucial intertexts for his own poetry, beyond Gaelic and Irish song, balladry and legend, are the sonnets of Shakespeare and Yeats's poems inspired by Maud Gonne.[4] No writing in either of Scotland's other languages can rival these as a source of inspiration and emulation, where MacLean's own love sequence *Dàin do Eimhir* (*Poems to Eimhir*) is concerned.

To insist on the importance, for the work of a Gaelic poet from Raasay, of poetry written in English elsewhere in the British Isles, beyond Scotland, is not necessarily to undermine the notion of a Scottish literature. At the simplest level, it means acknowledging that many, perhaps a majority, of the poets dealt with in this study received their schooling and, in most cases, their university education at a time when literature as a whole tended to be identified with English literature. Their acculturation, where books and examinations were concerned, took place against an English rather than a Scottish background. There are therefore no real grounds for surprise when Iain Crichton Smith, who spent his childhood and adolescence in a village on the Isle of Lewis, indicates that:

> Though I was brought up on an island where Gaelic was the dominant language, my reading was much the same as if I had been educated at Eton, rather than at Bayble Public School, that is to say, *Penguin New Writing*, among whose contributors were, of course, Auden, Spender and MacNeice.[5]

Does this imply that Crichton Smith is somehow a less 'Scottish' writer? Clearly not. What matters is to acknowledge the privileged role the work in English of English poets played in his intellectual and aesthetic formation. Douglas Dunn makes a related point in 'Audenesques for 1960', a wistful epistle to a not 'heterosexually inclined' older poet with whom he enjoyed imaginary dialogues while on his way to work in Renfrew County Library, but whom he lacked the nerve to approach on the one occasion when they might have spoken to each another:

> Nationality doesn't identify 'our side'.
> Muses are international, and mine is a Lady
> Who speaks all sorts of languages (in translation),
> Collects guidebooks, maps, timetables, menus,
> Wine lists, and other hedonistic souvenirs.
>
> So what if you were English? I speak that language,
> But not its nationality; I love your poetry,
> And our imaginary talks – I mean, remembering them –
> Please me as proof of how imagination side-steps
> Half-witted nagging about 'National Identity'.[6]

Where the 'question about Scottishness' and the investigation of a Scottish tradition are viewed as priorities, issues of this kind take on an awkward, even threatening quality. And yet it would be unduly restrictive to view the centuries-long symbiosis between writing in the non-Gaelic areas of Scotland (but not only there) and writing in England exclusively in terms of assimilation, domination or the throwing-off of cultural oppression. What matters is not the 'Scottishness' or the 'Englishness' of a given text but finding the appropriate context within which to read it, even discovering the extent to which different contexts can make unprecedented readings feasible.

In the end, the major justification for positing the existence of a Scottish Literature, from the point of view of readers and critics, has been that English Literature no longer offered an adequate, or even a possible context within which to read specific texts. But if one context has been set aside as superseded, it would be mistaken to seek a replacement in rigid, monolithic terms, or to refuse to contemplate further alternatives.

Comparative readings, readings which step across the boundaries between national or linguistic traditions, are of particular importance within the field of Scottish literature. It is more than likely that such readings will run contrary to attempts to define a Scottish tradition or to elicit the specific traits or characteristics which tell us that a text is Scottish. The preoccupation with identity and with nationalist ideology has, indeed, rendered many theoretical perspectives quite simply out of bounds. One could argue that the nationalist critic and the practitioner of literary theory are natural enemies. What the first is concerned to discern and to unearth, to construct or even to claim as preexisting, 'natural', is of minimal interest to the second. The insights offered by Bakhtin in *Discourse on the Novel*, or the alternative reading of the origins of the novel form offered in Margaret Ann Doody's *The True History of the Novel* take little note of national traditions, or the boundaries between them, nor is national belonging a significant consideration in the essay on Baudelaire's 'Les chats' by Roman Jakobson and Claude Lévi-Strauss, or Lacan's study of Edgar Allan Poe's 'The Purloined Letter'.[7] Theoretical approaches tend to move backwards and forwards across such boundaries, a crucial advantage of deploying literary theory being the way it encourages us to read side by side, or as reflecting one another, texts which a nationalist perspective would have prevented us from ever bringing into contact. To assert that the Scottish critical tradition has yet to acknowledge the challenge of literary theory to any significant extent would be only partially an exaggeration. In the chapters that follow, discussion of individual poets is consistently informed by a concern for different theoretical approaches, and for the light they can shed on the texts being examined. And comparative perspectives, rather than being shunned, will be brought into the argument wherever this seems both helpful and appropriate.

Agnosticism is quite different from atheism. To ask whether the most important feature of Scottish literature is indeed its 'Scottishness' is not to question the usefulness of positing a 'Scottish literature'. Within the educational institutions familiar to us, literature will continue to be marshalled under national headings for the foreseeable future. But the critical tradition associated with Scottish literature has surely reached a point in its evolution where the 'question about Scottishness', and the associated search for a national tradition can be set aside, not least because the answers these have come up with are riddled with ambiguities. This book does not attempt to set any single factor in place of national belonging as a privileged interpretive tool. That would mean simply replacing one constriction with another. If it is a study not only of *Modern **Scottish** Poetry* but of *Modern **Scottish** **Poetry***, then the boundary between poetry and prose should prove, at least in theory, to be no less important than that between what is and is not Scottish, though just as difficult to define. It might be helpful to shift the emphasis onto the second term, offering, if not a definition, then at any rate a discussion of what renders 'poetry' special, of its defining characteristics. If the task provokes a modicum of nervousness in whoever prepares to attempt it, that will be as nothing to the nervousness consistently exhibited by university students, and beyond them by the population at large, when asked to engage with 'poetry' rather than with the superficially less problematic realms of narrative fiction and non-fictive prose.

Some thirty years ago, I attended an outdoor performance of an Elizabethan tragedy, Middleton's *The Changeling*, to be precise, in the courtyard of a Cambridge college. The playing area lay along one of the shorter sides of the rectangle, against a background of regularly spaced windows, with staircase entrances to the right and to the left. Suddenly an incongruous figure wandered onto the stage. One of the college porters, busy on a banal errand, looked up to realise, with horror, that over a hundred pairs of eyes were following his every movement. Said personage scuttled back into the staircase from which he had emerged as quickly as he could.

What had made it so obvious that he did not belong in the play? His movements and his gestures *were not double*. When an actor performs on a stage, each movement that is made, each word spoken, has a double nature that distinguishes it from the same movements or words in everyday life. It is itself and something else as well, possessed of an additional layer of meaning. The doubleness is made possible by framing, by the designation of a particular space as the acting space, as the object of our gaze.

In an analogous way, poetry is 'language on a stage'. The words and sounds need not in themselves be different from those of ordinary speech, though very frequently they are. An analogy here could be the presence or absence of costume. It is the framing that gives them a double value. A new layer of meaning is created, over and above what the words would have meant without that frame. That extra, that plus, is available to an audience, now composed of readers rather than spectators, thanks to the altered context, to the existence of a frame.

Poetry then could be, as much as a kind of text, a way of reading. That is certainly what Valéry suggests when he notes that:

> Rhyme is an indication that we are confronting poetry. It stops anyone looking for prose – and tells them to read *in a special way* (which puts the *linked sequence of sounds* in the foreground – and not their cleanness or clarity; their heard totality and not what they add up to by *meaning*.[8]

The notion is useful for our understanding of the processes involved in 'found' poetry, or in the use MacDiarmid so clamorously, even scandalously, made of writing by other hands in the poetry of his later period. Where the poem 'Perfect' was concerned, which he excerpted from a short story by the Welsh writer Glyn Thomas, his practice led to a public controversy though not, in the end, to a legal suit for plagiarism.[9] MacDiarmid claimed to have copied the lines down and then forgotten the source. But what he did was not so very different from his excerpting of material from Jamieson's Scots language dictionary earlier in his poetic career. Coming upon a word or words, a sentence, a group of sentences, or even a whole stanza, he realised that, read in a different way, read poetically, they could have a different or additional meaning, could 'mean' in a different way.

What might be the characteristics of language read as poetry? It upsets, or redresses, the balance of language in 'ordinary' use, in everyday conversation or for the exchange of information, in at least two ways. When MacDiarmid adapted a section of prose for poetic reading, he divided it up into lines. Those with any experience of writing poetry themselves will know that the placing of the first line break is a crucial decision, with significant repercussions for everything that is to follow. While everyday speech, and even our reading of a novel or a newspaper article, resembles a ribbon, a horizontal flow, poetry breaks this up into segments, counterposing that horizontal flow with a contrary, vertical structuring. Lines are placed one beneath the other with the implication that, at some level, they are equivalents. Each line is, in its way, a new beginning, yet also a return, a repetition (like the *da capo* indication in a musical score). The ending of a line is correspondingly highlighted, as one of the 'louder' positions in a poetic text. Seen on the page, a poem, or a verse paragraph, can look like the drawing of a building, yet here we begin with the roof, while it is the last verse, the final one to be put in place, which constitutes the foundation, the basis upon which the rest can be hoisted up.

When we read language as poetry, we also redress the balance between 'signifier' and 'signified'. The terms are of course Saussure's, the first referring to the material aspect of a word, what can be perceived even by someone who does not know the language (listening to texts in a foreign language can be a useful training for the poetic ear), while the second refers to its meaning part, though this conceptual element does not necessarily entail a concrete manifestation in the visual world to which one can point and say, that is what the word designates.[10]

For Saussure, the relationship between the two was entirely arbitrary, in a fashion that anchored them all the more securely to one another, endowing verbal signs with a much needed stability.[11] If our habit is to ignore the signifier, to dedicate as little attention as possible to it in our hurry to detect the signified, when we read language as poetry the signifier is instead held up for our attention, refusing to dissolve and yield to the signified. Here again, Valéry's comments are illuminating:

> the meaning of the words . . . does not cancel out their materiality. – This is why, in passing, obscurity and poetry are so closely connected. What is obscure, if not a discourse that refuses to disappear in front of what it means?[12]

Patterns of sound and stress which, in a hurried conversation, might have the status of mere accessories, are themselves endowed with meaning. Poetry demands to be read, not just more slowly than prose, but again and again, thence its perceived 'difficulty' over and against prose. The effect is undoubtedly, though it cannot be restricted to, a 'defamiliarisation' in the sense given to that word by the Russian Formalists.[13] It also leads us to experience afresh a reality pinpointed by Tom Leonard in his essay on William Carlos Williams, namely 'that language is itself an object in the world – the world is not an object in it.'[14] In a celebrated discussion of the manuscript variants for one single word in Pushkin's *Eugene Onegin*, Lotman implies that, from a certain point of view, writing poetry can be easier than writing prose:

> in a poetic text a certain secondary synonymy arises: the words prove to be equivalent only by virtue of their isometrism [having the same number of syllables, and the same stress pattern]. 'Florentine', 'à la Rubens' and 'full-breasted' are conjoined with the word 'women' as interchanging epithets . . . the rhythmic structure of the text creates a secondary synonymy . . . Poetry does not describe the same world as prose through other means, but creates its own world.[15]

Whereas in prose it is the message, the thing wanting to be said, which dictates the choice of words, and the range of possible substitutions is determined semantically, on the basis of meaning, in poetry any term which meets the relevant requirements with respect to length, stress pattern and sounds can theoretically be a potential candidate. Valéry offers a similar insight before the fact rather than after the fact, from the point of view of the poet at work:

> The poet looks for a word which should be:
> feminine in gender
> of two syllables
> containing 'p' or 'f'
> ending in a silent vowel
> a synonym for breaking, falling apart
> not scientific or unusual
> 6 conditions – at least.[16]

Though Valéry includes a semantic requirement in his conditions,[17] the implication is nonetheless that, when writing poetry, one's potential choice of words is infinitely greater than when writing prose. Indeed, Lotman goes so far as to claim that 'In an extreme case, any word in poetic language may become a synonym for any other.'[18] This could be rephrased by saying that poetry, in returning importance to the signifier as against the signified, sets up a new kind of semantics, establishing an implicit link between any two words which resemble one another in their sound pattern or stress (a sort of paronomasia gone wild), so that shared phonetic features can imply a link in meaning. This is a major element in the degree to which, when we read language as poetry, words 'mean' in a different way.

Another significant feature of poetry, as against prose, is its potentially 'sacral' quality (much as the mention of such a function might horrify certain contemporary critics, who would see in it the return of an out-dated liberal humanism). In the Outer Hebrides, the notion of the poet as healer, as thaumaturge, survived until at least as late as the eighteenth century. It is said of the North Uist poet John MacCodrum that individuals would travel many miles on foot in order to confide in him a difficulty or a problem they were experiencing. The remedy he offered took the form of healing words, uttered secretly to the suppliants, which they were at liberty to carry away with them and treasure for as long as necessary. The words might be written down as an amulet, or conserved in the memory. While it is important to be extraordinarily tentative in ascribing a therapeutic function to poetry, there can be no doubt that, in moments of acute tension, whether this be the first experience of sexual love, a major bereavement, or dizzying ontological uncertainty, again and again isolated individuals have encountered, in a poem, normally within the space of a few lines or even in one single line, a formula, a spell almost, which helped them survive, a sort of talisman.

Faced with a class of alarmed students, one would be tempted to ask (if there was the slightest likelihood of getting an honest response) those who have *not* at *any* stage in their lives tried to compose a poem to rise to their feet. But attempts at composition of this kind, and the resort to poetry at times of unbearable stress, are such private, or indeed 'sacral' experiences, that public acknowledgement of them might be inappropriate. Such sacral or spiritual recourse to poetry is obviously at the opposite pole from the construction of a canon, or from the selection and modelling of texts and poetic careers in function of a narrative of national self-assertion. Yet if we wish to give honest consideration to how poetry subsists in contemporary society, how it is used, a sacral element cannot be overlooked.

If poetry is indeed framed speech, language on a stage, then the framing, often consisting in a regular pattern of metre or rhyme, may well render safe the articulation, the representation of taboo contents which might otherwise create excessive anxiety in listeners and readers. Yet the relation is more complex. Framing does more than make dangerous material safe. In the prologue to her cycle 'Requiem',[19] which deals with the Stalinist purges specifically associated with Chief of Police Yezhov, Anna Akhmatova describes herself standing in a queue outside the gates of Leningrad's 'Crosses' prison. When another woman recognises and names her, a third turns to ask: 'Can you describe this?' Receiving an affirmative answer, the woman smiles, albeit briefly.[20]

Indicated here is the capacity of representation to reduce unbearable levels of distress and offer solace, precisely because the representation is not 'the real thing', not tied to a place or a time or even to a specific language. While poetry does not have an exclusive claim to offer representations of this kind, bringing about the associated solace, it does have particular claims in terms of scale, given that the power exerted by a poetic text is not proportional, but can even be in inverse proportion, to its extent. Two lines can do the job as well as two hundred. And those two lines can be remembered, can be carried around inside one's head, in a way that does not occur with prose fictions (at least not in our society). The poems in Akhmatova's cycle were too compromising to be written down in 1938. Memorised by a group of women friends, they were not transcribed and assembled, physically, on paper and as a cycle, until 1956. Before then, one would be tempted to say they had existed inside those women's heads, however problematic the issues such a conception raises.[21]

Formal patterning and the regularity of a metrical grid have an important role to play in rendering unbearable contents approachable and accessible. Yet it is characteristic of a poem that the words themselves, the language, should refuse to become supine, to lie down and submit passively to metrical patterning. Rather than as a source of frustration, the gap between the metrical grid and its actual realisation, line by line, can be seen as crucial to the operation of a poem, as the origin of a dynamism without which it would risk death. If Russian poet Joseph Brodsky speaks, in the passage quoted below, of a 'soul', this is in part a question of his mischievous delight in refloating a word, and a concept, which Soviet censorship had rendered taboo for more than half a century. But it also indicates an urge towards transcendence which leads him, with fascinating perversity, to suggest that the dynamic conflict between metre and language can sketch for us a psychological portrait of the author:

> Anyone with some experience in composing verse knows that verse meter is the equivalent of a certain psychological state, at times not of just one state but of several. The poet 'picks' his way towards the spirit of a work by means of the meter. Lurking within the use of standard meters is, of course, the danger of mechanical speech, and every poet overcomes that danger in his own way, and the more difficult the process of overcoming, the more detailed – both for himself and for the reader – becomes the picture of a given

psychological state. Often the upshot is that the poet begins to perceive meters as animate – inspired in the archaic sense – entities, as certain sacred vessels. This is basically just. Form is even less separable from content in poetry than body is from soul, and what makes the body dear is precisely that it is mortal (in poetry the equivalent of death is mechanicalness of sound or the possibility of slipping into cliché). At any rate, every verse-maker has his own favorite, dominant meters, which would be regarded as his autographs, for they correspond to the most frequently repeated psychological state of the author.[22]

If one wished to add a proviso to this brilliant passage, it would be the suggestion that the 'psychological state' be conceived, not as an attribute of the writer at the moment of writing, but as an aspect of the poem itself. (The interpretation of Robert Garioch's 'Perfect' offered later in this study sees it as directly informed by the insights Brodsky outlines in this passage.)

Poetry is not a democratic art, any more than being a concert pianist is. One of the pleasures of attending a virtuoso recital is to see enormously difficult feats carried off with aplomb, and without apparent effort. A similar pleasure can be procured by the skilful deployment of metre and rhyme in a poem. Many would agree that Norman MacCaig's poetry lost when he abandoned the wondrously complex stanza patternings of his earlier volumes in favour of free verse, and of an unadorned *sermo pedestris*, in his later. One's delight in noticing such features (which may well be equally a source of pleasure for those who remain unconscious of them) is, in part, a delight in regularity, and regularity may be a crucial aspect of what we perceive as beautiful. (Such would certainly seem to be the case with the human face.) Metrical patterning and regular rhyme furthermore combine to offer the pleasure of anticipation without the dullness of predictable fulfilment.

What justification can be offered for the undoubted difficulty of poetry when set against prose, for all those extra rules and conventions? Returning to the simile of a theatrical performance, one could indicate how rule-bound the behaviour of an audience at such a performance is. They agree to remain in their places for the duration, not to get up and move around, not to trespass into the acting area unless specifically invited to do so, not to move around excessively in their seats or raise their arms, and not to talk, or at least, to keep their voices at a level which will cause only minimal disturbance to their neighbours. Without such rules or conventions, the performance could not happen, and if

observing them involves a degree of constraint, it is analogous to the
constraint involved in submitting to the undoubted ardours of reading
a poem. Lotman's view of the poetic text brings it into close proximity
with information science. A poem, he argues, is an outstandingly eco-
nomical way of storing and communicating information. But the rules
have a further justification. In Lotman's terms, literature in general, and
in particular poetry, is the result of imposing a secondary language, with
its own set of conventions, upon the primary language used in everyday
life: 'Literature speaks in a special language which is superimposed as
a secondary system on natural language.'[23] The payoff for the added
conventions is a near exponential increase in the quantity of information
that can be conveyed:

> [the artistic text] transmits different information to different readers
> in proportion to each one's comprehension; it provides the reader
> with a language in which each successive portion of information
> may be assimilated with repeated reading. It behaves as a kind of
> living organism which has a feedback channel to the reader and
> thereby instructs him.[24]

The rules are not there for their own sake, but as enablers. A poem,
indeed, can offer a sort of gradual release not dissimilar to what has
been claimed for certain brands of vitamin tablets, supposed to continue
exercising their beneficial effects on one's system as many as eight hours
after consumption. A poetic text may release a different meaning to the
same individual on successive readings, even after a gap of years or
decades, while also proposing a range of sometimes contradictory
meanings to each individual member of a class or seminar group. The
most successful seminar discussion can be one after which participants
split up in total disagreement, rather than having reached factitious
agreement on crucial issues. Students, especially when cramming for an
examination, can be frustrated when they realise that no one meaning
of a text can be taken as definitive and final. They may even interpret
as a failure on their teacher's part what is, in reality, an inalienable
feature of poetic texts:

> What interests us here is that large intermediate zone which lies
> between the comprehension and non-comprehension of an artistic
> text. Differences in the interpretation of works of art are common
> and, despite general opinion, do not arise from attendant and
> easily obviated causes, but rather are organic to art. It should at

least be apparent that the aforementioned property of art, its ability to correlate with the reader and provide him with just the information he needs and is prepared to receive, is related to the possibility of diverse interpretation.[25]

Poetic texts are both protean and promiscuous, different every time we return to them, impatient of demands that they should refrain from responding to readers other than ourselves with equal generosity and eagerness. And for this reason they will constantly and consistently elude the grasp of rigidly nationalist critics and of canon formers, of those who place a primary value on Scottishness, making it, implicitly or explicitly, the ultimate goal of their examinations.

The perspectives offered in the course of this chapter are not specifically Scottish, though they are as applicable to poetry in one of the three languages of contemporary Scotland as to that in any other European language. Once more it may be worth emphasising the 'agnostic' stance of the present book, designed to balance, counterpose and counteract rather than to challenge. Within Scotland, and further afield in the British Isles, it is unlikely that in the foreseeable future a viable alternative to the grouping of literary products by and large in terms of the perceived nation of origin, when not specifically in terms of a single language, will emerge. Just as the knowledge and understanding of one's own language is as essential, perhaps more essential, to the translator than expertise in the language being translated from, a valid basis for the study of literature in the broadest sense is study of texts with an obvious relation to one's own place, one's own language or languages and one's perceived historical and cultural predicament. This is the best way to obviate the dangers highlighted by Margaret Atwood in her *Survival: a Survey of Canadian Literature*, of coming to believe that literature can only be produced by foreigners, and by dead foreigners at that.[26] Texts that can be described as Scottish, for one reason or another, therefore deserve to be assigned a pivotal role in literary and cultural studies within Scotland, even if at times their role will be to catapult individual readers effectively into texts originating from very different cultural surroundings. Such enabling, however, must never become oppressive. Scottishness must not become a straitjacket, nor should texts be minimised or distorted in the interests of establishing a national canon which all too soon risks mimicking that which it aimed to replace. The concepts of nation, national belonging and national identity demand that our relationship to them should also be one of play, of imagination, invention and paradoxical renewal and reversal.In this manner alone can such concepts enable rather than restrict, can they open doors in our formation and perception, rather than banging them shut.

Notes

1. Boris Pasternak / Marina Tsvetayeva / Rainer Maria Rilke *Letters Summer 1926* eds Yevgeny Pasternak, Yelena Pasternak and Konstantin M. Azadovsky, trans. Margaret Wettlin and Walter Arndt (London, Jonathan Cape 1986) pp. 169–70. Tsvetayeva wrote this letter in German: the original can be found in Konstantin Asadowski [*sic*] ed. *Rilke und Russland* (Frankfurt am Main, Insel Verlag 1986) pp. 409ff.
2. *Sobranie sochinenii v semi tomakh* (Moscow, Ellis Lak 1995) VII: pp. 387–8 (my translation).
3. Kurt Wittig *The Scottish Tradition in Literature* (Edinburgh, Mercat Press 1978, facsimile of the original 1958 edition) pp. 5–6.
4. See Somhairle MacGillEain/Sorley MacLean *Dàin do Eimhir* ed. Christopher Whyte (Glasgow, Association for Scottish Literary Studies 2002) esp. pp. 25, 29, 143, 144, 147, 148.
5. Iain Crichton Smith *Towards the Human: Selected Essays* (Edinburgh, Macdonald 1986) p. 27.
6. Douglas Dunn *New Selected Poems 1964–2000* (London, Faber & Faber 2003) p. 273.
7. See M. M. Bakhtin in 'Discourse in the Novel' in *The Dialogic Imagination* ed. Michael Holquist, transl. Caryl Emerson & Michael Holquist (Austin, University of Texas Press 1981) pp. 259–422, Margaret Anne Doody *The True History of the Novel* (London, Harper Collins 1997), '"Les Chats" de Charles Baudelaire' in Roman Jakobson *Questions de Poétique* (Paris, Éditions du Seuil 1973) pp. 401–19, Jacques Lacan 'Seminar on "The Purloined Letter"' transl. Jeffrey Mehlman in *Yale French Studies* 48 (1972) pp. 38–72.
8. Paul Valéry *Cahiers* ed. Judith Robinson (Paris, Gallimard 1974) II p. 1103 (my translation).
9. See Alan Bold *MacDiarmid: a Critical Biography* (London, John Murray 1988) pp. 423–4.
10. Ferdinand de Saussure *Course in General Linguistics* translated and annotated by Roy Harris (La Salle, IL, Open Court 1983) pp. 65–7.
11. Saussure, p. 67.
12. Valéry, p. 1087.
13. See *Russian Formalist Criticism: Four Essays* translated with an introduction by Lee T. Lemon and Marion J. Reis (Lincoln, NA, and London, University of Nebraska Press 1965) pp. 13–22, 85–7.
14. 'The Locust Tree in Flower, and Why it had Difficulty Flowering in Britain' in Tom Leonard *Intimate Voices 1965–1983* (Newcastle upon Tyne, Galloping Dog Press 1984) pp. 95–102, here p. 102.
15. Jurij Lotman *The Structure of the Artistic Text* trans. Ronald Vroom (University of Michigan, MI, Ann Arbor 1977) p. 116.
16. Valéry, p. 1068.
17. Several items from the *Cahiers* could be cited here in the role of correctives, for example the observation that 'In submitting to metre, the poet has to sacrifice his

initial line of thought' (p. 1061) or that 'With a poet, "ideas" are not fixed elements which language has to come up with the closest possible expression for. They are one of the variables' (p. 1124).

18. Lotman, p. 29.
19. The actual title is 'Instead of a Preface'.
20. See *The Complete Poems of Anna Akhmatova* translated by Judith Hemschemeyer, edited and with an introduction by Roberta Reeder (Somerville, MA, Zephyr Press 1990) II p. 95, and the sensitive and penetrating discussion in Susan Amert *In a Shattered Mirror: the Later Poetry of Anna Akhmatova* (Stanford, CA, Stanford University Press 1992) pp. 31ff.
21. For the circumstances of the cycle's preservation, see Amanda Haight *Anna Akhmatova: a Poetic Pilgrimage* (Oxford and New York, Oxford University Press 1990) p. 98.
22. From 'Footnote to a Poem' in Joseph Brodsky *Less Than One: Selected Essays* (Penguin, Harmondsworth 1987) pp. 195–267, here pp. 208–9.
23. Lotman, p. 21.
24. Ibid., p. 23.
25. Ibid., p. 24.
26. See Margaret Atwood *Survival: a Thematic Guide to Canadian Literature* (Toronto, Anansi 1972) p. 15.

3

The Story So Far

Heilanman – *Tell me all about the Scottish Renascence.*
Makar – *Och, no in the High Street.*
ROBERT GARIOCH

*Die nationale Mystik ist Bespiegelung des
Selbst, in ein Totem verlegt.*
HUGO VON HOFMANNSTHAL

How seductive would be the prospect of discussing modern Scottish literature without mentioning MacDiarmid! Seductive, but also impossible. At the very least, to have a single figure occupy so many different roles produces confusion. What is the relation of the biographical figure to the poet? And of the poet to the movement he launched, and christened as the Scottish Renaissance Movement? How does the poetry he wrote relate to the programme and to the ideology with which he supplied the movement? Since the latter cannot be identified with any single figure or with that figure's plans for it, how does it relate to MacDiarmid's blueprint? Did it turn out as he would have wanted it to be? What would MacDiarmid's poetry look like if we were to 'liberate' it from the Scottish Renaissance Movement and even from his own pronouncements, and instead sought to evoke the context or contexts which would allow it most effectively to release its meaning, and to release the most meanings possible?[1]

Dedicating a chapter to the interwar period in a study whose declared focus is the period from the outbreak of the Second World War to the close of the century might seem unnecessary. But it is not until the affirmation of Edwin Morgan as a major figure on the scene at the end of the 1960s that a significant area in modern Scottish poetry emerges which need not, indeed cannot be defined in terms of its relation to MacDiarmid, whether as polemicist, aspirant politician or poet. For each of the other poets in the next two chapters either a literary or a personal relationship to MacDiarmid can be charted, as if encountering him on their path were an inevitable stage in both development and self-definition for MacLean and Campbell Hay, for Muir, MacCaig and Goodsir Smith. MacDiarmid had to be grown out of, when he could not be grown out from, in the years immediately following the war. However faithful or unfaithful differing perceptions of the man's actual works and his conduct might prove to be, that maddening figure demanded attention, even resolution, if a more broadly based literature were to affirm itself. A literature, that is, which could call itself Scottish with a limited degree of self-doubt or self-consciousness. Returns to his legacy proved necessary and arrived as successive waves, of which the most important was heralded by the 1962 festschrift edited by Kevin Duval and Sydney Goodsir Smith and Duncan Glen's monograph of 1964. The 1980s were particularly productive in this respect, as part of the movement of cultural reassessment provoked by the débâcle of the 1979 referendum which found expression in the pages of the quarterly review *Cencrastus*.[2] As might have been expected, the rereading prompted, from certain quarters, a passionate disavowal of the man and what he stood for.[3] A distinct lull, however, set in as the 1990s progressed. Though both the poet and the movement he had initiated continued to demand attention, there was by that stage much in Scottish poetry that could no longer be explained in terms of either MacDiarmid's influence or reaction against it, and which drew on different strengths and sources.

It is inevitable that the literature on MacDiarmid should assume at times a hagiographical tone. Hagiography means the writing of saints' lives, and an essential part of such lives is that there should be, not just miracles, but a conversion, a movement from light to darkness. The equivalent of Saul's falling from his horse on the road to Damascus, and rising up as Paul, was the process by which a relatively obscure journalist, named Christopher Murray Grieve, who had come out in print against attempting to extend the life of an apparently moribund Scots language poetry into the twentieth century, invented a second self named Hugh MacDiarmid who would, in the course of time, come to be identified primarily with his poems in that language, despite the fact that these represented considerably less than half of his overall output.[4] Rather than letters or a gospel, MacDiarmid provided his nation with a founding poem, *A Drunk Man Looks at the Thistle*.[5] The tale of how, on a visit to the poet in his Montrose home, the composer Francis George Scott helped MacDiarmid arrange its scattered elements, written on scraps of paper and the backs of envelopes, on the kitchen table, then assembled these into something like a coherent whole no doubt has a basis in fact.[6] It certainly retains an attractive sheen of the hagiographic, dutifully mirroring in a more northern climate the role Ezra Pound is said to have played in settling the final form of Eliot's *The Waste Land*.

MacDiarmid spent most of the 1930s living in poverty and in a kind of internal exile in Shetland and, though one might confer an element of hagiography on this period by speaking of it in terms of the forty days and nights in the desert which preceded Christ's supreme sacrifice, to do so would be misleading. If any resurrection followed, it was only partial and long delayed. The celebratory narrative of MacDiarmid's feats could well extend from the appearance of the first Scots lyrics bearing his name in the *Dunfermline Free Press* in September 1922 to the founding of the National Party of Scotland, out of four hitherto distinct formations, in May 1928; or even to October of that same year, when the poet spoke at a public meeting in Glasgow's St Andrew's Halls, after R. B. Cunninghame Graham had failed by a margin of thirty-six votes to win Glasgow University's rectorial election.[7] What is most striking in the years that follow is the speed with which this founding figure was sidelined, indeed ostracised, where the development of political and cultural nationalism in Scotland was concerned. The movements he had helped to spawn betrayed him, though some might argue that MacDiarmid effectively rendered further coexistence impossible by abandoning Scots for an 'aggrandised' English in his poetry and by his increasing and explicit fascination with Lenin, Marxism and undisguisedly totalitarian political systems. It did not help that he came to see Scottish Gaelic as the native tradition which should henceforth assume the greatest weight and importance.[8]

The hagiography went wrong. By the middle of 1942 the national poet who ought to have been a national hero was doing manual work in a munitions factory in Glasgow, almost a leper if not merely an embarrassment. With the passage of time, he acquired the status of a well-kept secret among the few who really mattered. The reception and appreciation of MacDiarmid's work did not shake off this vaguely conspiratorial air till well into the 1960s. As late as the 1980s, a Scottish university would decline to accept the gift of his papers from two well-meaning benefactors because of the corollary requirement that a Chair of Scottish Literature be set up bearing his name. By 1939 much of his work was out of print, and there was little prospect of him publishing any of the large scale projects he had embarked on, even the ones he managed to finish.

One consequence of the vicissitudes in the man's existence has been an invidious periodisation of his work, a parcelling out of MacDiarmid as not one but three poets. The first writes in Scots and is at the centre of a movement for political and cultural revival, active on a bewildering range of fronts, as agitator, poet, prose writer, journalist and founder of reviews. He can be identified with the period from 1922 to the publication in 1930 of the transitional long poem *To Circumjack Cencrastus*, a fascinating yet uneven sequel to *A Drunk Man Looks at the Thistle*. The second prefers dense and even impenetrable extended intellectual poems in English, where Scotland, national revival and indeed the concept of the nation itself disappear progressively from view. The culminating achievement of this period is 'On a Raised Beach', and a major difficulty in its interpretation is that, if its imagery of stones and resurrection links it to the miraculous short lyrics of the early 1920s, it demands a different range of skills and responses from its readers. Indeed, the poem contemplates a radically different audience, to the extent that it contemplates any audience at all. The third period saw the production (some might say compilation) of a mass of materials, consisting to a staggering extent of lifted and modified versions of texts by other hands and intended to constitute a series of book length poems. These in turn may have been intended to compose a larger whole. Though basically to be identified with the later 1930s, this phase culminated in the publication of *In Memoriam James Joyce* in 1955, a project to be discussed in the fourth chapter of the present study.

Bringing these distinct phases to bear on one another, and working towards a reading of MacDiarmid which would be neither piecemeal nor marred by excessive periodisation; one which could, so to speak, rescue his work from its chronology, has been problematic in part because the MacDiarmid of the first period, the one most closely associated with cultural nationalism and the Scottish Renaissance Movement, has been effectively hijacked by the hagiographers. He is busy elsewhere, and unavailable for comment. One possible way out of this apparent impasse is to propose more complex readings precisely of that first period, so as to demonstrate the difficulty of doing justice to the richness of its implications with any single approach. The effect will hopefully be to render more of MacDiarmid available for interaction with the remainder of his work, while at the same time opening up spaces in the interwar period which need not be related primarily to the nationalist ideology he had engaged with so passionately in the 1920s.

His poetry, from *Sangschaw* of 1925 to *To Circumjack Cencrastus* of 1930, demands to be viewed within at least two distinct, not ultimately conflatable contexts, neither of which can offer anything like a full account of its range of possible implications. The years after the First World War have been referred to as a spring of nations. A number of independent states with recognised international boundaries appeared, or reappeared, on the map of Europe as a direct consequence of the collapse of two imperial formations, the Russian and the Austro-Hungarian, which had played dominant roles in the politics of the previous century. National governments in Finland, Estonia, Latvia, Lithuania and Poland faced the task of implementing fully the use of a national language which had never had, or had been deprived of official status, and of mobilising a corps of committed intellectuals in the construction, both retrospective and prospective, of a national culture which would include a literary canon as its backbone. Something analogous took place in the 1990s with the collapse of the Soviet Union, the emergence of an independent Ukraine as the second Slavic state in terms of population, the peaceful dissolution of Czechoslovakia and the bloody dissolution of Yugoslavia as then known, indicating both the difficulties inherent in the process of delimiting national groups and fostering their self-affirmation, and the extent to which the process had been left incomplete during the interwar period. The effective obsolescence of the term Serbo-Croatian, and the emergence on the Balkan scene of what was apparently a new language, Bosnian, are only the superficial and external markers of an extraordinarily complex process, and one which offers interesting yet unexplored parallels with that of Scotland.

The year in which MacDiarmid's first lyrics came into print, 1922, also saw the establishment of the Irish Free State. It may, at that time, have appeared perfectly plausible that yet another imperial formation was in the process of breaking up, and that Britain's predicament could be Scotland's opportunity:

> the Scottish psychology differs from the Irish, and, nationalistically laggard as Scotland has been in comparison with other countries, there are grounds for anticipating that, once it does waken up, it will redeem the leeway at a single stride and be the first to penetrate into that arcanum which still foils even Mr de Valera with its intangible and ubiquitous barriers.[9]

After all, MacDiarmid had read his Spengler,[10] and was familiar with the notion of the alternating rise and fall of different and competing cultural centres. In the nations mentioned earlier, it was perfectly normal (though the process started in the previous century) that writers and intellectuals educated and acculturated in the language and literature of a more dominant nationality, one which might well have been easier and more 'natural' for them to use in their own work, should choose instead to revive and, where necessary, transform their 'own' national language, one that had survived in its richest form in uncultivated, peasant use, bringing it into line with current international trends and fitting it out for 'national' deployment.

Oral, popular culture was not infrequently the subject of emotive and even mythical projections, relevant to the discussion of William Soutar and his possible debt to Scottish balladry later in this chapter. This would seem a valid context in which to view MacDiarmid's activity, as poet and polemicist, throughout the 1920s. Looking back from the threshold of the twenty-first century, it is difficult to believe that Scotland could have moved towards independence shortly after the twenty-six Irish provinces, and without their history of bloodshed and division. At the time, however, it may well have seemed perfectly plausible that this should happen.

But there is another, competing, and equally plausible context within which to view MacDiarmid's poetic activity. It is the crisis in the modes and language of specifically English literature which accompanied the emergence of Modernism. With respect to Latvia or to the Czechs, he appeared to be skipping crucial stages in laying the bases for and nourishing a specifically national culture. There had been no collecting, editing and disseminating of oral literature to a broader, literate public. Against its background of a united Britain neither the dissemination in printed form of the border ballads nor James Macpherson's Ossianic prose poems can be interpreted as phenomena of 'nation-building' in a specifically Scottish sense. Nor had significant sections of the bourgeoisie been won over to, or reinforced in their use of the national language in writing and in day to day existence, or involved in its rehabilitation for prose and non-imaginative uses. The poetry MacDiarmid wrote was not popular in its aims or its conception, either in the sense of reproducing the modes and styles of pre-existing, orally circulating poetry, or of aiming to reach a wide public. On the contrary, his Scots poetry of the 1920s has all the half-contemptuous élitism, the self-advertising and, at times, self-defeating difficulty of the work of Eliot and Joyce, or of Pound's *Cantos*. That poetry should then be read not as part of the emerging literature of a nation reborn, but as one more manifestation of the crisis of Modernism in the English language, a crisis not confined to the geographical boundaries of England.

Were this to be the case, then MacDiarmid's adoption of Scots would be a reaction to that very collapse of the accepted Victorian and Edwardian linguistic *koiné* which prompted Eliot to pepper *The Waste Land* with quotations from a variety of languages, and motivated the linguistic allusiveness of the *Cantos* and the alchemical manipulations

of language in *Ulysses*. MacDiarmid's foregrounding of Russian literature (the first volume of Scots lyrics has a version from Merezhkovsky)[11]
and his gestures towards German Expressionism[12] would then be
attempts to redefine, and ultimately destabilise the canon, along the lines
of Eliot's championing of the English Metaphysicals, or Pound's fascination with the Provençal troubadours and the Italian poets of the *dolce
stil nuovo*. More than with the ballads or with any clearly definable
national tradition, MacDiarmid's work of the 1920s seeks to establish
links with European Decadentism in the broadest sense. After all, one
way of explaining the transformation of English poetry brought about
by Pound and Eliot is that writers in English had at last become aware
of what had been happening in French poetry since the time of
Baudelaire.[13] In so far as MacDiarmid was able to draw on the achievements of European Symbolism, this came about thanks to the work
of Aleksandr Blok, rather than of Baudelaire. But not for nothing did
MacDiarmid choose Dostoevsky as the presiding spirit of *A Drunk Man
Looks at the Thistle*, setting alongside the Russian novelist's fascination
with epilepsy and other sicknesses, and how these could alter consciousness, the Scottish shibboleth of drunkenness, and the psychic or
spiritual states associated with sexual intercourse and orgasm.[14]

While it would be inaccurate to claim that MacDiarmid's manifesto
poem of 1926 makes use of a stream of consciousness, the fiction of
subjectivity which permeates it is akin to that found in the novels of
Virginia Woolf or in Joyce's *Portrait of the Artist as a Young Man*. It is
a subjectivity stretched to bursting point, barely skirting the dangers of
collapse, encyclopedic and yet self-obsessed, raising its own viewpoint
to the status of window on the world, as if any casual, fortuitous
sequence of sensual and nervous stimuli, free-wheeling associations,
memories and speculation could attain to a species of universal truth: an
exasperated subjectivity which, through the very fact of self-exhibition,
hopes to attains the status of the objective.

To restrict MacDiarmid's production of the 1920s to either of these
perspectives would be to diminish and misrepresent it. Although, where
Englishness is concerned, he was no more of an outsider than Joyce or
Eliot or Pound, his fate has been different from theirs. As late as the
1960s, his work was largely unobtainable in print, and the space
dedicated to him on the curricula of university English departments
negligible. He had all the appearance of a loser, his strategies condemned
to failure, the path he followed leading to a wilderness. The work he
produced subsequent to the 1920s had been met on the whole with
hostility or indifference. Today, in a situation where the greater part of

MacDiarmid's production continues to be unknown even to the poetry-reading public in Scotland and throughout the British Isles, it would nonetheless be difficult to view him as a loser. Proust argued, with respect to Beethoven's late quartets, that artworks have the ability to educate their readers, offering them all the guidelines needed in order to appreciate and assimilate them, as if an innovative text could somehow encapsulate its own induction course.[15] The school is in the works themselves. MacDiarmid was aware, in producing *A Drunk Man Looks at the Thistle*, that he had written an extended poem in a language no one could read, and for a public that did not then exist ('Nor cared gin [*if*] truth frae me ootsprung/ In ne'er a leed [*idiom*] o' ony tongue/ That ever in a heid was hung' [lines 2,410–12]). For it to come into being, Scottish Literature as a distinct and independent entity had to be either posited or revived. That this occurred must be attributed in no small measure to MacDiarmid's influence.

Whereas Joyce, Eliot and Pound could be drawn into the ambit of English Literature (or at least, our understanding of English Literature could be modified so as to accommodate their work, or even transformed in terms of it). MacDiarmid's poetry has resisted such assimilation. His greatest gift to later poets and their readers was that a new critical framework had to be made available if even just his work of the 1920s were to become accessible. And to this extent it is valid to attribute to that work a foundational role in the emergence, or the re-emergence, of a specifically Scottish literature, not only in terms of the texts themselves, but of the associated paraphernalia: critical readings, investigations of the tradition, and engagement with a range of different kinds of cultural nationalism.

Though it sets out to be a foundational poem, the position at which *A Drunk Man Looks at the Thistle* comes to rest, with regard to nationalism, national identity, and the establishment or the resurrection of a national literature, is an undisguisedly agnostic one. The 'question about Scottishness' remains an open question. Perhaps the speaker in the poem will choose, or accept, that nationality. Perhaps he will reject it. All he can do is take the issue 'to avizandum', the formula used when a Scottish judge takes a case home for private consideration outside a court.[16] The conclusion is paradoxical and, indeed, the re-emergence of a Scottish literature under MacDiarmid's aegis is veined with paradoxes. Among the most striking of these is that the literary movement he spearheaded, only to be extruded by it, is as memorable today for its failures as for its successes.

The first of these was its relentless pastoralism. What hope of success could a political and cultural movement have which told a numerical majority of the population they were not actually living in Scotland? For, as far as the Scottish Renaissance Movement was concerned, the 'true' Scotland was to be found, not in Glasgow, or Motherwell, or Greenock, but in Caithness or the Mearns, the Western Isles or the Border counties. Though it would be misleading to view him in any straightforward sense as a spokesman for the movement, Edwin Muir's reflections about Glasgow in his *Scottish Journey* (first published in 1935) shed a fascinating light on the rejection of the realities of industrialised Scotland which so consistently characterised it:

> Glasgow is in every way the most important city in modern Scotland, since it is an epitome of the virtues and vices of the industrial regions, which comprise the majority of the population. A description of Scotland which did not put Glasgow in the centre of the picture would not be a description of Scotland at all.
>
> Yet at the same time Glasgow is not a typically Scottish town; the worst of the many evils with which it festers were not born of the soil on which it stands or of the people who live in it – a mixed population of Lowlanders, Highlanders, and Irish – but of Industrialism; and in writing about it I shall be writing about a particular area of modern civilisation which is independent of national boundaries, and can be found in England, Germany, Poland, Czechoslovakia and most other countries as well as on the banks of the Clyde. This No Man's Land of civilisation comprises in Scotland an area which, though not very large in extent, is very densely populated. In one way it may be said that this area *is* modern Scotland, since it is the most active and vital part of Scotland as well as the most populous: the proof of its vitality being that it influences rural Scotland in all sorts of ways, while rural Scotland has no effective influence on it. But from another point of view one may say that it is not Scotland at all, or not Scotland in particular, since it is merely one of the expressions of Industrialism, and Industrialism operates by laws which do not recognise nationality.[17]

Muir gets entangled by the paradoxes of his own position. If his acknowledged agenda concerns Scotland, the country's distinctiveness, that which makes it different from other nations and constitutes a national character, Glasgow and the industrial central belt cannot enter into his argument. As economic and cultural phenomena, these communities, for Muir, are the product not of a national movement but of forces which recognise no national boundaries – industry and international capital. So there can be nothing 'typically Scottish' about Glasgow. Yet he cannot help admitting that to leave Glasgow out of his account of Scotland would be in effect to abandon any valid attempt at talking about the country.

He gave eloquent expression to the unequal relationship obtaining between industrial and rural Scotland in his autobiography, first published as *The Story and the Fable* in 1940, and then revised and extended (but with certain omissions) as *An Autobiography* in 1954. Here Muir speaks of his experience when employed in Greenock, at the time an industrialised outlier of Glasgow on the south shore of the Firth of Clyde, an unlovely township he ironically rechristens Fairport:

> The job I took up in Fairport and kept for two years was a job in a bone factory. This was a place where fresh and decaying bones, gathered from all over Scotland, were flung into furnaces and reduced to charcoal. The charcoal was sold to refineries to purify sugar; the grease was filled into drums and dispatched for some purpose which I no longer remember. The bones, decorated with festoons of slowly writhing, fat yellow maggots, lay in the adjoining railway siding, and were shunted into the factory whenever the furnaces were ready for them. Seagulls, flying up from the estuary, were always about those bones, and the trucks, as they lay in the siding, looked as if they were covered with moving snowdrifts. There were sharp complaints from Glasgow whenever the trucks lay too long in the siding, for the seagulls could gobble up half a hundredweight of maggots in no time, and as the bones had to be paid for by their original weight, and the maggots were part of it, this means a serious loss to the firm. After one of these complaints the foreman, an Irishman, would go out and let off a few shots at the seagulls, who would rise, suddenly darkening the windows. But in a little while they would be back again.
>
> The bones were yellow and greasy, with little rags of decomposed flesh clinging to them. Raw, they had a strong, sour, penetrating smell. But it was nothing to the stench they gave off when they were shovelled along with the maggots into the furnaces. It was a gentle, clinging, sweet stench, suggesting dissolution and hospitals and slaughter-houses, the odour of drains, and the rancid stink of bad, roasting meat. On hot summer days it stood round the factory like a wall of glass.[18]

This passage alone could support the contention that Muir's prose is consistently more daring, experimental and effective than his poetry. At first glance, with the details of the maggots and the seagulls, and the ineffectual sallies of the Irish foreman, one might be tempted to view the mode as realist. Yet the disgust evoked is such that realism moves in the direction of expressionism. For all its descriptive precision, the passage, in a fashion characteristic for Muir, cries out for symbolic interpretation.

On one level, this could be economic. The maggots gathering on the loads of bones would stand for the plus value accruing to goods thanks to capitalist manipulation, and the seagulls for the entrepreneurs themselves, located elsewhere, aloof from the stinking mess they have created and merely turning up from time to time to cream off its produce. On a second, however, the passage images the relationship Muir perceived between a new, industrial, international Scotland and an old, vivid, agricultural world which had preserved its national character, albeit precariously. After all, the factory dealt in dead animals, so that the wealth it produced depended on the slaughter and the exploitation as commodity, rather than as living beings, of the creatures which populated that older Scotland.

One would be hard pressed to come up with a more eloquent expression of the rejection of Glasgow and industrial Scotland which characterised the Scottish Renaissance Movement. It was a logical consequence of its nationalist ideology. One might find grounds for asserting that, where representation is concerned, until the late 1960s and 1970s Glasgow was not a part of Scotland at all. A sort of *cordon sanitaire* surrounded it. (The metropolis in *Grey Granite* (1934), the third novel in Lewis Grassic Gibbon's *A Scots Quair* trilogy (1932–4), which constitutes a significant exception, is interestingly located in eastern Scotland rather than on Clydeside.)

An ideology which placed a premium on delimiting and affirming national character was bound to have difficulties embracing pluralism and hybridity. Muir encountered in Glasgow 'a mixed population of Lowlanders, Highlanders, and Irish', and the 1931 'Introduction' to the first volume of the *Scottish National Dictionary* excluded Glasgow speech from the data on which it would draw, since 'the influx of Irish and foreign immigrants' meant that 'the dialect has become hopelessly corrupt'.[19] Original purity, the clear fount of national speech, must be sought in rural environments untainted by the operation of international capital. William Soutar (1898–1943), a poet from the town of Perth only six years MacDiarmid's junior, who wrote in both English and Scots, attempted to match the older man's achievement in *A Drunk Man* with his extended Scots poem 'The Auld Tree'. At its heart lies a sequence where William Wallace, hero and martyr of the national struggle for independence at the end of the thirteenth century, wields his mighty sword to free a tree, representing national tradition and poetical inspiration, from the parasites infesting it:

Whaur derk against thc lift upstüde	*sky*
The Eildon tree: about its wüd	*wood*
(Deathly as ivy on an aik)	
Was wuppit a twa-heided snake . . .	*wrapped*
He sklent it strauchtly into twa	*cleft*
And kelterin' they skail'd awa;	*quivering; dispersed*
The ane haud'n southard to his hame,	
The ither wast owre Irish faem.[20]	

Like *A Drunk Man*, Soutar's poem is a programmatic text about the possibilities for a national revival. But it lacks the tentative, agnostic stance of the earlier poem. A corrupt culture has to be liberated and purified from the alien agency, not just of dominant English culture, but of the Irish immigrants who had come, by the time Soutar wrote, to form a significant element in the population of west central Scotland. In the years immediately preceding the writing of Soutar's poem, Scotland's national church had made urgent representations to the Westminster government along exactly these lines. MacDiarmid quotes, in *Albyn: or Scotland and the Future* (1927), the Church of Scotland's Committee on the Church and Nation as follows:

There are only two explanations of the great racial problem that has arisen in Scotland – the emigration of the Scots and the immigration of the Irish people . . . The outlook for the Scottish race is exceedingly grave. If ever there was a call to the Church of Scotland to stand fast for what men rightly contend dearest – their nationality and their traditions – that call is surely sounding now, when our race and our culture are faced with a peril which, though silent and unostentatious, is the gravest with which the Scottish people has ever been confronted.

Here, as elsewhere, and intriguingly for the man who set the movement for national revival in motion, MacDiarmid's position was more complex than that of his contemporaries. He declares that, as far as the Scottish Renaissance Movement is concerned, 'the growth of Catholicism, and the influx of the Irish, are alike welcome, as undoing those accompaniments of the Reformation which have lain like a blight on Scottish arts and affairs', adding that 'just as many of the great figures in the Irish literary movement have been Protestants, so, on the other hand, if there is to be cultural progress in Scotland, must many of the emerging artists be Catholics'.[21] MacDiarmid welcomed the Catholic immigration, assigning to it a pivotal role in the recreation of an independent and recognisably Scottish culture which he hoped was taking place. The role was to be analogous to that of the Irish Ascendancy, where a group differing from the majority of the population in terms of religion, linguistic background and perceived ethnicity could significantly further the drive for separation from England and Britain. Their Catholic belief, far from representing a threat to the preservation of the national character, could help to undo the nefarious influence of centuries of Calvinism, forging a new link with the pre-Reformation Scotland of Henryson and Dunbar to which MacDiarmid constantly harked back.

The view of national identity implied here is a dynamic one, with opposing and contradictory qualities interacting in a process that will never quite attain fixity or stabilisation. In so far as MacDiarmid did come up with a definition for the Scottish national character, this was in terms of a dynamic and unstable oscillation, a backwards and forwards movement between opposites which could never actually be reconciled. In a study published just after the end of the First World War, G. Gregory Smith had found Scottish literature to be 'remarkably varied', becoming, 'under the stress of foreign influence and native division and reaction, almost a zigzag of contradictions'. In this very 'combination of opposites' Smith perceived 'what either of the two Thomases, of Norwich and Cromarty, might have been willing to call "the Caledonian antisyzygy"'. One pole was 'not merely the talent of close observation, but the power of producing, by a cumulation of touches, a quick and perfect image for the reader'. The other was 'the airier pleasure to be found in the confusion of the senses, in the fun of things thrown topsy-turvy, in the horns of elfland and the voices of the mountains'.[22] By definition an 'antisyzygy' is a union of opposites *sui generis*, a refusal to yoke discordant elements together or force them into any kind of synthesis. In other words, the 'Caledonian antisyzygy' as adopted by MacDiarmid could hardly be converted into a stereotype. The terminology, however, has managed to bewilder generations of readers and university students, provoking a delightfully irreverent squib from Robert Garioch, who took no trouble to disguise a marked intolerance of MacDiarmid's intellectual pretensions.[23]

MacDiarmid's role as exemplary bard of the Scottish Renaissance Movement was devolved, as the 1930s proceeded, upon Soutar, though the Perth-based poet's gift was hardly of dimensions to fit him out for the succession. If the relationship of MacDiarmid, and of the movement he spawned, to European Modernism was rendered problematic by unwillingness or inability to attempt a poetry of urban life, Soutar (in this respect resembling Muir) wrote as if a Modernist revolution had not taken place. A more appropriate context in which to view his work would be that of the English Georgian poets and their pastoral forerunners, of Edward Thomas or Walter de la Mare. Though Housman's work belongs to a still earlier period, a pervasive, elegiac tone of erotic suppression and lack of fulfilment, combined with faithful depiction of the charms of a specific region, gives the two poets much in common. It therefore comes as a surprise to find Soutar dismissing Georgian poetry as 'an escape – a kind of truancy into the country', claiming that 'this flight from industrialism and its problems could be but a phase', since 'a turning away to a rural lyricism is no longer a pardonable truancy but a cowardly retreat'.[24] And yet it is precisely such 'rural lyricism' which characterises Soutar's most successful poems.

His diaries, source of the above remarks, were penned in the bed to which a spinal illness condemned him for the greater part of his adult life, and from which he could look out through a specially constructed window onto a garden and the hills behind.[25] Written in a self-consciously correct and even academic English, they make an odd linguistic impression on the reader. It is as if the poet should insist on wearing evening dress even when alone, although there was no prospect of his issuing forth from that one room in his parents' home. His distance from Modernism and from its fascination with the supposed stream of conscious self-talk emerges unequivocally in the following entry:

> The only logical alternative to a God is the isolated individual; for if we deny that life is a unity and is purposive, we can set up no comparable integrity other than the unification of experience in the individual mind. But to accept this necessity is to accept only the reality of the self and its moment; and such a polarized cosmos can claim no validity beyond the isolated self.[26]

There could hardly be a more rotund rejection of the concept which lies at the basis, not just of the mature fiction of Virginia Woolf or of James Joyce, but of MacDiarmid's *A Drunk Man Looks at the Thistle*. MacDiarmid has been the subject of attack both for the choice of poems in the collected Soutar volume which he edited five years after the younger poet's death, and for the remarks made in the preface to it, not least that Soutar had always shrunk from taking the 'mad flight into the symbol'.[27] Leaving value judgements aside, the remark can be interpreted more or less factually. MacDiarmid, in his work of the 1920s, had demonstrated a knowledge and understanding of the achievements of the European Symbolist and Decadent Movements profound enough to let him supersede them. Indeed, it is problematic to speak of *A Drunk Man* as Symbolist in any real sense, its principal images (the thistle and the moon) being so tired and hackneyed as to preclude any potential for shimmering, ungraspable suggestion. Soutar's use of symbols like the cuckoo, the whale or the unicorn, on the other hand, is first and foremost allegorical. The approach links him once more to Edwin Muir who, in poems like 'The Combat',[28] was to conceive of mythological creatures that might have sprung from the pages of a medieval bestiary. 'The Auld Tree' makes explicit the debt to medieval dream poetry which was implicit in *A Drunk Man*, albeit cast somewhat into shadow by the presence of an even more crucial intertext, Burns's 'Tam o' Shanter'. Yet if MacDiarmid absorbs and supersedes this model, Soutar goes some way towards reinstating it.

The manifesto poem 'Birthday', a nationalist fable in which reincarnations of the three Magi behold a newborn child descend from the Grampian hills upon the back of a unicorn, indicates how direct and unironic Soutar's symbolism could be. It may have been the conjunction with nationalist ideology that prompted this simplification, for his use, in more personal terms, of the 'gowk' or cuckoo is much more fluid and elusive. The emergence of a symbol such as the unicorn can be read as symptomatic of the direction the Scottish Renaissance Movement took after MacDiarmid's ostracisation.

Soutar, with his effectively sexless existence (no mention of masturbation in the diary extracts so far printed),[29] strongly evangelical background and steadfast dedication to his art, could appear to be a more suitable candidate for hagiography (one is tempted to write 'canonisation') than MacDiarmid. The importance of his religious background for his poetry awaits adequate treatment. He aspired to produce 'parables after the fashion of the gospel'.[30] Though a populism hardly surprising at the time led him to claim the traditional ballad as 'the most stimulating source of inspiration for the modern writer in Scots' and to add (somewhat forlornly, seen with hindsight) that this indicated 'the social implications of the vernacular revival',[31] it is likely that his metrical practice owes just as much to the English versions of the psalms used in Presbyterian worship, which utilise an identical stanza form, as to folk tradition.[32]

MacDiarmid had been alive to the potential of hybridity, and had clamorously struggled to link the new Scottish poetry to areas still farther afield than those opened up by Eliot and Pound. Russian poetry and philosophy of the period immediately preceding the Bolshevik Revolution, the so-called 'Silver Age', was of primary importance here. In addition, in so far as he was prepared to offer a theory of Scottishness, this was a highly cerebral one, one which defied formulation in a rigid model capable of constraining subsequent poetic practice. Soutar, in contrast, deploys an organicist rhetoric which is disturbingly reminiscent of racial and racist cultural theorising in the dictatorships of mainland Europe at roughly the time he was writing:

> One cannot hope to isolate the true tap-root of nationalism, it goes down too deeply into the racial unconsciousness, but sometimes one can sense as if a portion of oneself has flowered upon the strength which rouses along a fibre of this root. One begins to be more conscious of the atavistic constitution of one's being; life still flows up from the loam of the past and stimulates the branches of one's blood.[33]

The lines just quoted are peculiarly damning as regards the rationale behind Soutar's longing to purge Scottish culture of both English and immigrant Irish influence. Being unconscious, the reservoir of cultural memory referred to here cannot be interrogated. It cannot even be represented. His distaste for the exasperated subjectivity of the Modernists leads him to posit an organic model for poetical inspiration. The individual poet is the latest shoot on a tree whose roots draw nourishment from a past beyond recorded history ('atavistic'). The sap of the tree is the blood running through the poet's veins (though the occurrence of terms like 'strength', 'rouses' and 'fibre' indicate a possible male colouring, suggesting that the liquid might indeed be sperm).

It comes as no surprise to find that these attitudes were linked to outright linguistic essentialism. Continuing the same entry, Soutar writes that:

> English is *not* natural to me; and I use it 'consciously' even in conversation; it is always something of an effort for me to find my words; and not uncommonly I labour as if I were speaking in a foreign language. It is as if one had come out of the past with only a fragmentary memory of one's true tongue, and yet this broken speech remained as rocks which disturb the flow of modern speech.

One is tempted to rejoin that poetry, of its very 'nature', is 'unnatural' or distorted speech and that, if both Scots and Gaelic failed, in the course of Soutar's century, to produce an extended body of prose of significant literary merit, this is because written prose constitutes a still more 'unnatural' form of language than poetry. There is no need to elaborate on the problems involved in reconciling such attitudes with MacDiarmid's espousal, during this decade, of increasingly idiosyncratic English registers in his verse; or on how the differing practice of the two poets pinpoints the breaking up of the Scottish Renaissance Movement into two distinct, irreconcilable streams.

If 'The Auld Tree' is as much a rejection of the gains of *A Drunk Man Looks at the Thistle* as a homage to MacDiarmid's poem, a debt to the tone and lexical practice of MacDiarmid's first two Scots collections, *Sangschaw* (1925) and *Penny Wheep* (1926) is unmistakable in many of Soutar's lyrics.[34] What distinguishes them, however, is a vagueness, a shimmering, flickering quality of imprecision. MacDiarmid made extensive use of the available philological materials in Scots, to the extent that his early collections abound in 'found poems', poems which seem to have been constructed, not to integrate disused lexical items in a larger whole where they can lose their strangeness and blend in with one another, but rather to exhibit them, to give them the glittering, unyielding quality of a chunk of quartz. Any such notion would have been foreign to Soutar's practice. Hand in hand with vagueness, in his case, goes an undeniable infantilisation. The term is harsh, yet one would look in vain in Soutar's lyrics for the complexity of intellectual and cultural reference which underpins MacDiarmid's. Soutar argued explicitly for such an infantilisation, in a celebrated passage from a letter of 1931 to MacDiarmid where he insists that 'If the Doric is to come back alive, it will come on a cock-horse.'[35] The art he aimed to fashion, and which would typify the Renaissance in which he believed he was participating, must be 'simple in the sense that all the basic truths of life are simple', must 'grow out of the experience of humble folk and their daily toil'.[36] So much for the resolute, aggressive, perennially fraught élitism of the Modernists.

A degree of linguistic essentialism also underlies a vexed passage from Edwin Muir's extended essay of 1936 entitled *Scott and Scotland*. It offered the grounds for a definitive estrangement between him and MacDiarmid, and continued to exert a degree of influence for decades afterwards, not just in reactions to choices subsequently made by Scottish poets, but in assessment of the linguistic choices of eighteenth-century poets such as Ramsay, Fergusson or Burns. The very notion of a 'vernacular revival' serves to denationalise the work in English of these poets, and of figures such as James Thomson, author of *The*

Seasons, or James Beattie, whose *The Minstrel* was a significant text for both Byron and Wordsworth. Thomson and Beattie, indeed, have been derided in some quarters as 'Anglo-Scots', Scots whose writing is somehow less than Scottish. Such attitudes are clearly indebted to Muir's analysis of the linguistic 'predicament' facing Lowland Scottish writers:

> Scots has survived to our time as a language for simple poetry and the simpler kind of short story... all its other uses have lapsed, and it expresses therefore only a fragment of the Scottish mind. One can go further than this, however, and assert that its very use is proof that the Scottish consciousness is divided. For, reduced to its simplest terms, this linguistic division means that Scotsmen feel in one language and think in another; that their emotions turn to the Scottish tongue, with all its associations of local sentiment, and their minds to a standard English which for them is almost bare of associations other than those of the classroom... Scottish poetry exists in a vacuum... Hugh MacDiarmid has recently tried to revive it by impregnating it with all the contemporary influences of Europe one after another, and thus galvanize it into life by a series of violent shocks... but he has left Scottish verse very much where it was before. For the major forms of poetry rise from a collision between emotion and intellect where both meet on equal terms; and it can never come into existence where the poet feels in one language and thinks in another, even though he should subsequently translate his thoughts into the language of his feelings. Scots poetry can only be revived, that is to say, when Scotsmen begin to think *naturally* in Scots. The curse of Scottish literature is the lack of a whole language, which finally means the lack of a whole mind.[37]

Muir's hypothesis was, of course, a deft and probably unconscious reworking, in the Scottish context, of the dissociation of sensibility Eliot diagnosed in English poetry from Milton onwards. Its facile oppositions of 'thought' and 'feeling', 'head' and 'heart', 'English' and 'Scots' proved attractive. It offered theoretical justification for the linguistic power relations actually obtaining, and which were and are a forceful element in social practice and in the bias of state-funded, compulsory education. The hypothesis thus acquired a certain bogus validity which has not abandoned it even today. The paradoxical nature of Muir's assertions becomes evident when one realises he is claiming that, not just the individual, but the writer who has experience of more than one language is at a disadvantage when compared to the hypothetically pure individual who knows only one. Although he gives a different meaning to the term 'thought', the pronouncement of a fastidious craftsman such as Paul Valéry can serve, not just to counterpoise Muir's position, but to indicate how out of joint with the times it was:

> What makes poetry so beautiful and so powerful is that it cannot be thought, that is, it never comes to one fully balanced and perfect, combined, liquid, musical and dense. Thought of its nature cannot make poems but at most fragments.[38]

In other words, spontaneous and unmediated utterance, of the kind Muir longed for but believed to be impossible in Scots, was no less impossible for the 'natural' English speaker he so much envied, and with whom he wished to contrast his own situation. The most appropriate interpretation of Muir's views may be as *a taking in of the colonial wound*, whereby Muir places himself in the position of the colonised with respect to canonised English authors, choosing to view himself as lacking, as divided and fissured when set against the wholeness he attributes to the culture of the coloniser. To trace a 'wholeness' of the kind Muir hankers after in the work of Eliot, Pound, Yeats or Auden would, of course, be a fruitless task.

Perverse as it was, Muir's hypothesis can be seen to have had a liberating influence. If, in the eyes of committed nationalists, writing in English became a 'quisling' choice, then branding English, in the work of Scottish poets, as an alien medium paradoxically freed writers like Norman MacCaig or Edwin Morgan from the need to handle issues of national belonging in their poetry. Not only his Glasgow origins, but his choice of language gave the impression that Morgan had arrived from 'somewhere else'. MacCaig got the chance to develop his own very personal poetics without specific reference to the ideas or the productions of the Scottish Renaissance Movement. The position of those who chose to write in Scots was, however, more problematic. The medium, due in no small measure to the influence of Soutar, lost the position at the vanguard of innovation it arguably held at the time of the Depression. Both Robert Garioch and Sydney Goodsir Smith were confronted with a language not just powerfully stigmatised in terms of its social use, but also burdened with an overpowering weight of specific national identification. Choosing Scots for their poetry meant they had to seek accommodation with the ambiguous heritage of the Renaissance Movement, with its awkward combination of passionate ambition and ambivalent achievement. For them, writing in Scots was fraught with problems from the very start. Goodsir Smith's way forward lay through reinventing the language unscrupulously in terms of a strongly personal idiolect, one which bore little relation to cultural or social realities. Garioch's path was a longer and slower one. Identification with the eighteenth century and a consistent urge to refine his linguistic medium to a degree of standardisation meant that he distanced himself more and more from his immediate predecessors. Painstaking and, in the end, outstandingly successful toil as a translator was a not insignificant element in this process.

Among Soutar's most enduring achievements is his lyric 'The Tryst'. Much can be learnt from it about his actual practice, whether conscious or unconscious, and about the extent to which his poetics differed from those of MacDiarmid. What makes the lyric so appealing is the more or less irresistible temptation of a biographical reading, in terms of the frustrations experienced by the man Soutar, and the extent to which his illness condemned him to what was effectively the life of a eunuch. The female figure in the poem, in the last analysis, belongs in the company of 'La Belle Dame Sans Merci' of Keats's poem, elusive, ungraspable and haunting, a kind of succubus who can never be possessed and whose ultimate legacy, as with the knight waking on a cold hillside, is one of loss and abandonment. Soutar would almost certainly have been familiar with Keats's poem, yet his deployment of the vernacular and a characteristic vagueness, a suffusing of contours, give the Scots lyric a popular allure.

The motif of the night visitor crops up in a range of different folk traditions and in the cultivated poems composed as calques of these. It can be found in 'Wo die schönen Trompeten blasen' ('Where the Beautiful Trumpets Blare', though the original title was 'Unbeschreibliche Freude' or 'Indescribable Joy'), a poem from the *Des Knaben Wunderhorn* collection put together by Clemens Brentano and his brother-in-law Achim von Arnim and published in 1805–8.[39] Some readers will be familiar with it in the musical setting by Gustav Mahler. A girl gets up as dawn is breaking to admit her lover to the house. He claims to be going off to the wars, but the ending of the poem, in which he refers to his home of green turf, is ambivalent. There is a clear implication that he has already died.

A still more significant instance of the night visitor is 'Mir träumte von einem Königskind' ('I Dreamt of a King's Daughter'), poem XLI from the 'Lyrisches Intermezzo' in the *Buch der Lieder* of German Jewish poet Heinrich Heine (1797–1856). The poem is worth quoting in full:

Mir träumte von einem Königskind',
Mit nassen, blassen Wangen;
Wir saßen unter der grünen Lind',
Und hielten uns liebumfangen.

'Ich will nicht deines Vaters Thron,
Und will nicht sein Scepter von Golde,
Ich will nicht seine demantene Kron',
Ich will dich selber, du Holde!'

Das kann nicht seyn, sprach sie zu mir,
Ich liege ja im Grabe,
Und nur des Nachts komm' ich zu dir,
Weil ich so lieb dich habe.[40]

A more or less literal translation could be:

I dreamt about a king's daughter,
With wet, white cheeks;
We sat beneath the green lime tree,
And embraced one another lovingly.

'I do not want your father's throne,
I do not want his golden sceptre,
I do not want his diamond crown,
It is you I want, beautiful one!'

That cannot be, she told me,
I am already lying in my grave,
And I only come at night to you,
Because I love you so much.

It is worth repeating that what concerns us at this point is the relevant framework within which to read Soutar's poem, and what this reveals about his practice. A bourgeois or petty bourgeois poet, residing in a city or a large town, imitates the modes and tone of folk poetry as he perceives them, but for a different audience, and with diffusion through the very different medium of print in mind. No matter how much his lyric aims to resemble, to appear the same as its model, it is radically other. Soutar's relationship to the ballads, or to Scottish oral tradition, is no more simple or straightforward than Heine's to German folk poetry. To speak merely of influence is misleading. If anything, this is an appropriation which takes place, not just across a boundary between the urban (or the small town) and the rural, but also, and more crucially, across a boundary of class.

Excessive preoccupation with issues of national regeneration and national identity means that an analysis of Scottish literature during the interwar period, and of the Scottish Renaissance Movement, in terms of class agency and class antagonisms, has not yet been attempted. Nor will it be here! Even to enter upon such a discussion would risk extending this book beyond all reasonable bounds. Preliminary speculations in this direction, though, suggest that to idealise the relationship of a poet such as Soutar to popular balladry, and to use the latter as a means of validating his work, is a risky and a problematic enterprise. That relationship stands at the very heart of European Romanticism, yet it is one we must be wary of 'believing in' as its practitioners may have believed in it. One advantage of referring to the German-speaking countries rather than to the British Isles is that one can thus highlight the anomalous interchange between a fascination with oral literature and effective nation-building which characterises Scotland. It is as if the two phases had occurred at a considerable distance of time from one another. Though Soutar's aspirations might link him to the early nineteenth century, they cannot but be read within the context of the period between the wars.

The simplicity of Soutar's work, and the point bears repeating, is a deceptive simplicity. His lyrics are condemned to an underlying complexity, to a longing backward glance towards the unattainable. This is, indeed, the fate of much pastoral writing in the European languages. Yet if such pastoralism is characteristic of the Scottish Renaissance Movement, it cannot serve to conceal the chasm that opens up between the aesthetic practices of Soutar and other cultivated balladeers like him and the Movement's founder and spokesman, Hugh MacDiarmid. Rarely can two such friends and associated figures have exhibited such divergent tendencies.

The framework proposed here for reading Soutar's lyrics is largely speaking valid for the work of Violet Jacob (1863–1946) and Marion Angus (1866–1946).[41] Both women were well into middle age by the time MacDiarmid's first lyrics appeared in print. Both appropriated lyrical tones and modes to which they were alien in terms of both class and linguistic medium. Jacob came from an aristocratic landowning family, the Kennedy-Erskines of Mar, whose splendid mansion, the House of Dun, can still be visited in its position above the basin of Montrose, within view of the North Sea. The daughter of a United Free

Presbyterian Minister, Angus may well have been born south of the border in Sunderland. She came from a poorly paid stratum of the professional classes, condemned to vagrancy by the very nature of their employment. Her gender made a vagrant and an exile of Violet Jacob. Unable to inherit the family estate, she followed her hussar husband to India in the service of the British Empire and then to the Welsh Marches, before returning to her native Angus in the last years of her life.

MacDiarmid examines the work of both these poets in a series of essays surveying the state of Scottish culture in the mid-1920s, literary, musical and visual, published in collected form as *Contemporary Scottish Studies* in 1926. Marred by a degree of sexism and by the self-promoting, Wagnerian egocentrism which characterised MacDiarmid's polemical writings throughout his life, his assessment nonetheless constituted the only serious discussion of either poet for nearly half a century. He views Jacob's work as 'far from being merely sentimental' even if 'she may seem through her choice of subject and angle of treatment to be merely a belated and etherealised Kailyairder', and perceptively links her to the tradition of aristocratic women whose work had imitated and sought to blend with the tones of popular poetry: 'Mrs Jacob belongs by birth and breeding to the company which includes Lady Grisel Baillie, Lady Nairne, Lady Ann Lindsay, Lady Wardlaw, Jean Elliot...'[42] Though the content of her work 'for the most part belongs to a mass which is so bad as to be beneath criticism', nonetheless Jacob's 'technique raises it, ever so unobtrusively, to a plane upon which it acquires a definite if almost indefinable value'.[43] Jacob played a significant role in prising Scots poetry away from the tyranny of the Burns stanza. Even if he turned what he learnt to very different ends, MacDiarmid's debt, or even dependence, on her is easily seen when comparing the ending of her 'The Guidwife Speaks':

> An' yet, an' yet, I dreid tae see
> The ingle standin' toom; oh, then   *fireside corner; empty*
> Youth's last left licht wad gang wi' ye –   *go*
> What wad I dae? I dinna ken.   *know*

with that of MacDiarmid's 'The Widower':

> For Guid's sake, Jean, wauken up!
> A word frae your mou'
> Has knit my gantin' timbers   *yawning*
> Thegither or noo.[44]

One need only, however, read 'Tam i' the Kirk' alongside Goethe's 'Heldenröslein', or 'The Wild Geese' alongside the 'Lied vom Winde' written in 1828 by the Swabian poet Eduard Mörike (1804–75) to see that her debt to Romanticism is no less than Soutar's.[45] Her 'The Northern Lichts' reads like a gentler, no longer tragic return to Goethe's 'Erlkönig'. There is no basis for thinking that a woman of Jacob's class and education would not have been familiar with Goethe's poems and with their musical settings by Schubert. An aspiration to become song once more is, of course, typical for artificially simple, cultivated lyrics of this kind.[46] Like Jacob's, Mörike's poem is cast as a dialogue with the wind, where the speaker first enquires about its homeland, and then about the homeland of love. At the close, the wind, rushing on impatiently, promises to greet the speaker's beloved if it should come across her. The comparison need not diminish our understanding of Jacob's achievement. She introduces new elements into the inherited, or imitated, pattern. One is the by now familiar polemic against industrialism and the way in which it has uprooted rural populations, absorbing them into towns and cities. London, the pulsing centre of the imperial enterprise so many Scots had chosen to take part in, is a focus of specific animus in Jacob's work. Another is national displacement, the loss of homeland and language:

> 'Oh, tell me what was on yer road, ye roarin' norlan' wind
> As ye cam' blawin' frae the land that's niver frae my mind?
> My feet they trayvel England, but I'm deein' for the north . . .'[47]

Though the speaker may well be conceived of as male, it is not hard to imagine Jacob identifying strongly with his position. Jacob's technical skill is evident in the way the two voices are handled, that of the wind coming to occupy nearly all of the last stanza, till the questioner breaks in and asks it to be quiet.

If the Romantic background to Jacob's practice is unquestionable, and her distance from Modernism no less than Soutar's, Marion Angus's case is somewhat different. With her the borrowed modes are moulded, wittingly or unwittingly (and the limited evidence available hardly indicates that Angus realised the radical potential of her work) into a vocabulary for expressing a profoundly troubled subjectivity, one which foregrounds its female gendering without seeking confirmation through opposition to the male. The dynamics of Angus's poetry are intragender rather than between genders. Its eerie fascination comes from juxtaposing manifestations of the self, in different roles and at different stages in existence, presented as distinct and separate people. In

'Hogmanay', one cannot be sure whether the young girl knocking at the door is anything other than the fantasy of an unrecoverable self, now vanished into time gone past:

> And tho' an auld wife maun awhilie greet   *weep*
> Ye'll aye gang limber an' licht an' free –   *go*
> Canny bit lassie that aince wis me.[48]   *shrewd*

The three figures of 'Candlemas', the old woman, the young girl who has in her turn become old, and the new youngster who passes by, are portrayed as distinct from one another, yet one's impression on reading the poem is of a fluidity which prevents clear boundaries being defined. 'Waater o' Dye' is perhaps Angus's most startling lyric. Any imputation of lesbian undercurrents is likely to be as inaccurate as it would be anachronistic, given the environment in which the poet spent most of her life. The blending into another woman, who lived at a time in the distant past and whose experience of love and childbirth the speaker is able in this fashion to penetrate and even appropriate, does, however, go beyond conventional understanding of what interpersonal relationships can bring:

> Waater o'Dye, whaur ye rin still
> On me she warks her auncient will;
> What I hae niver kent, I ken –   *known; know*
> The feel o' babes, the luve o' men.[49]

And 'The Eerie House', which makes the acceptance, introjection and maintenance of prohibition the very cornerstone of subjectivity, shows us Angus struggling to find words for an experience of being which, if it takes its point of departure in gender specificity, ranges far beyond in its search for some kind of stability. The end result, in poems such as 'Huntly Wood' or 'The Sea Graveyard', is disembodiment. One need only read the latter poem alongside MacDiarmid's 'Crowdieknowe'[50] to perceive how Angus has moulded similar material with admirable subtlety, in the direction of an imagery of absence with its own inimitable link to Modernity.

    Neither Jacob nor Angus identified either privately or in public with the Scottish Renaissance Movement. Helen Burness Cruickshank, often grouped with these two though perhaps a lesser poet, acted as host and handmaiden to it, taking a practical interest in MacDiarmid's welfare after the collapse of both his first marriage and his career in journalism.[51] As the Movement itself remained overwhelmingly male in self-conception and in focus, the work of these marginalised female figures was affected by an amnesia not totally dispelled today. Their poetry is still not available in published form other than in anthologies. This marginalisation was a further shortcoming of MacDiarmid's planned regeneration. Its effects during the latter half of the postwar period should not be underestimated. When, in the person of Liz Lochhead, a woman at last came to occupy an uncontested space on the poetic scene, she had little awareness of Scottish predecessors, and had to invent herself, and her speaking position, more or less from scratch. Notwithstanding Lewis Grassic Gibbon's outstanding impersonation of a female perspective in his fictional trilogy *A Scots Quair*, an impressive instance of 'cross-writing', as opposed to 'cross-dressing', nonetheless surrounded by an aura of androgynous ambivalence, the Movement had little to offer women writers of subsequent generations. Not until the century's last two decades was reassessment of the legacy of MacDiarmid, Soutar and Muir counterpoised by consideration of the achievements of Jacob, Angus and Cruickshank, and of the novelists Catherine Carswell, Willa Muir, Nan Shepherd and Naomi Mitchison.

Before proceeding further, it will be useful to summarise the assessment this chapter offers of the interwar years, and of the complex and ambiguous legacy of the Scottish Renaissance Movement. MacDiarmid's political and cultural radicalism was increasingly marginalised after 1928. Though it cannot match MacDiarmid's in either range or depth, Soutar's poetry, with its rejection of the literary avant-garde and its proposal of a purist and essentialist view of national identity and culture, not without a distinct racial element, is emblematic of the change. If Scottish poets, and writers more generally, failed at this time to grasp the advantages of hybridisation and impurity, they also failed to conceptualise the linguistic situation of Scottish poetry other than in terms of the necessary hegemony of one single language. Here MacDiarmid's championing in turn of Scots and Gaelic is symptomatic. The rejection of industrialism and of the associated urban society drove writers in the direction of a timeless pastoralism. This was a further aspect of the problematic nature of the Movement's relationship to Modernity and moreover disenfranchised large segments of Scotland's population in terms of cultural representation. Their lives were judged unfit to image Scotland. In gender terms, the work of women poets suffered a marginalisation which effectively continues to this day. Though each of these points would require adjustment if the discourse were broadened to embrace prose fiction, they would nonetheless retain a degree of relevance. Such an assessment, while sobering, is not unduly critical, and offers a valid point of departure for considering the work of the wartime and postwar poets. Those who chose to move on from the bases laid by the Scottish Renaissance Movement were forced to tussle with its powerful yet ambiguous legacy. Others, among them MacCaig, Morgan and Crichton Smith, adopted a tangential approach, or else created for themselves a poetics and a cultural stance to which that movement had only minimal relevance.

Notes

1. The standard edition is the *Complete Poems* edited by M. Grieve and W. R. Aitken (2 vols. London, Martin Brian and O'Keeffe 1978). MacDiarmid's correspondence is published in Alan Bold ed. *The Letters of Hugh MacDiarmid* (London, Hamish Hamilton 1984) and Dorian Grieve, Owen Dudley Edwards and Alan Riach eds *Hugh MacDiarmid: New Selected Letters* (Manchester, Carcanet 2001). See also Duncan Glen ed. *Selected Essays of Hugh MacDiarmid* (London, Jonathan Cape 1969), Alan Riach ed. *Selected Prose* (Manchester, Carcanet 1992) and Angus Calder, Glen Murray and Alan Riach eds *The Raucle Tongue: Hitherto Uncollected Prose* (3 vols. Manchester, Carcanet 1996–8). Extensive sections of MacDiarmid's autobiographical writings have been published as *Lucky Poet* (London, Methuen 1943). The standard biography is Alan Bold *MacDiarmid: a Critical Biography* (London, John Murray 1988). See also Gordon Wright *MacDiarmid: an Illustrated Biography of Christopher Murray Grieve* (Edinburgh, Gordon Wright Publishing 1977).
2. See K. D. Duval and Sydney Goodsir Smith eds *Hugh MacDiarmid: a Festschrift* (Edinburgh, K. D. Duval 1962) and Duncan Glen *Hugh MacDiarmid and the Scottish Renaissance* (Edinburgh and London, Chambers 1964), also Paul H. Scott and A. C. Davis eds *The Age of MacDiarmid: Essays on Hugh MacDiarmid and his Influence on Contemporary Scotland* (Edinburgh and London, Scottish Academic Press 1972). The available monographs include Edwin Morgan *Hugh MacDiarmid* (Harlow, British Council 1976), Anne Edwards Boutelle *Thistle and Rose: a Study of Hugh MacDiarmid's Poetry* (Loanhead, Macdonald 1980), Kenneth Buthlay *Hugh MacDiarmid* (Edinburgh, Scottish Academic Press 1982), Alan Bold *MacDiarmid: the Terrible Crystal* (London, Boston, Routledge and Kegan Paul 1983), Catherine Kerrigan *Whaur Extremes Meet: the Poetry of Hugh MacDiarmid* (Edinburgh, Mercat Press 1983), Nancy K. Gish *Hugh MacDiarmid: the Man and his Work* (London and Basingstoke, Macmillan 1984), Harvey Oxenhorn *Elemental Things: the Poetry of Hugh MacDiarmid* (Edinburgh, Edinburgh University Press 1984), Roderick Watson *MacDiarmid* (Milton Keynes, Open University Press 1985), Peter McCarey *Hugh MacDiarmid and the Russians* (Edinburgh, Scottish Academic Press 1987) and, in the 1990s, Alan Riach *Hugh MacDiarmid's Epic Poetry* (Edinburgh, Edinburgh University Press 1991) and W. N. Herbert *To Circumjack MacDiarmid: the Poetry and Prose of Hugh MacDiarmid* (Oxford, Oxford University Press 1992).
3. See for example Aileen Christianson, 'Flyting with *A Drunk Man*' in *Scottish Affairs 5* (Autumn 1993) pp. 126–35.
4. A very rough calculation would suggest not more than 400 pages in the nearly 1,450 pages of the *Complete Poems*.

5. See Kenneth Buthlay ed. *A Drunk Man Looks at the Thistle: Annotated Edition* (Edinburgh, Scottish Academic Press 1987).

6. See Bold *MacDiarmid: a Critical Biography* (Note 1), pp. 180–6 on the genesis of the poem. Scott's account is contained in an autobiographical letter dated 20 May 1945 and deposited in the Maurice Lindsay archive at the National Library of Scotland. See also Maurice Lindsay *Francis George Scott and the Scottish Renaissance* (Edinburgh, Paul Harris 1980) pp. 54–5.

7. See Bold ibid., pp. 231–8.

8. Important in this respect is the essay 'English Ascendancy in British Literature', first published by T. S. Eliot in *The Criterion* in 1931, reprinted in *Selected Prose* pp. 61–80.

9. From the last paragraph but one of *Albyn: or Scotland and the Future* (1927), now in Hugh MacDiarmid *Albyn: Shorter Books and Monographs* ed. Alan Riach (Manchester, Carcanet 1996) p. 38.

10. See Kerrigan (Note 2), pp. 87–9, 98–9.

11. *Complete Poems*, p. 29.

12. See the version from the German of Else Lasker-Schuler incorporated in the text of *A Drunk Man* (lines 401ff.)

13. Ruth Z. Temple *The Critic's Alchemy: a Study of the Introduction of French Symbolism in England* (New York, Twayne 1953) and the anthology edited by Cyrena N. Pondrom *The Road from Paris: French Influence on English Poetry 1900–1920* (Cambridge, Cambridge University Press 1974) are helpful in this respect.

14. On MacDiarmid and Dostoevsky see Chapter 1 of McCarey (Note 2).

15. Marcel Proust *À la recherche du temps perdu* II *À l'ombre des jeunes filles en fleurs* (Paris, Gallimard 1954) p. 111.

16. See Buthlay's edition p. 190.

17. Edwin Muir *Scottish Journey* with an introduction by T. C. Smout (Edinburgh, Mainstream 1980) p. 102.

18. Edwin Muir *An Autobiography* (London, Hogarth Press 1954) pp. 130–1. The passage comes just after the opening of Chapter 4.

19. William Grant ed. *The Scottish National Dictionary* vol.1 (1931) p. xxvii.

20. Carl MacDougall and Douglas Gifford eds *Into a Room: Selected Poems of William Soutar* (Glendaruel, Argyll Publishing 2000) pp. 88–9. Poems are quoted from this source unless otherwise stated.

21. *Albyn*, pp. 29, 4.

22. G. Gregory Smith *Scottish Literature: Character and Influence* (London, Macmillan 1919) pp. 4, 5, 19.

23. See 'Ane Guid New Sang in Preise of Professor Gregory Smith, Inventor of the Caledonian Antisyzygy': 'the richt word in a Scotsman's mouth/ is Antisyzygygygy' (Robert Garioch *Complete Poetical Works* (Edinburgh, Macdonald 1983) p. 153).

24. William Soutar *Diaries of a Dying Man* ed. Alexander Scott (Edinburgh and London, Chambers 1954) p. 74 (entry for 18 October 1934).

25. See the description in the biography by Alexander Scott *Still Life* (Edinburgh and London, Chambers 1958) pp. 88–9.

26. Soutar's *Diaries*, p. 113 (entry for 14 June 1937).

27. See for example the 'Introduction' to *Into a Room*, pp. 20ff. The remark occurs on p. 17 of William Soutar *Collected Poems* ed. with an introductory essay by Hugh MacDiarmid (London, Andrew Dakers 1948). Earlier on the same page

MacDiarmid also insists that, in speaking of Soutar as a 'minor classic . . . The adjective "minor" must be stressed.'

28. See Edwin Muir *Collected Poems 1921–58* (London, Faber 1984) p. 179.

29. The question merits precise discussion. Soutar writes of 'moments of magnanimous lust' (*Diaries*, p. 108, entry for 1 January 1937) and sees himself as 'blessed . . . with a full-blooded virility which is incompatible with my stagnant bodily state' (p. 55, entry for 2 May 1933). Rather than being a sexless individual, Soutar was one whose sexuality was rigorously restricted and restrained in its expression by the conditions of his life (no less rigorously than by any potential vow of chastity). The issue is dealt with sensitively in Chapter 4 of Scott's biography.

30. Soutar's *Diaries*, p. 50 (entry for 28 January 1933).

31. Ibid. p. 157 (entry for 11 October 1940).

32. Scott quotes (*Still Life*, pp. 65–6) a diary entry from 22 July 1924 describing how Soutar's father, about to lead family worship, launches spontaneously into Burns's 'The Lea Rig', 'leaning back in his chair with the Bible clasped in his hands; Mum with eyes shut and myself with head going from side to side'. The effortlessness with which worship of the Creator blends into worship of the national bard is eloquent of a specific structuring of religious affiliation and national identity.

33. Soutar's *Diaries*, p. 118 (entry for 2 November 1937).

34. See, for example, 'Apotheosis', from 1931, with clear echoes such as 'yowdendrift', 'watergaw' and 'auld-farand blethers/ O' gowdan feathers', and 'The earth hings like a keekin'-glass', from 1933, which makes the same attempt to counterfeit the 'cosmic' lyrics from MacDiarmid's collections. That this was not a passing phase is shown by 'Bairntime' from 1941, the year of Soutar's death, with its echoing of 'O Jesu Parvule' from *Sangschaw* (*Complete Poems* I, 31). For these Soutar lyrics see W. R. Aitken ed. *Poems of William Soutar: a New Selection* (Edinburgh, Scottish Academic Press 1988) pp. 207, 217, 239.

35. See *Still Life*, p. 116.

36. Soutar's *Diaries*, p. 50 (entry for 28 January 1933).

37. Edwin Muir *Scott and Scotland: the Predicament of the Scottish Writer* with an introduction by Allan Massie (originally 1936; Polygon, Edinburgh 1982) pp. 8–9. An indication of the attention Muir's arguments continued to command, at the time of this reprinting, is that a double number of literary magazine *Chapman* was given over to a debate on 'The State of Scotland: a Predicament for the Scottish Writer?' See *Chapman* 35–6 (vol. VII nos. 5–6, July 1983).

38. Paul Valéry *Cahiers* ed. Judith Robinson (Paris, Gallimard 1974) II p. 1061 (my translation).

39. Clemens Brentano *Sämtliche Werke und Briefe* (Stuttgart, Berlin, Köln and Mainz, W. Kohlhammer 1977) vol. 8, p. 113.

40. Heinrich Heine *Buch der Lieder* ed. Ralph Tymms (Manchester, Manchester University Press 1967) pp. 68–9.

41. The work of neither poet is currently in print, though Carol Anderson has edited *Jacob's Diaries and Letters from India 1895–1900* (Edinburgh, Canongate 1990) and her novel *Flemington* (Glasgow, Association for Scottish Literary Studies 1994). Jacob's best known collection is *Songs of Angus* (London, John Murray 1915); her work may be consulted in *The Scottish Poems of Violet Jacob* (Edinburgh and London, Oliver and Boyd 1915). For Marion Angus, see *Selected Poems of Marion Angus* ed. Maurice Lindsay with a personal memoir by Helen

B. Cruickshank (Edinburgh, Serif Books 1950), also Christopher Whyte 'Marion Angus and the Boundaries of Self' in Douglas Gifford and Dorothy McMillan eds *A History of Scottish Women's Writing* (Edinburgh, Edinburgh University Press 1997) pp. 373–88.

42. For samples of the work of all but one of these predecessors see Catherine Kerrigan *An Anthology of Scottish Women Poets* (Edinburgh, Edinburgh University Press 1991).

43. From an article first published in 17 July 1925, now in Hugh MacDiarmid *Contemporary Scottish Studies* ed. with an introduction by Alan Riach (Manchester, Carcanet 1995) pp. 27–34.

44. *Scottish Poems*, p. 10 and *Complete Poems* I, p. 56.

45. The poem dates from 1828 and was set to music by Hugo Wolf. See Eduard Mörike *Sämtliche Werke* (München, Carl Hanser 1954) p. 49.

46. 'The Wild Geese' (alternative title 'The Norlan' Wind'), as well as 'Rohallion' and Helen Burness Cruickshank's poem 'Up the Noran Water' are all set to music in Jim Reid's 1984 album *I Saw the Wild Geese Flee* (Springthyme Records, Kingskettle, Fife).

47. *Scottish Poems*, p. 82.

48. *Selected Poems*, p. 30.

49. Ibid., p. 19.

50. Ibid., p. 7 and *Complete Poems* I, p. 26.

51. See Helen B. Cruickshank *Octobiography* (Montrose, Standard Press 1976) and Bold (*Letters*) pp. 283–4, 291–2.

4

The 1940s
(Sorley MacLean, Edwin Muir,
George Campbell Hay)

Few people would argue with the assertion that English poets writing about the Second World War (where are they?) failed to match the achievements of Owen, Sassoon or Rosenberg in their treatment of the First. The reverse is true for Scotland. Though it may be hard to believe, the finest poetry inspired by the conflict to emerge from the British Isles was undoubtedly written in Gaelic, by Sorley MacLean (1911–96) and George Campbell Hay (1915–84).

War service had a dramatic effect on the lives of both men. While *Dàin do Eimhir agus Dàin eile* (*Poems to Eimhir and Other Poems*) (1943) was being prepared for the press, MacLean was seriously wounded at the battle of El Alamein, in North Africa. At the time the book appeared, he was convalescing in a military hospital near Inverness. Responsibility for editing the volume devolved largely upon Douglas Young, who had suffered a prison sentence for refusing to accept conscription on the basis of his nationalist beliefs. MacLean later increasingly distanced himself from the collection and its contents and even expressed a degree of indifference in the run-up to publication. His attitude to the sequence which is the backbone of the book remained ambivalent and, with the exception of one missing item, it was not published in its entirety until 2003.[1]

Campbell Hay eluded the call-up for as long as possible, taking to the Argyllshire hills until he was finally rounded up. His attitude to Britain's war was bound to have an effect on his life within the ranks. It was a considerable time before his outstanding talents as a linguist and interpreter were put to use and an application for transfer to the Intelligence Corps met, predictably, with a rejection. Nevertheless, it can be argued that contact with the Arab world of North Africa was the single most important event in his career as a poet.

It served to give a wider and sobering context to the unthinking, radical nationalism that informed so much of his work. His crowning achievement ought to have been *Mochtàr is Dùghall* (*Mokhtâr and Dougall*), an extended poem in which he planned to set two ordinary soldiers, an Arab and a Scottish Gael, side by side – two marginal figures, in their different ways alien to the banner under which they fought. Hay, however, suffered a nervous breakdown in Thessaloniki, northern Greece in May or early June 1946.[2] He was convinced that his life was in danger because he had regularly fraternised with the local republicans and witnessed a violent attack on a group of these. The experience precipitated what may well have been a latent mental instability. Only sections of the project which, interestingly, in the main concern the Arab soldier, had been completed at this stage.

Despite the catastrophe of the blitz on Clydebank, Scotland was distant, in geographical terms, from the theatres of conflict. The adhesion of poets and intellectuals to a war which saw British troops pitted against the forces of totalitarianism across the globe, while in eastern Europe the forces of another totalitarian regime fought as their allies, was anything but unanimous. Norman MacCaig (1910–96) remained a conscientious objector throughout the war years. Edwin Morgan (1920–), having initially resolved to do the same, changed his mind and served in the Medical Corps, given that he would not be required to take human life there. His experience of the military was liberating in a sexual and personal sense. The period spent in the Middle East inspired what is probably his most enigmatic collection, one to which little attention has so far been paid, *The New Divan* (1977). Hugh MacDiarmid abandoned his Shetland exile to work in a munitions factory in Glasgow. His archives had to be packed away, and sections of the manuscript of *In Memoriam James Joyce* were lost or damaged in the process. A completed version of the poem saw the light in 1955.

The translating work on which Edwin Muir (1887–1959) and his wife had relied for their livelihood came to an end in 1940. In March 1942 he began working for the British Council in Edinburgh, organising programmes for the centres established there to bring together refugees from the occupied nations of central and eastern Europe. Appointed to take charge of the British Institute in Prague in the aftermath of the war, he made a journey by car through a devastated Germany which acquires an epic quality in the powerful description in his *Autobiography*.[3] Rather than the experience of conflict, it was seeing the longer-term effects of the postwar settlement that marked Muir's poetry. The fate of Czechoslovakia, and by analogy the fate of other countries which fell under Russian domination, gave him a theme that could activate quite naturally his knowledge of German language writers such as Kafka and Hölderlin. It also linked in with his memories of a small community in his native Orkney. The result was a body of poems which penetrate central European experience in a manner that would be unthinkable without Muir's Scottish background. His understanding of the histories of disappeared or disappearing nations was both profound and sympathetic because he came from such a nation himself.

Iain Crichton Smith described *Dàin do Eimhir agus Dàin eile* as 'the greatest Gaelic book of this century'.[4] This is no exaggeration. As an individual, MacLean was both bilingual and bicultural.[5] He exploited his position in a poetic sequence which draws on the achievements of high Modernism and European Symbolism. It revives tropes and attitudes of the Provençal troubadours in a manner indebted to Pound, while also taking note of Scottish Modernism in MacDiarmid's work of the 1920s. At the same time, it mobilises elements of the Gaelic tradition, in particular anonymous song and the work of the eighteenth-century love poet William Ross. Although MacLean was very much cast as a representative of Gaelic Scotland when his writing was rediscovered and justly celebrated in the 1980s and afterwards, the resulting mix is comparatively unGaelic, élitist rather than populist, and permeable only with difficulty to the community which uses the language in its day to day existence.

The Eimhir poems were printed in 1943 in a numbered sequence from I to LX, with fourteen gaps, followed by a 'Dimitto'. Three of the omitted poems were released in 1970.[6] Their theme, alluded to rather than directly expressed, appears to be the effects of a problematic abortion, and this may have motivated their exclusion. In 1977 MacLean included a limited, and in 1989 a more generous selection from the sequence in retrospective volumes. But their source was not explicitly named, and they were supplied with titles. Not until after his death could the sequence as a whole be republished. Yet it is only in this larger context that the meaning and implications of individual items can be fully grasped.[7]

More or less concurrently with the sequence, which seems to have been written down with the immediacy and spontaneity, the naturalness of Petrarch's *rime sparse*, MacLean worked on an ambitious project entitled 'An Cuilithionn'. Its concerns are the culture and history of the island of Skye, and the traditions of political radicalism there and on the broader European scene. Conversations with Sydney Goodsir Smith in Edinburgh about the abortive 1944 rising in Warsaw and the ambivalent conduct of the Russian forces in that context brought MacLean's disillusionment with communism to a head, making any resumption of the project unthinkable. He allowed 'what I think tolerable of it' to be published in *Chapman* magazine between 1987 and 1989. One is left with the impression that his conscious, politically engaged self was busy with 'An Cuilthionn', the kind of poetry he felt he ought to be writing, while the Eimhir sequence, one of whose themes is the manner in which even unrequited love can eat away at, and ultimately undermine, political commitment, emerged almost of its own accord, an unplanned and (by the poet) unacknowledged masterpiece.

Born in 1911 on Raasay, a small island to the east of Skye, MacLean, second son of a family of seven, was brought up in a household where details of piping technique and niceties of Gaelic grammar and expression were frequent topics of conversation. His grandmother, a Matheson by birth, lived with the poet's family until her death in 1923, and was a fine tradition bearer. Her family had brought with them to Skye many songs from the nearby mainland areas of Lochalsh and Kintail. His father was an excellent singer, while the rich store of songs of Peggy, his father's sister, went some way to compensate for her right-wing political beliefs. Among his mother's siblings were two pipers, three fine singers and a poet. The islanders predominantly belonged to the Free Presbyterian church, whose fundamentalist approach to predestination, the role of grace in election and the consequent impotence of all human action where salvation was concerned, inspired the poet with both untiring radicalism and a persistent pessimism. Shelley and Wordsworth were early enthusiasms. Studying for a degree in English literature at Edinburgh University, MacLean heard Herbert Grierson lecture on the Metaphysicals, and produced some English verses in the style of Eliot. He nevertheless judged his Gaelic voice to be more authentic.

James Caird and the philosopher George Davie were contemporaries, and it was thanks to them that MacLean made MacDiarmid's acquaintance. A photograph from a visit to Whalsay in 1935, taken shortly before the older poet's breakdown, shows the two reclining on a grassy bank, no doubt deep in conversation about projects which included the translations of eighteenth-century Gaelic poets Duncan Bàn MacIntyre and Alasdair Mac Mhaighstir Alasdair they had undertaken. In Edinburgh MacLean also met Robert Garioch, who issued their joint pamphlet from a hand press in 1939, under the unassuming title of *17 Poems for 6d*.

The Eimhir sequence was written across a decade between 1931 and 1941. Though as many as three different women are grouped under the name of Cuchulainn's beloved, who figures largely in the Red Branch Irish epic tales, there is good reason to believe that the woman in the opening poem can be identified with the Scotswoman who later comes to dominate the cycle. Eimhir functions as a pseudonym or *senhal* after the fashion of the troubadours. Such pseudonyms were employed because the Provençal poets had specific aristocratic ladies and patronesses in mind, who may well have constituted part of the original audience in front of which their compositions were to be performed. It is peculiarly appropriate that MacLean should have activated links to the period of European literature when, for perhaps the last time until the modern age, Gaelic and Irish language poetry participated on terms of normality and equality in the broader international scene. His sequence is a *canzoniere* in the manner of Petrarch, or of Guido Cavalcanti, but nonetheless with echoes of Ovid and Propertius in the background.

The sequence has four principal themes: unrequited love; the siren call of the struggle against fascism in Spain and Germany; the conflict set up between these two in the speaker's mind, with the subsequent, unconditional victory of the former; and, last but not least, his awareness that, by the very fact of annotating his predicament in verse, he is acquiring the status of a major poet.

That fourth theme must be crucial to any reading of the sequence. Written between 1938 and 1940, *Requiem,* by the Russian poetess Anna Akhmatova, also concerns a profound interior crisis, inspired by tragic personal and political circumstances. In discussing it, Joseph Brodsky highlights the scission as a result of which the writer both experiences painful emotions and distances them, rendering them other and less real, by the very fact of writing:

> Akhmatova is describing the state of the poet who is looking at everything that is happening to her as if she were standing off to one side. For the poet, the writing of this is no less an event than the event she is describing.

Achieving this distance can seem an abomination:

> The writer can suffer his grief in a genuine way, but the description of this grief is not genuine tears or gray hair. It is only an approximation of a genuine reaction, and the awareness of this detachment creates a truly insane situation.[8]

Division is, of course, a recurrent motif throughout the *Dàin do Eimhir* and MacLean has indicated unambiguously that too autobiographical an interpretation of the sequence can be misleading. For all their passionate rhetoric, there is a violently cerebral quality to these poems.

By no stretch of the imagination could they be described as arousing or erotic, and they stretch the definition of 'amorous' to the limit. Literary artifice is constantly and consciously employed. Indeed, the coming into being of the work is one of its principal themes, as has already been stated.

A poem such as XXII offers a helpful example of how biographical details were touched up and heightened in the interests of literary effect. MacLean never faced a clear choice between enlisting as a volunteer in the International Brigade in Spain and enjoying the love of the woman he adored. But here he creates an intellectual double bind which is symptomatic of the speaker's constant, tormented self-analysis. The mental knots he ties himself in are, in their very personal way, a homage to the conceits of Donne and his school. Were he to go to Spain, he would surely die, losing Eimhir as a result. But if he stays, he renders himself unworthy of her love:

> Cha d' ghabh mise bàs croinn-ceusaidh
> an èiginn chruaidh na Spàinn
> is ciamar sin bhiodh dùil agam
> ri aon duais ùir an dàin?

> *I did not take a cross's death*
> *in the hard extremity of Spain*
> *and how then should I expect*
> *the one new prize of fate?*

So he will lose her in any case. The lyric opens with a split, between the speaker and his intellect (gendered as feminine in Gaelic) who always remains 'a little distance' from him. The two engage in a pitiless intellectual debate in which no emotion, no underlying vulnerability is spared. The conclusion insists that, given another chance, the speaker would make a choice which would be wholehearted:

> Ach nan robh 'n roghainn rithist dhomh
> 's mi 'm sheasamh air an àird,
> leumainn à nèamh no iutharna
> le spiorad 's cridhe slàn.

> *But if I had the choice again*
> *and stood on that headland,*
> *I would leap from heaven or hell*
> *with a whole spirit and heart.*

The Gaelic word for 'whole', slàn, also means 'healthy', and represents a kind of unreachable talisman, here as elsewhere in the cycle.

There is an underlying Puritanism in these poems, as if to be preoccupied with personal and sexual fulfilment were indefensible in such a tumultuous historical period. Poem IV presents the beloved, identified here as elsewhere through her 'gold-yellow' hair, singing a traditional song, perhaps in the course of a ceilidh. But it is as if her performance were intended perversely to deaden awareness of the killing of the Asturian miners and the rise to power of tyrants such as Hitler and Mussolini:

> An tugadh t' fhonn no t' àilleachd ghòrmhor
> bhuamsa gràinealeachd marbh nan dòigh seo,
> a' bhrùid 's am meàirleach air ceann na h-Eòrpa
> 's do bhial-sa uaill-dhearg san t-seann òran?

> *Would your song and splendid beauty take*
> *from me the dead loathsomeness of these ways,*
> *the brute and the brigand at the head of Europe*
> *and your mouth red and proud with the old song?*

The speaker cannot chase these events from his mind. They could almost be projected onto a cinema screen behind her. Poem XXX makes a similar point in a more light-hearted way. Even if the speaker were to obtain the republican, post-revolutionary Scotland he desires, he would proclaim his beloved its queen. Love would be enough to make of him a monarchist when all such hereditary distinctions had been abolished.

Poem XXIX, 'Coin is Madaidhean-allaidh'('Dogs and Wolves') is one of two which MacLean claimed, in a letter to Douglas Young, to have written in the middle of the night, in a species of trance, without changing a single word afterwards.[9] It deploys the traditional Gaelic imagery of the hunt in repeated, incantatory syntactic parallelisms:

> gadhair chaola 's madaidhean-allaidh
> a' leum thar mullaichean nan gàrradh,
> a' ruith fo sgàil nan craobhan fàsail,
> a' gabhail cumhang nan caol-ghleann,
> a' sireadh caisead nan gaoth-bheann . . .

> *lean greyhounds and wolves*
> *leaping over the tops of the dykes,*
> *running under the shade of the trees of the wilderness,*

taking the defile of narrow glens,
making for the steepness of windy mountains. . .

Because the hunt represents a psychological process, MacLean is solving a problem faced by all users of a language insufficiently deployed in modern life. In the absence of new vocabulary, it becomes necessary to charge what is available with different resonances, to 're-semanticise' it. If the white deer is Eimhir's beauty, however, and the pack in untiring pursuit of her is his unwritten poems, the implication is clear. Were he to produce these poems and entrap her in them, she would be torn to pieces.

Images of stripping, flaying, laying bare and fragmentation pervade the cycle. The speaker's stated ambition is to write a poetry whose starkness would satisfy the canons of Socialist Realism (Poem XXXII):

> Sgatham le faobhar-roinn gach àilleachd
> a chuir do bhòidhche 'nam bhàrdachd,
> 's dèanam dàin cho lom aognaidh
> ri bàs Liebknecht no daorsa

> *Let me lop off with sharp blade every grace*
> *that your beauty put in my verse,*
> *and make poems as bare and chill*
> *as Liebknecht's death or slavery.*

Yet hair and tree imagery will not be excised. Though the hunt continues ('tòir' and 'tòrachd', which carry this meaning in Gaelic, are recurring terms) what proves most important is, not bringing his chosen quarry to ground, but rather a precious object found by chance, a 'faodail' – the cycle itself. The triumph of the cycle is its own completion, which MacLean unashamedly compares to the finest lyrics of the oral tradition recorded in the nineteenth century by the compiler of the *Carmina Gadelica*, Alexander Carmichael (Poem LIX).

The *Dàin do Eimhir*, however, reach their culmination just before this, in an extended poem (LVII) of exhausting intellectual speculation and heart-searching. Now that Eimhir is lost beyond recovery, and only the memory of his love for her is left, the speaker addresses the problem of forgetfulness, of how to confer immortality on her and his obsession with her by means of verbal art. The exploits of the Red Army on the Dnieper have lost all interest for him. All he can think of is her face, which persists in haunting him.

Within a matter of months of writing that poem, MacLean was fighting in the desert war. A little-known quatrain dated June 1942 and entitled 'Knightsbridge, Libya' suggests that the bleakness of his war poems derives at least in part from the realisation that the woman he loved had deceived him.[10] But they are also informed by a ubiquitous and very masculine compassion, which can even be extended to dead enemies ('Glac a' Bhàis'/'Death Valley'). This led MacLean to pen an elegy to, of all people, a physically insignificant English gunner, in 'Curaidhean' ('Heroes').

A persistent, gentle irony tempers the poem's warmth, rendering it all the more affecting. Explicit reference is made to the traditional praise of a Gaelic warrior in Silis na Ceapaich's seventeenth-century elegy for Alasdair of Glengarry, hero of the battle of Sheriffmuir.[11] Though good looks and physical prowess were expected in a Highland chieftain, MacLean insists that the Englishman, devoid of both, deserves no less than they to have the old, heroic vocabulary applied to him:

> Fear beag truaigh le gruaidhean pluiceach
> is glùinean a' bleith a chèile,
> aodann guireanach gun tlachd ann –
> còmhdach an spioraid bu tréine.

> *A poor little chap with chubby cheeks*
> *and knees grinding each other,*
> *pimply unattractive face –*
> *garment of the bravest spirit.*

The tenderness of this tribute is never allowed to descend into sentimentality. The rephrasing of a line from the earlier poem is telling in this respect. 'Thug thu 'n-diugh gal air mo shùilean', says the model ('You forced weeping on my eyes today'). MacLean writes, at the conclusion of his elegy, 'Thug thu gal *beag* air mo shùilean', that is, 'You forced *a little* weeping on my eyes' (my italics).

No subsequent period in the poet's life was to match the productivity of the years before 1942. Two landmarks stand out among his later writings: 'Hallaig' (first published in the quarterly magazine *Gairm* in 1952) and the elegy for his brother Calum, ethnographer and convert to Catholicism, who died of cancer in 1960, at the premature age of 45.

The 'Cumha Chaluim Iain MacGill-Eain' consistently deploys short lines and paragraphs, and makes pervasive use of understatement, in such a way as nearly to give one the impression of reading prose. Its stylised repetitions produce an appropriately liturgical quality. If the comparison can be forgiven, the poem constitutes a litany of place names, clan names and personal names. Men and women known to the poet and his brother are remembered as if they must be equally familiar to the reader, who is temporarily elected to membership of the same cultural community. As the ethnographer is said to have done, the elegy turns its back resolutely on the contemporary world, addressing a Gaelic homeland portrayed as still intact. In doing so, it envisages a kind of utopia, where the divisions between Scots and Irish are negated, along with the old tribal hostilities that set MacLeods, MacLeans or MacDonalds at war with one another. Even that most longstanding of hatreds, between Gaelic-speaking and non-Gaelic-speaking Scots, is dissolved, thanks to Calum MacLean's painstaking, affirmative researches:

> On bu mhùirnean thu do 'n Ghàidheal
> bu mhùirnean thu do 'n Ghall.
> On bha t' ùidh anns an duine
> 's nach b' aithne dhut an fhoill,
> no sliomaireachd no sodal stàite,
> rinn thu Gàidheil dhe na Goill.

> *Since you were a favourite with the Gael*
> *you were a favourite with the Gall.*
> *Since you cared for the man*
> *and did not know guile*
> *or sleekitness or fawning for place*
> *you made Gaels of the Galls.*

The elegy's opening mood of puzzlement, though not quite distress, at the idea of the poet's brother being buried in an unfamiliar place, issues in an impulse of generosity, thanks to which his remains become a heartfelt gift to the people and the traditions of Uist.

It was daring of MacLean to attempt with 'Hallaig' a poem on the Clearances, the forced eviction of the Gaelic-speaking peasantry from their ancestral lands at the end of the eighteenth and throughout much of the nineteenth century, since there is no more hackneyed subject in Gaelic poetry. His Eimhir sequence had broken with tradition by linking the personal and the political, setting the two on a collision course, while its verse structures eschew the facile, clinking rhymes of many songs from the Victorian period. Here he returns to a traditional theme, bringing to it the riches gained from completing the love sequence and from his acquaintance with Modernism more generally.

The Gaelic language possesses a characteristic structure by which someone who is a doctor or a lawyer is defined as being 'in his doctor' or 'in her lawyer'. The preposition and possessive adjective are combined

in a single word, ''na' (plural form ''nan' or ''nam'). The Clearances on
Raasay are a distant memory now, and trees have had time to grow
since the former inhabitants were forced onto ships. MacLean uses the
structure to identify these people with the trees which have taken their
place ('tha 'n nigheanan 's am mic 'nan coille', 'their daughters and sons
are a wood'). He suggests that, given the power of his individual
imagination, the deported villagers can continue to be present, on a
mystical, magical level. It is a hugely sad poem, with its celebration of a
landscape eloquent of human injustice and tragedy, and its incantatory
recitation of local toponyms, all but forgotten now. The poet's enemy in
this evocation is time, whose reality he is able to cancel out thanks to
an intimate act of love and piety. The epigraph identifies time with a
deer rooting in the woods round Hallaig. The poem's close suggests
that the miracle it embodies is dependent on the poet's individual consciousness. Its operation will be nullified once he has died:

> 's nuair theàrnas grian air cùl Dhùn Cana
> thig peileir dian á gunna Ghaoil;
>
> 's buailear am fiadh a tha 'na thuaineal
> a' snòtach nan làraichean feòir;
> thig reothadh air a shùil 's a' choille:
> chan fhaighear lorg air fhuil ri m' bheò.
>
> *and when the sun goes down behind Dun Cana*
> *a vehement bullet will come from the gun of Love;*
>
> *and will strike the deer that goes dizzily,*
> *sniffing at the grass-grown ruined homes;*
> *his eye will freeze in the wood,*
> *his blood will not be traced while I live.*

Edwin Muir was obsessed by time throughout his life.[12] He characterised the journey which brought him, as a 14-year-old adolescent,
from his native Orkney to the port of Leith, and thence to Glasgow in
Scotland's industrial heartland, as a paradoxical journey through time:

> I was born before the Industrial Revolution, and am now about
> two hundred years old. But I have skipped a hundred and fifty of
> them. I was really born in 1737, and till I was fourteen no time-
> accidents happened to me. Then in 1751 I set out from Orkney for

Glasgow. When I arrived I found that it was not 1751, but 1901, and that a hundred and fifty years had been burned up in my two days' journey. But I myself was still in 1751, and remained there for a long time. All my life since I have been trying to overhaul that invisible leeway.[13]

Though it only lasted three days, the journey took him across a lapse of a century and a half, from the cooperative, communal society of an island of farmers, to the individualistic, competitive jungle of a capitalist metropolis. If it is understandable that this perspective should have prompted a backward-looking, at times facile deployment of the pastoral mode, prompting analogies with the myth of the Fall and the consequent expulsion of Adam and Eve from the garden of Eden, it is to be regretted that Muir's own poetic practice all too often subsisted in a kind of time warp. By common consent, he reached maturity with *The Labyrinth*, published in 1949, when he had entered on his seventh decade. His earlier work sets off unabashedly from the diction and ideology of the English Romantics at the turn of the eighteenth century. Where prosody is concerned, he wrote during much of his life as if Eliot, Pound and the Modernist generation had not existed. His work is symptomatic of the fact that, within Scotland, innovation and experimentation, until the 1950s, were to be found predominantly in poetry written in Scots and Gaelic rather than English (a situation which subsequently underwent radical change).

Muir's autobiography contains what read like prose sketches for poems subsequently completed. The prose is consistently more imaginative, effective and contemporary than the poems. The paragraph which formed the nucleus of 'The Combat', from the 1949 collection, is a good example, as well as being a helpful corrective to the tendency to interpret Muir's work along the obvious series of binary axes: childhood/ adulthood, innocence/ experience, Orkney/ Glasgow, agriculture/ industry, state of grace/ state of sin:

Another dream also points back to Wyre, but even less directly than these two . . . I was walking with some people in the country, when I saw a shining grey bird in a field. I turned and said in an awed voice, 'It's a heron.' We went towards it, but as it came nearer it spread its tail like a peacock, so that we could see nothing else. As the tail grew I saw that it was not round, but square, an impenetrable grey hedge of feathers; and at once I knew that its body was not a bird's body now, but an animal's, and that behind that gleaming hedge it was walking away from us on four feet padded like a leopard's or a tiger's. Then, confronting it in the field, there appeared an ancient, dirty, earth-coloured animal with a head like that of an old sheep or a mangy dog. Its eyes were soft and brown; it was alone against the splendid-tailed beast; yet it stood its ground and prepared to fight the danger coming towards it, whether that was death or merely humiliation and pain. (end of Chapter One)

The dream is said to date from Muir's time in Orkney, indicating that he had already gained awareness of positive and destructive forces, and of the conflict between them. This awareness cannot therefore be interpreted as a consequence of his expulsion from a rural paradise.

The journey from his native island to the metropolis supplied him with an underlying pattern which he was able to exploit in a variety of ways throughout his writing career. In it, two worlds are separated by a journey. Given that the move from the first to the second is experienced as traumatic, the journey acquires a potential moral significance. Did it come as retribution for sins committed? Was the exchange of one world for the other a consequence of something the speaker did, of guilt incurred, rather than an inexplicable act of God, a decree of destiny?

In 'The Good Town' Muir can be seen applying this pattern to the changes he witnessed in Prague during the years spent there after the Second World War. This was the only one of the Soviet bloc countries where the Communist Party came to power in the wake of a democratic election, rather than through a coup. Muir first saw the city in 1921, during the initial flush of enthusiasm at the establishment of a nation state, after decades of campaigning and struggle by both Czechs and Slovaks within the framework of the Austro-Hungarian empire. The contrast with the city he was forced to leave in 1948, in a state close to mental and physical collapse, could not have been stronger.

The poem falls into four sections, which could conveniently be labelled 'before', 'after', 'how it happened' and 'why it happened'. Yet it is not possible to limit its resonances to Czechoslovakia or to Prague. That city was left miraculously untouched by the war, whereas in the city depicted in the poem bridges are left gaping across a river, as happened, for example, with the bridges across the Danube in Budapest, at the culmination of a protracted and terrible siege.

The town, in its prewar incarnation, cannot be viewed as prelapsarian, lacking knowledge of sin. There is a prison, though it has fallen out of use, and the ravages of time are evident, though mitigated, thanks to a notional pact arrived at by the inhabitants. The damage inflicted in the course of the fighting is presented as if a body had been mutilated:

> Look well. These mounds of rubble,
> And shattered piers, half-windows, broken arches
> And groping arms were once inwoven in walls
> Covered with saints and angels, bore the roof,
> Shot up the towering spire. These gaping bridges
> Once spanned the quiet river . . .

In the town's postwar incarnation, the organic bonds that link human communities have also been severed. Normal intercourse has stopped. The friendliest people are the least to be trusted.

The poem's third section is the most interesting, for the manner in which it presents the perception of political processes typical of a small nation, one to which no role seems to have been assigned in the unfolding drama of world history. Such a nation does not itself wage war. Its men are conscripted in the service of a larger power's interests. Victory, under these circumstances, is an impossibility. War brings with it little more than impotent submission to invasion ('a herd/ Of clumsy-footed beasts on a stupid errand/ Unknown to them or us'). Muir seems to refer to the odd shape of the Czechoslovak state as it emerged from the First World War, with its famously extended and indefensible boundaries, in lines where history is likened to a game of cards, subject to no superior meaning or direction:

> Our fields were like a pack of cheating cards
> Dealt out at random – all we had to play
> In the bad game for the good stake, our life.

There is no way of influencing the hand one will be dealt.

The final section, however, moves beyond passivity, to question what part the city's inhabitants may have played in their fate. The speaker, who counts himself among them, and would appear to be showing a visitor around, repeats his opening words at the close, as if to signal both that we have arrived at the crux of the matter and that his speculations lead nowhere, only round in circles. He puts forward a number of hypotheses: that disaster arrived from elsewhere; that the governed take on the moral and spiritual characteristics of those who govern them; that the scales of good and evil are irrevocably weighted in favour of evil; and, last and most disturbingly, in a sentence that culminates in fine mirror-structure or chiasmus, that one cannot battle against evil without acquiring some of its characteristics:

We have seen
Good men made evil wrangling with the evil,
Straight minds grown crooked fighting crooked minds.
Our peace betrayed us; we betrayed our peace.

'The Interrogation' belongs to the same nightmarish world of a Central Europe forcibly incorporated into the Soviet bloc. It could be an episode from a *film noir* situated at the Iron Curtain. The speakers have only just failed to escape to freedom. Their journey, which aimed to bring them to a better, more desirable world, and should therefore have been the reverse of Muir's from Orkney to Glasgow, has been interrupted. Now they are poised maddeningly on the dividing line between the two, in a predicament which seems to be unending. The imagery hints at a neurosis.

Muir's finest exploitation of this motif of the journey between worlds comes in 'The Labyrinth'. The poem draws on the storehouse of classical Greek myth, rather than on history taking place before the poet's eyes. Its resonances are more personal than communal. In it, the persistent neuroses of which Muir speaks in his autobiography bear fruit. They achieve consummate expression, though no resolution is proposed. The tale of Theseus, who with the help of Ariadne, daughter of King Minos, escaped from the Cretan labyrinth after killing the monstrous creature, half-man half-bull, imprisoned there, provides a starting point. Ariadne, and the thread she gave the hero to help him find his way out from the maze, have however been excised. The poem's first, truly labyrin-thine sentence extends through thirty-five lines. We are told three times (at lines 1, 11 and 23) that the speaker has emerged. Yet if we pay attention to where the utterance locates us, we will see that the sentence enacts a helpless movement out of, then back into, then again out of the underground maze. In consequence the two worlds, which ought to represent a clear opposition, conflate so that 'all seemed a part/ Of the great labyrinth'. The maze is, after all, the ultimate perversion of the motif of the journey. Inside it, unceasing movement roots one to the spot. The description of the daylight world, with its criss-crossing roads and monstrous interiors (reminiscent of totalitarian architecture) shows a debt to Kafka.

If the two worlds have fallen together, the obvious strategy is to create a third one. This is what the speaker does. The vision of a peace-ful, pastoral existence on an island archipelago makes one think of Orkney, but also of the idealised vision of classical Greece in the work of Hölderlin. Once again, what the poem says has to be set against what it enacts. 'That was the real world. I have touched it once.' If he has spent so little time there, how can the speaker describe this world as more real than the one he normally inhabits? He says he could not survive if the maze were not a dream, implying that he engages in a kind of self-delusion in order to continue living. The poem's conclusion brings us back to underground entrapment. When the speaker wakes, one would expect him to find himself in an 'other' world, one different from the maze. His disorientation and displacement imply that no such escape is possible. ('Last night I dreamt I was in the labyrinth,/ And woke far on. I did not know the place.')

It is the tension between assertion and enactment, between what the poem states and what it actually does, that makes 'The Labyrinth' a high point in Muir's poetic career. Though basically deploying traditional blank verse, the opening sentence at last moves beyond the inheritance of the English Victorians to attempt something more modern and experimental.

None of the poems of resolution which followed, in the last collection published during his lifetime, *One Foot in Eden* (1955), has the same tension or ring of truth. The title poem identifies Muir's underlying pattern of worlds and journeys with the Christian doctrine of the *felix culpa*, according to which our first parents' transgression was part of God's larger scale plan, resulting in a world which is, in the last analysis, superior to the one they could have preserved through obedience to his word:

> What had Eden ever to say
> Of hope and faith and pity and love
> Until was buried all its day
> And memory found its treasure trove?

'The Difficult Land', like so much of Muir's work, is couched in the first person plural, and expresses the history of a community which has come to terms with the adverse forces threatening it, in a manner reminiscent of the opening section of 'The Good Town'. One is left with the impression that Muir has turned away from the contemporary world, taking refuge in a pre-existent, comforting ideological system, in a slightly flaccid quietism. All is well, he would appear to say. There was no real reason for the earlier panic and heartsearching.

Such weaknesses can be detected in the most attractive of these late poems of conciliation, 'The Horses'. It shares its title with a poem from Muir's first published collection which contains clear verbal echoes of Coleridge's 'The Rime of the Ancient Mariner', adumbrating a similar philosophy of redemption through closeness to, and spontaneous immersion in, the created, animal world:

And oh the rapture, when, one furrow done,
They marched broad-breasted to the sinking sun!
The light flowed off their bossy sides in flakes;
The furrows rolled behind like struggling snakes.

Little seems to have changed in the poem written three decades later, though evocation of the spectre of an unleashed nuclear conflict, and apparent advocacy of a 'back to the soil' return to subsistence farming, place it firmly in the postwar period.

The first part of the poem sounds not unlike the thunderous preaching of a revivalist minister, with its Biblical language, repetitions and peroration, and the conscious mimicking of the seven days in which God was said to have created the world. The narrative is undermined, however, by a troubling awareness on the reader's part that nuclear war would be unlikely to leave such unaffected pockets here and there along the temperate latitudes, especially if these were connected with bigger land masses in such a way as to render the arrival of the horses possible. What is more, in a poem that purports to deal with moral regeneration, the community is consistently inactive. They are spared, they wait, and the horses arrive. One has no sense of the inner turmoil or perplexed decision-making that go hand in hand with major change, at an individual and a communal level. When at the end we are told that these men and women would not choose to get their old world back, one cannot help reflecting that they are not likely to be consulted. Everything that happened acted upon them rather than through them. They have not contributed to their own fate in any significant way.

Only son of the novelist John MacDougall Hay, George Campbell Hay lost his father at the age of 4.[14] Tarbert Loch Fyne, portrayed in thinly veiled fashion in MacDougall Hay's novel *Gillespie* (1914), was also the place where the poet began picking up Gaelic, in residual use by a pair of maiden aunts, as well as from the local fishermen. He proceeded from Fettes College in Edinburgh to Corpus Christi at Oxford, emerging with a disappointing fourth class degree. Hay translated from different European languages, not disdaining the use of cribs, and tried his hand at writing in several of them. Though he published poems in both Scots and English, his knowledge of Gaelic vocabulary was well nigh encyclopedic, and his work in Gaelic is pre-eminent as a literary achievement. The contents of his four major collections (*Fuaran Sléibh* (*Hillside Springs*) and *Wind on Loch Fyne* (both 1948), *O Na Ceithir Àirdean* (*From the Four Airts*) (1952) and the long poem *Mochtàr is Dùghall* (*Mokhtâr and Dougall*), which lay undiscovered until Derick Thomson brought out a nearly complete edition in 1982) had been written by the time Hay entered a mental institution in 1948. He spent the next twelve years there. Given the mental health problems and alcoholism which dogged him for the remainder of his life, the extent of his continuing productivity, in all three languages, is remarkable.

Hay was a learner of Gaelic. In contrast to MacLean, he does not offer an account of his own experiences or place a projection of himself at the core of his poems. At one level, he is a verbal artist whose feats are resistant to translation. He constellates lines and stanzas in a meticulous and nearly obsessive fashion, making rich use of the assonances between stressed vowels which are the Gaelic equivalent of rhyme, and which can occur in the middle as well as at the end of a line. In this second stanza from 'Siubhal a' *Choire*' ('The Voyaging of the *Corrie*', dating from 1936) a lovingly detailed description of a ship tossed by a storm, assonating vowels are italicised. The spelling itself may be a sufficient indicator to readers who have no Gaelic of the intensity of the verbal music. Little or nothing can be done to reproduce such virtuosity in another language:

> Shìn i a sgòd le cr*ua*s na cr*ua*dhach,
> shìn i 'taobh ri taobh nan st*ua*dhan,
> shìn i 'ce*u*m a che*u*madh ch*ua*ntan.
> > Bh*ua*il i be*u*m le 'be*u*l 's i 'tu*a*irgneadh,
> > thug i s*a*d le sg*a*r a g*ua*ilne,
> > gheàrr i leòn le 'sròin 's i 'l*ua*sgan.

> *She stretched her sheet as hard as steel,*
> *she stretched her side to the sides of the [breakers],*
> *she stretched her stride to pace the oceans.*
> *She struck a blow with her gunnel as she buffeted,*
> *she struck a dunt with the seam of her shoulder,*
> *she clove a wound with her beak as she lurched.*

On another level, Hay is a doctrinaire nationalist, with an intransigent fervour characteristic of the newly converted, who developed a type of poem that was to be enormously influential on both Thomson and the younger generations of Gaelic poets. A picture is presented to us and then imbued with didactic and allegorical significance, frequently by means of a closing caption. The process, with Hay, tends to culminate in an overt moral exhortation to his audience.

'Feachd a' Phrionnsa' (The Prince's Army) describes the forces of Charles Stuart, in the course of the 1745–6 rebellion, setting foot on

English soil for the first time. They unsheath their weapons, turn back to look on Scotland, and make a silent vow of loyalty. The implications for the contemporary world are obvious:

> Is e bu chòir dhuinn stad is tionndadh,
> amharc air ar tìr le dùrachd,
> le gealladh blàth gun bhòst, gun bhùitich,
> is lann ar spioraid theth a rùsgadh,
> seann lann lasairgheal ar dùthcha;
> 's a liuthad bliadhna meirg' is dùsail
> a mhaolaich i san truaill dhùinte.
> B'e 'n dùsal dubh e – seo an dùsgadh.

> *Now is the time when we should stop and turn,*
> *look upon our land with affection and devotion,*
> *with a warm promise without either boasting or threats,*
> *and unsheath the blade of our hot spirit,*
> *the old white-flaming sword of our country;*
> *so many years of rusting and slumber*
> *it has been growing blunt, set fast in its sheath.*
> *It was a wretched slumber – this is the awakening.*

Given the political and historical circumstances, it is hardly surprising that a backward-looking militaristic rhetoric of this kind, with its strikingly phallic imagery, failed to encounter general support. One has a suspicion that, if it had, it might have aligned Scotland with those nationalisms on mainland Europe which failed to resist the temptation of reaching a compromise with the Axis powers, in the hope of emancipating themselves from those they viewed as their oppressors. Though the poet's precarious isolation casts a sobering light on his attitudes, it is clear that his ideological stance placed him in the reactionary, rather than the radical camp. But then, this was a phase of European history in which the task of wedding a commitment to national self-determination in terms of language, politics and culture with the prevalent left-wing ideologies proved insoluble, even where the range of options for theoretical elaboration and debate was infinitely broader than in Scotland.

The very titles of poems such as 'Na trèig do thalamh dùthchais' ('Do not Forsake your Native Land') or 'Fhearaibh 's a mhnài na h-Albann' ('Men and Women of Scotland') assign them to a similar strand in Hay's production. In 'Stoc is Failleanan' ('The Stump and the Shoots') the same allegorical method is deployed to put forward a programme for cultural renewal. Not until the sixth and final stanza are we instructed how to interpret the image it presents. The stump of a tree cut down the previous year is now hidden by the fresh shoots which have grown up around it. It is only a matter of time until birdsong (presumably the equivalent of literary production) will be heard among its leaves:

> Ar cainnt 's ar cultar, car sealain
>   ged rachadh an leagadh buileach,
> cuiridh am freumhan 's an seann stoc dhiubh
>   failleanan snodhaich is duilleach.

> *Our speech and our culture,*
>   *though they should be wholly cast down for a time,*
> *their roots and their old stock will put forth*
>   *sappy shoots and leaves again.*

The botanical imagery here is exploited in a very different fashion from its caustic and ironic use in MacDiarmid's *A Drunk Man Looks at the Thistle*. The implication is that both languages and cultures (and the undisguised English borrowing 'cultar' sounds strange in such a context) proceed organically like trees and plants. Their resurgence is an equally 'natural' phenomenon. At the same time, the imagery has ecological implications which connect Gaelic to a pure, more genuine world. The strategy is dangerously double-edged, as it risks validating the language's exclusion from a society moulded by industry, techno-logical innovation and, in due course, the informatics revolution. This aspect of Hay's approach was to be characteristic of much Gaelic verse until the end of the century.

Writing about the war, Hay evinces an agnosticism similar to that of the third section in Muir's 'The Good Town', but without the evident sense of involvement, or the speaker's speculations as to the guilt he himself may carry. Hay is not a warm poet. The emotions that inform his verse rarely concern individually realised human beings, but rather larger groupings and political causes. The detachment that runs through his war poetry may therefore depend as much on personal disposition as on intellectual convictions. Yet, as we shall see in 'Bisearta' (Bizerba), it does not exclude a passionate championing of the ordinary people caught up in a catastrophe which, in Hay's eyes, is little more than a cynical plot against them on the part of their rulers.

'Truaighe na h-Eòrpa' (Europe's Piteous Plight) refuses to make a dis-tinction between one side and the other in the conflict, or so much as to enter upon the motives which may have led them to engage in combat.

The poem laments a ruined continent, whose ravaged cultural traditions are no less deserving of attention than the very human sufferings of its inhabitants:

> Is luaineach, làn airce,
> oidhch' is latha a daoine.
>
> Chaidh geurghuth an truaighe
> thar cruaidhghàir a gaothan.
>
> Dh'fhalbh bhàrr na h-Eòrpa
> trian de 'bòidhchead sèimh aosta.
>
> Sean teàrmann na h-ealain,
> cridhe meachair na daondachd.
>
> *Without ever rest, full of need,*
> *are the nights and days of her folk.*
>
> *The shrill voice of their pitiful complaining*
> *drowns the hard roaring of her winds.*
>
> *Gone from Europe*
> *is a third of her tranquil, aged beauty.*
>
> *The old sanctuary of the arts,*
> *the tender heart of humanity.*

O Na Ceithir Àirdean features seven of Petrarch's sonnets in strikingly effective Gaelic translations, and the metre of 'Bisearta' is one that Petrarch used. Dated 1943 in the collection, but 16 January 1945 in a manuscript notebook, the poem describes the battle for the town on the North African coast. It draws inspiration from the work of the fourteenth-century religious agitator and preacher Girolamo Savonarola, which Hay read late in 1944, and where the same metrical pattern occurs. Savonarola, who counted the painter Sandro Botticelli among his admirers, was burned in Florence in the public square. His merciless castigation of contemporary vices offered a suitable model for Hay's inflexible, unquestioning devotion to what he saw as the interests of his country. The poem is a *canzone* (to be more exact, a *canzone antica* or *petrarchesca*), alternating lines of seven and eleven syllables. The metre adapts well to Gaelic. All the long lines in each section share a final rhyme, while the last vowel in each short line is echoed, in characteristically Gaelic fashion, in the course of the long line following.

Earlier cultural artefacts can acquire a talismanic quality in epochs of wholesale destruction. 'Say, is there a country where someone still knows the hexameter?' asked the Hungarian poet Miklós Radnóti, in a poem found in his address book when his body was dug up twenty months after his execution.[15] The *recherché* source and venerable origins of Hay's metre are no less eloquent, in their way, than the 'ancient high tranquillity of the stars' ('àrsaidh àrd nan reultan') which constitutes the backdrop of the scene that he depicts.

A soldier on night guard sees flames darting along the skyline. Unable to hear any sound, he uses the power of his own imagination, in the poem's second and third sections, to evoke the human reality that corresponds to this eerie spectacle. MacLean envisaged war as a struggle which tested male courage, endurance and dignity to the full. For Hay, war subjects defenceless civilians to meaningless violence. The plight of this bombarded population is emblematic of the way in which ordinary people have suffered across the planet and through the ages, with all the regularity of an annual tax levy. It is simply that their turn has come:

> Is cò a-nochd tha 'g atach
> am Bàs a theachd gu grad 'nan cainntibh uile,
> no a' spàirn measg chlach is shailthean
> air bhàinidh a' gairm air cobhair, is nach cluinnear?
> Cò 'a-nochd a phàigheas
> seann chìs àbhaisteach na fala cumant?

> *And who tonight are beseeching*
> *Death to come quickly in all their tongues,*
> *or are struggling among stones and beams,*
> *crying in frenzy for help, and are not heard?*
> *Who to-night is paying*
> *the old accustomed tax of common blood?*

The final section charts, with horrid fascination, the movements of the flames across the sky, seeing in them an embodiment of the evil which has provoked the destruction of the city. However much it tries, though, it cannot profane the august, impassive and superhuman tranquillity of which the stars are a pledge.

'Clann Adhaimh' ('Adam's Clan') indicates how strongly Hay was attracted by pseudo-medieval habits of allegorical thinking and imagery. It revives the idea of a 'ship of fools', inhabited by personifications of opposing qualities (another of the poet's typical traits) whose commotion is drained of all meaning by the indifference of the surrounding ocean. The view of the human predicament expressed in the poem is grim indeed. 'Meftah Bâbkum es-Sabar?', which takes its title from a line of an Arab poem asserting that 'patience is the key to your door' (presumably a prison door) uses opposites in a more hopeful way. The poem claims that, for the Arab culture of North Africa, human actions are as incapable of influencing fate as the ship's passengers. But here that quietism is exploited as the converse of Hay's programme for Gaelic:

> A ghliocais mar chluig mhall' an fheasgair,
> chan ann dhuinne do leithid!
> Oir sgrìobhadh roghainn fa leth dhuinn,
> an t-sìth 's am bàs no gleac 's a' bheatha.

> *Wisdom like the slow bells of evening,*
> *not for us is your like!*
> *For a choice apart has been written for us:*
> *peace and death, or struggling and life.*

The colonialist appropriation of an alien culture to represent what the white man must not and cannot be is unmistakable. Islamic fatalism functions as the springboard for a very different resolve. The chosen battlefield of Hay's audience must be:

> an talla a fhuair sinn gun cheilear,
> is far an cluinnear moch is feasgar
> ceòl ar sinnsre is gàir ar seinne;
> an leabhar far an sgrìobhar leinne
> bàrdachd ùr fon rann mu dheireadh
> a chuireadh leis na bàird o shean ann . . .

> *the hall we found without melody,*
> *and where will be heard, early and evening,*
> *the music of our forebears and the clamour of our singing;*
> *the book where we will write*
> *new poetry below the last verse*
> *put in it by the poets of old . . .*

Rather than the war effort on an international scale, it is a national revival that demands and deserves our energies, one ultimately aimed at achieving continuity with an interrupted tradition.

Hay's interest in Arab culture was, however, more profound and complex than the use he makes of it in 'Meftah Bâbkum es-Sabar?' might suggest. Faced with the torso of a planned long poem, readers are inevitably spurred on to imagine what the completed text might have looked like, and to view the available sections in this light. The interpretive problems that arise may well, however, be insoluble.

The main body of *Mochtàr is Dùghall* concerns the Arab soldier, viewing him in terms of what might be called 'vertical culture'. Not, that is, of his contemporaries (with the exception of his wife, whose brief, ritualistic lament opens the section) but of his father, grandfather and great-grandfather. The poem's ending mourns the children whom he never had:

> Mort nam marbh is mort nan naoidhean
> nach do ghineadh – crìoch dhà shaoghal.

> *Murder of the dead, murder of the children*
> *never begotten – the end of two worlds.*

Mokhtâr's great-grandfather Ahmed returned heartbroken from a lost war with Christian armies. His son Òmar tells a gripping tale (reminiscent, in its way, of Stevenson's adventures of action at their best) about Tuareg plunderers in the desert and how he brought off a third of his booty from an encounter with them. Mokhtâr's father Obayd is a very different character, a visionary with a strong religious spirit who scorns the pleasures and conflicts of the material world.

Hay's presentation of Arabic culture and lore in Africa is enthusiastically ethnocentric, punctuated by scornful expressions applied to the Christian aliens. The text is characterised as spoken, and is scattered with religious interjections and with references to usages and superstitions. The tones of virulent contempt in which Obayd describes the barbaric Tuaregs suggest that cultural antagonism or, more hopefully, cultural difference is one of the springboards of Hay's poetry. Òmar wins over the band's chief by offering him mint tea, which the foolish man misunderstands as the milk of a species of goat unknown to him ('"Is math an gobhar a shìl a leithid,/ ge b'e càite no cò leis e"' p. 132). Exchange between cultural groups which are hostile to one another, or merely ignorant of each other's ways, is mediated through a captive interpreter, yet the successful outcome of the encounter depends as

much on misinterpretation as on effective communication. By choosing
to write in Gaelic, in a language used neither by his parents nor in his
own social ambience, Hay had himself crossed a cultural boundary. The
experience of becoming or impersonating an 'other' may well have
encouraged a leap in the direction of other 'others'. His fascination with
Arab culture is the most prominent instance of this phenomenon.

Would the corresponding sections of the poem dealing with the
Scottish soldier have adopted a similar approach, using the notion of
'vertical culture' to convey his heritage to the reader, and thus indicating
that which (in a nearly untranslatable phrase – 'bu dual da'), was to be
expected of his mother's and his father's child? There is no way of
telling. They begin with heady verbal music, evoking a misty morning
in the Western Highlands rich in raindrops, a highly effective contrast
to the preceding desert landscapes. The tones in which Dougall is
addressed have an intimacy and a familiarity which are also new,
hinting that he would have been treated differently from the Arab
soldier. But as the poetic diptych was left incomplete, such speculations
must remain mere speculations.

Before leaving these two Gaelic poets behind, it is worth pausing to
reflect on how they subsist within the larger body of Scottish poetry.
The audience for their work in Gaelic cannot number much more than
ten thousand readers, and may be infinitely smaller. As a result, they
participate in the Scottish cultural field primarily in the form of English
translations, and self-translations, to boot. The danger with self-translation is that it can be deemed a substitute for the original in a way
impossible for translations done by other hands. In a polemical essay
Wilson McLeod tellingly pinpoints the dangers of presenting such texts
face to face:[16]

> The two texts can be understood as two functionally equivalent
> versions of the same thing, the same ideal 'original' – the difference
> being essentially one of format, like the difference between the
> compact disc or vinyl version of 'the same' record. Or the two
> texts can be seen as two distinct and different compositions, two
> 'originals' of essentially identical legitimacy and importance, each
> the fruit of the author's labour, and not essentially dependent on
> each other. What no longer seems a realistic interpretation is the
> most obvious one – that the Gaelic texts are the originals, and their
> English translations are ancillary and mediated compositions in
> whose production 'something has been lost'.[17]

Any translation must choose between a number of possible resonances. When, as is the case with Sorley MacLean, the poet himself does this, the effect can be to produce an official interpretation, one that restricts and deadens the range of possible readings of the poem. Under these conditions, translation, which ought to be an enlivening, enriching practice, especially when it takes place within a small but linguistically various culture such as Scotland's, strays from its purpose of disseminating and diffusing meaning. If translation can be defined paradoxically as a form of creative misunderstanding, the facing English versions by the original author which have become more or less mandatory in the case of Scottish Gaelic poetry cannot be regarded as translations in the true sense. The Gaelic originals risk being excised as an excrescence. The volume of *Critical Essays* on Sorley MacLean which appeared in 1986 was marred by its editors' failure to specify which contributors were discussing MacLean's English translations, and which the Gaelic poems he wrote first. Was the implication that no relevant distinction could be made between the two?

Rather than being an embarrassing reality in need of concealment, translation has a crucial role which needs to be highlighted without detracting from the Gaelic text's pre-eminence. After all, it alone is capable of spawning renewed versions to speak to the sensibilities of a changing society or a different century. And anyone requiring evidence of how translation can fructify and broaden our relationship to a poem need only compare, for example, the versions of LVII from the Eimhir sequence, in English by Sorley MacLean and Iain Crichton Smith, and in Scots by Douglas Young.[18]

Notes

1. See / Somhairle MacGill-Eain *Dàin do Eimhir* / Sorley MacLean *Poems to Eimhir* ed. Christopher Whyte (Glasgow, Association for Scottish Literary Studies 2003) with an introduction and extensive notes.
2. Michel Byrne ed. *Collected Poems and Songs of George Campbell Hay* (*Deòrsa Mac Iain Dheòrsa*) (Edinburgh, Edinburgh University Press 2003) pp. 483–4.
3. See *Edwin Muir: an Autobiography* (London, Hogarth Press 1974), beginning of Chapter 12.
4. 'Modern Gaelic Poetry' in *Towards the Human* (Loanhead, Macdonald 1986) pp. 97–107, here p. 98.
5. Items from the *Dàin do Eimhir* sequence are quoted from the edition cited above, which contains an extensive bibliography of secondary literature on MacLean on pp. 276–8. All other poems are quoted from Somhairle MacGill-Eain/Sorley MacLean *O Choille gu Bearradh* / *From Wood to Ridge* (corrected edition Manchester, Carcanet and Edinburgh, Birlinn 1999). Joy Hendry's essay 'The Man and his Work', clearly written in close collaboration with the poet, and published

in Joy Hendry and Raymond J. Ross eds *Sorley MacLean: Critical Essays* (Edinburgh, Scottish Academic Press 1986) pp. 9–38, is an important biographical source. See also 'My Relationship with the Muse' in William Gillies ed. *Ris a' Bhruthaich: the Criticism and Prose Writings of Sorley MacLean* (Stornoway, Acair 1987) pp. 6–14, Angus Nicolson (now Aonghas MacNeacail) 'An Interview with Sorley MacLean' in *Studies in Scottish Literature* XIV (1979) pp. 23–36 and Ray Burnett 'Sorley MacLean's *Hallaig*' in *Lines Review* 92 (March 1985) pp. 13–22.

6. See *Lines Review* 34 (September 1970).

7. This case is argued at length in Christopher Whyte 'The Cohesion of *Dàin do Eimhir*' in *Scottish Literary Journal* vol. 17, no.1 (May) pp. 46–70.

8. Solomon Volkov *Conversations with Joseph Brodsky* (New York, Free Press 1998) p. 227.

9. MacLean's letters to Douglas Young, a precious source for information about the cycle, are deposited in the National Library of Scotland, Accession 6419, Box 38b. The letter referred to here is dated 30 March 1942.

10. First published in *Poetry Scotland* 2 (1945), and reprinted in *Four Points of a Saltire* (Edinburgh, Reprographia 1970) p. 121, the poem is not included in MacLean's collected volume.

11. Reprinted with facing English translation in Ronald Black ed. *An Lasair: Anthology of Eighteenth-Century Scottish Gaelic Verse* (Edinburgh, Birlinn 2001) pp. 100–5.

12. Poems are quoted from Edwin Muir *Collected Poems 1921–1958* (London, Faber 1960, new edition 1984). Alongside Muir's *Autobiography* (London, Hogarth Press 1954) (of which an earlier version was issued as *The Story and the Fable* (London, Harrap 1940)), Peter Butter *Edwin Muir, Man and Poet* (Edinburgh and London, Oliver and Boyd 1966) may be consulted. Butter has also edited the *Complete Poems* (Aberdeen, Association for Scottish Literary Studies 1991) and *Selected Letters* (London, Hogarth Press 1974). Monographs include James Aitchison *The Golden Harvester: the Vision of Edwin Muir* (Aberdeen, Aberdeen University Press 1988), Elizabeth Huberman *The Poetry of Edwin Muir: the Field of Good and Ill* (New York, Oxford University Press 1971), Margery McCulloch *Edwin Muir: Poet, Critic and Novelist* (Edinburgh, Edinburgh University Press 1993), George Marshall *In a Distant Isle: the Orkney Background of Edwin Muir* (Edinburgh, Scottish Academic Press 1987) and Christopher Wiseman *Beyond the Labyrinth: a Study of Edwin Muir's Poetry* (Victoria, BC, Sono Nis Press 1978). C. J. MacLachlan and D. S. Robb have edited *Edwin Muir: Centenary Assessments* (Aberdeen, Association for Scottish Literary Studies 1990)

13. *The Story and the Fable*: 263.

14. Hay's poems are quoted from Michel Byrne ed. *Collected Poems and Songs of George Campbell Hay (Deòrsa Mac Iain Dheòrsa)* (Edinburgh, Edinburgh University Press 2003), which includes a short biography and two critical essays. See also R. A. Rankin's memoir 'George Campbell Hay as I knew him' in *Chapman* 40 (Winter 1984) pp. 1–12; Angus Martin 'George Campbell Hay – Bard of Kintyre' in his *Kintyre – the Hidden Past* (Edinburgh, John Donald 1984) pp. 48–71; Donald Meek 'Land and Loyalty: the Gaelic Verse of George Campbell Hay' in *Chapman* 39 (Autumn 1984) pp. 2–8; William Neill 'The Poetry of George Campbell Hay' in *Scotia Review* 8 (1974) pp. 50–6; and Christopher Whyte 'George Campbell Hay: Nationalism with a Difference' in

Derick S. Thomson ed. *Gaelic and Scots in Harmony* (Glasgow, Department of Celtic 1990) pp. 116–35.

15. *Foamy Sky: the Major Poems of Miklós Radnóti* selected and translated by Zsuzsanna Ozsváth and Frederick Turner (Budapest, Corvina 2000) p. 189.

16. The case is argued further in Christopher Whyte 'Against Self-Translation' in *Translation and Literature* vol. 11, pt 1 (Spring 2002) pp. 64–71.

17. Wilson McLeod 'The Packaging of Gaelic Poetry' in *Chapman* 89–90 (1998) pp. 149–51.

18. Iain Crichton Smith's 1971 English versions have now been reissued alongside the Gaelic texts, with an introduction by Donald Meek, as *Eimhir* (Stornoway, Acair 1999). MacLean found Douglas Young's version (in his *A Braird of Thristles* (Glasgow, Maclellan 1947) pp. 34–7) 'remarkably good, I think the best of your versions of my stuff which I have seen . . .' (*Dàin do Eimhir* p. 265).

5

The 1950s
(Hugh MacDiarmid, Norman MacCaig, Sydney Goodsir Smith)

The inclusion of Hugh MacDiarmid's *In Memoriam James Joyce* at this juncture in our study is a controversial move.[1] As if the text were not already surrounded by sufficient controversy! Completed before the outbreak of the Second World War, MacDiarmid (1892–1978) found gaps in the manuscript of the poem when he retrieved it from his damaged archives in anticipation of publication. Therefore, though one can argue that it is mainly a product of the 1930s, the actual text we have is the result of re-elaboration and patching together carried out in the first half of the 1950s. This is the timing of its entry onto the Scottish cultural scene.

The poem as a whole shows us MacDiarmid moving, at a surprisingly early stage, from the Modernism of his earlier production to positions that can clearly be identified as Postmodernist. Whether this trajectory was facilitated or hampered by the isolation he suffered in the years after his move to Whalsay, Shetland in 1933 or was, indeed, a response to it, is hard to say.

The text is in the nature of a compilation. Perhaps that is a gentle way of recording the consternation of a wide spectrum of champions, critics and readers of MacDiarmid when it became increasingly clear that large sections of the manuscript, far from being his own work, had been cobbled together from a bewildering variety of different sources. The discussion which follows offers a theoretical framework for coming to terms with, and even deriving enjoyment from, MacDiarmid's magpie practice. It cannot obfuscate the underlying ethical issues, in a society where the institution of copyright and the notion of intellectual property have the task of defending the interests, and facilitating the livelihoods, of writers, inventors and creative people generally.

During the period between the outbreak of war and the 1970s, the audience for MacDiarmid's work was in large measure restricted to Scotland, and to a minority within Scotland at that. Although both the Scottish National Party and the Communist Party of Great Britain had excluded him from their ranks early in the 1930s, reception of his work continued to be coloured by his association, in the minds of readers and critics, with the movement for a national cultural revival which he launched in the 1920s. An approach of this kind cannot offer an adequate framework for understanding *In Memoriam James Joyce* or, indeed, much of the poet's work after the completion of *To Circumjack Cencrastus* (1930). What was one to do with a national hero who abandoned his chosen language, Scots, in favour of the language of the oppressor, English? What could one say of a man who dismissed his "'enchanting early lyrics'" in favour of a 'Communist poetry that bases itself/ On the Resolution of the C.C. of the R.C.P./ In Spring 1925' (p. 615)? Who rejoined the Communist Party in the wake of the 1956 Soviet invasion of Hungary and stated in public, on one memorable occasion, that nothing could be set right in Scotland until the streets were awash with English blood?

The upshot was that, with only a few exceptions, those who promoted his work with such unselfish determination (thereby gaining him, in the course of the 1960s and 1970s, the recognition he deserved, with the result that, by the 1980s, he became a figurehead ripe for contesting and contextualisation) performed a wholesale amputation. His writing from the 1930s and afterwards was often ignored or overlooked. Yet what strikes one at this historical distance is the consistency of his practice, from the Scots lyrics of *Sangschaw* (1925) and *Penny Wheep* (1926) right through to *In Memoriam James Joyce*. The early lyrics are in many respects 'found poems', embedding phrases and sentences from Jamieson's dictionary and other works of Scots language philology in a context of MacDiarmid's own.[2] The crucial concluding section of *A Drunk Man Looks at the Thistle*, couched in eighty-two three-line stanzas with only one rhyme each (a stunning display of technical virtuosity) has its origin in a review of Yeats's *A Vision*, published in the *Irish Statesman* in February 1926.[3]

MacDiarmid had from the very outset sought to depersonalise his poetry. The process reached a climax with *In Memoriam James Joyce*. Basic assumptions about the making of poetry, associated with the Romantic period, having much earlier roots, and still endemic to a significant portion of the reading public, are put in question. These include originality as a requirement; the notion that the page the poet writes on is blank, making it feasible for his utterance not to overlap with that of any other poet; the notion of writing as expressing a subjectivity, a pre-existent body of experience or emotions, having clear boundaries and capable of being communicated to the reader; and the idea that any poetic text will be underpinned by a coherent psychological reality, associated with the biographical figure of the poet and at least partially valid as a means of explaining what he has written. Concepts such as originality, subjectivity and intellectual property collapse in the maelstrom of MacDiarmid's compilation which, though it can sound both overwhelming and forbidding when described like this, is at the same time an entertaining and enormously playful text.

Its play takes the form of turning accepted ideas and procedures on their heads, and this is nowhere more evident than in the poem's approach to language. Language has traditionally been viewed as secondary to the world, as a means of making the world accessible to thought and to discussion. But instead of using language to talk about the world, *In Memoriam James Joyce* upsets that hierarchy by using the world to talk about language. The world is the means and language is the end:

> But whatever language we use
> We must command its *Wesen* at its deepest,
> That element that cannot express itself
> More than dimly in man's everyday life,
> For in the aesthetic experience
> Instead of language meaning the material of experience
> – Things, ideas, emotions, feelings –
> This material means language. (p. 752)

The effect is to destabilise a series of binary oppositions, linked to a vulgarisation of Saussure's theory of the sign: signified/signifier, material/spiritual, content/form and so forth. As will become clear in our discussion of the work of Norman MacCaig, the freeing of language from those subservient functions of representation and mirroring which had hitherto been ascribed to it, though differently perceived by the two poets, was a preoccupation they shared at this time. It also reflects a new way of looking at words and how they mean, expressed with particular clarity in the work of Jacques Derrida around 1970.

Kenneth Buthlay offers one of the most devastating exposés of MacDiarmid's collage-like mode of proceeding, in an essay on his use of *Orchardford*, an undistinguished novel by a little-known author published in 1924.[4] Walter Perrie, by close textual analysis, has attempted to get an idea of how MacDiarmid sought, with what degree of success is still a matter of debate, to turn the prose of other authors into poetry of his own.[5] His essay represents a brave attempt to chart the English prosody of a modern Scottish free verse poet. There has been no follow-up, though further work is urgently needed, for instance, on the prosody of Edwin Morgan's poetry, which at certain points shows its own distinctive debt to late MacDiarmid.

In Memoriam James Joyce, then, breaks free of dependence on the idea of a writer, and even of writing as traditionally conceived. To accuse MacDiarmid of plagiarism is to insist on remaining within a rigid framework of concepts the text works to destabilise. Alan Riach and W. N. Herbert have struggled to clarify its relation to the numerous projects for long poems of epic dimensions which MacDiarmid entertained from the 1930s onwards.[6] Their efforts highlight the extent to which *In Memoriam James Joyce* is an open text, one in a state of constant becoming. It seems fair to assume that, had a serious opportunity for publication presented itself at any stage during the previous two decades, what emerged would have been a closely related, yet different compilation. For example, it is likely that the dedication to James Joyce was an afterthought, added when large sections of the poem had been completed. Who knows what form the poem might have taken had its publication been delayed for five, or ten years longer? Nothing could be further from a fetishistic concept of the perfected masterwork, no single iota of which can be changed without upsetting its achieved inner balance and harmony.

Though the book stages a death of the (Romantic) author figure, anticipating by some thirteen years Barthes's complaint that '*explanation* of the work is still sought in the person of its producer',[7] the role of the person whose name appears on the title page cannot wholly be discounted. This is not an example of the kind of irresponsible Postmodernism posited by reactionary critics, dissolving all existing boundaries and criteria in an inartistic free-for-all. The choice of sources, their excerpting and, most crucial of all, the ordering of the excerpts within a new, concerted structure, are MacDiarmid's responsibility. There is no need to underline that the meaning of any segment of a text is not wholly self-contained or self-present, but conditioned by the context in which it appears, by what precedes and follows.

Linda Hutcheon has described the dynamics of a Postmodernist aesthetic as 'a questioning of commonly accepted values of our culture (closure, teleology, and subjectivity), a questioning that is totally dependent upon that which it interrogates.'[8] MacDiarmid's book introduced to the field of Scottish literary production a range of interrogatives to which no answer has been found and for which, it may be, no answer is available. It is a transitional text, however, and what distances it from

Postmodernism as more generally conceived, despite its unmistakably ludic quality, is a resolute élitism of Modernist ascendancy. While it may well be erroneous to assume that the reader is expected to match or measure the poem's dazzling erudition (indeed, the most competent reader could be one who refuses to make any attempt to come to terms with its range of references), the issue is raised in a manner symptomatic of the collapse of a shared cultural humus perceived in the wake of the First World War. The poem is incomprehensible, in the strict sense of resisting being assembled and synthesised within the reader's mind. Whether incomprehensibility, in the more commonly used meaning, is simply one of the games it plays, remains an open question.

In spite of its marginalised, even proscribed status, MacDiarmid's later work has had a traceable influence on the practice of younger poets. Among its most enthusiastic champions is Edwin Morgan, who admires the urge towards a poetry of fact which will bridge the gulf between the humanities and the empirical disciplines lamented by Wordsworth, while at the same time aspiring to a similar impersonality.[9] Such impersonality, however, in Morgan's case, can be linked to his ambivalent gender status, to the need for self-censorship under a regime which criminalised his sexual orientation. This is a point we will return to in dealing with his poetry.

Rather than aiming to embrace the whole of *In Memoriam James Joyce* (itself presented as an excerpt from a larger work, 'A Vision of World Language') the remaining discussion focuses on a single section, the opening one, some 2,300 lines in length, in order to characterise the texture of the text, the variety of tones and elements encountered in it, as well as picking out instances of transition and cardinal points, with metatextual gestures offered at intervals as clues or guidance to the reader.

The tone is that of a very male discussion between learned, even pedantic friends, in a room piled high with books which have the contours of a storm at sea, and punctuated by ample clouds of tobacco smoke. The identity of the interlocutor is never clear. If one is prepared for it to be Joyce, it several times turns out to be Yeats, and probably it is unhelpful to want to pin it down to any single name. What matters is the feeling of direct, urgent, even intimate address, and the inconspicuous flattery by which the reader is subsumed into the enormously erudite company envisaged by the speaker. First person pronouns recur constantly, for example, in the space of merely four pages (pp. 752–6): 'Once again we seek . . .', 'We are for . . .' (both heading new paragraphs), 'We will away with . . .', 'We have the privilege . . .', 'So, like him, we cry . . .' The possibility of dissent or incomprehension on the

reader's part is never envisaged. The sharing of knowledge and enjoyment, with its undisguised gender bias, is particularly evident in passages
such as that on page 762, where in the space of barely twenty lines the
reader comes upon 'we delight in . . .', 'to men like us', 'We who have
sat . . ./ And talked with', 'We, who know intimately. . .', 'even as we
know. . .', 'Knowing them as . . .', 'Knowing that . . .'.

Articulation through personal pronouns is matched by a constant
syntactical device which offers a crucial key to the poem's construction –
the use of 'as' or 'even as' as a connector. Tonally, the effect is of
someone highlighting analogies so familiar to the reader that they are
axiomatic, hardly requiring a movement of assent. Structurally, the
words indicate that the poem proceeds sideways, rather than using
blocks of lines to contrast with or supersede one another. Repetition
and similarity, rather than supersession and contradiction, are the stuff
of the poem, one more aspect of its beguiling ploy of appearing to state
the obvious.

The screeds of evidence being marshalled before our eyes, if they
dazzle or daunt us, risk blinding us to the fact that this can be an
extremely easy poem to read. And its sensuousness, though of a very
special kind, should encourage us to sit back and relish the sequence of
sounds, of familiar and unfamiliar lexis, in a passage such as this one:

Or, brooding over the world history of the dance,
Review with the mind's eye all the forms,
Passecaille, chaconne, sarabande,
The dances of the Dinka, the Naura, the Nilotic Nanda,
The Toba of the Gran Chaco,
To the maxixe, tango, charleston,
Shag and big apple, and, *en route*,
Rejoice, in a philological parenthesis,
To analyse the Hebrew verb *rakad*
And find thence that King David *skipped*
Rather than *danced* before the Ark.
The Russian *Trepak* and the Georgian *Lekuri*,
The French *Bourée* and Spanish *Fandango*,
The dizzy *Moldavanesca* with its circular movements,
The slow *Hora* languid as the strains of the Moldavian *doina*,
The men's fiery *Ciocarlia* dance, the *Coasa suite*,
And the charming Tadjik *Non-Boza*.
(Compare the dance passages in Dynnik's *Skazanniya o Nartakh*
and in Dozon's *Bulgarski Narodni Pesni*) (p. 761)

The quotation is a lengthy one, and length is one of *In Memoriam James Joyce*'s most salient characteristics, both in the text as a whole and in segments such as this. Parallelism is a crucial strategy. It is fair to say that, in the course of this extended passage, nothing happens. The reader may baulk at the invitation to 'Rejoice, in a philological parenthesis', until he or she realises that MacDiarmid's poem is a source of rich, unending and mischievous fun. That this parading of extremely *recherché* lore should also be experienced as light-hearted, entertaining, even frivolous, is a noteworthy attainment.

The biography, the emotional experiences, the psychological state of the man behind the poetry could hardly be less relevant. It does not seek after self-expression, or immortality, or to reproduce within the reader what the writer felt, by pinning down an appropriate 'objective correlative'. MacDiarmid gives the impression that he has succeeded in changing the agenda of modern poetry, or at least in offering an alternative agenda. And part of that is the way the world of facts, of data, a sheer welter of information, overwhelms the text, as if a flooding river had broken the banks separating it from everything it had failed to, but now can, embrace.

The danger of chaos is kept at bay thanks to structural organisation. In so far as these masses of information are analogous to something else, and the poem works by an untiring accumulation of similes, they appear to be present by virtue of that which is not, but which they point to. And at a strikingly early stage, MacDiarmid confesses that this is indeed the case. He does so in lines that are haunting, elusive, while at the same time confirming one's sense of being in the presence of a conjuror, a player of games, someone who will not and cannot communicate directly, but must instead use analogy and allusion:

> – And all this here, everything I write, of course
> Is an extended metaphor for something I never mention. (p. 745)

The gesture is reminiscent of the French philosopher Jacques Derrida's words about the unconscious:

> A certain alterity – to which Freud gives the metaphysical name of the unconscious – is definitively exempt from every process of presentation by means of which we would call upon it to show itself in person . . . the unconscious is not, as we know, a hidden, virtual, or potential self-presence. It differs from, and defers, itself; which doubtless means that it is woven of differences, and also that it sends out delegates, representatives, proxies, but without any

chance that the giver of proxies might 'exist', might be present, be 'itself' conscious.[10]

Those two lines of MacDiarmid's represent the poem's core. The huge disparity between their terseness and the outsize means deployed throughout *In Memoriam James Joyce* is part of its playfulness. The flouting of traditional notions of economy can be viewed as quintessentially poetic, if Valéry is to be trusted:

> The practical universe amounts to a number of *ends*. When an end is achieved, speech dies. This universe excludes ambiguity, eliminates it; it instructs us to proceed by the shortest paths ... But poetry demands or suggests a very different 'Universe' ... Thus, in the art of the dance, the state of the dancer ... being the object of this art, the movements or displacements of bodies in the dance have ... no visible object; no *thing* which, once achieved, cancels them out; and nobody would dream of imposing upon choreographic actions the law of *non-poetic* and *useful* acts, namely that their end should be achieved *with the greatest economy of forces*, and *by the shortest route*.[11]

When MacDiarmid attempts to be more traditionally 'poetic', as in the 'hawthorn tree' passage (pp. 756–7), laboriously seeking out rhymes in his prose original (from the novel *Orchardford*), the effect is less convincing, not to say embarrassing. As it is, too, in those passages where he appears to forget the metaphorical procedure of the poem as a whole, stating his meaning baldly instead:

> (The so-called 'unknowable' was the semantic result
> Of identification, of semantic unbalance,
> Which posits for knowledge
> Something 'beyond' knowledge.
> But has such a postulation any meanings
> Outside of psychopathy? Of course not,
> As it starts with a self-contradictory assumption,
> Which, being senseless, leads to senseless results!) (p. 784)

Against such a method, one can invoke MacDiarmid's own words, at a slightly later stage in this section:

> Whether the aesthetic is right after all
> For which the simple constitutes the very climax

> Of admirable achievement, when in living Nature,
> From the point of view of success and fitness
> It is the complicated which is that climax. (p. 793)

Language is, naturally, a major preoccupation, for example in the extended discussion of the work of Karl Kraus (pp. 767ff.), with its claim that crimes against humanity, whether current or in preparation, will also or primarily be expressed as crimes against language.

MacDiarmid's fascination 'With every language, dialect, usage of words,/ Even any sort of gobbledygook,/ The mode despised, neglected or rejected' which 'May become the corner stone of a miracle of expression' (p. 752) exhibits a characteristic appropriation of Biblical language for his own ends (a trick Morgan was to learn, and use to consummate effect) and echoes the words with which, in a Scottish provincial newspaper in far-off 1922, he had presented his poetic *persona* to the world. The poem's ultimate triumph, however, is its ability to move effortlessly, dizzyingly between levels, as in this justly celebrated paragraph:

> (Silence supervening at poetry's height,
> Like the haemolytic streptococcus
> In the sore throat preceding rheumatic fever
> But which, at the height of the sickness,
> Is no longer there, but has been and gone!
> Or as 'laughter is the representative of tragedy
> When tragedy is away.') (p. 771)

While poeticising the apparently unpoetic with dazzling success, those lines enforce one's impression of the poem as a protracted, ludic act of deferral, a celebration of *différence* which works by means of *différance*, a representative of something else that is (temporarily?) 'away'. Moving between levels further facilitates its metatextual content, aimed at characterising the kind of poetry the speaker wants to write and may well be managing to. Indeed, the principal comparable achievement of MacDiarmid's later period is entitled *The Kind of Poetry I Want*, a phrase that crops up in the body of *In Memoriam James Joyce*.

Not Morgan alone, but a sizeable group of younger poets (among them Robert Crawford) have aspired to take up the challenge offered by MacDiarmid's poem. Interesting as the use made by later generations of an aggrandised Scots, or an aggrandised English may be, vital elements in *In Memoriam James Joyce* have been overlooked, not least its sheer length. But then, to offer achieved length as a triumph rings strangely, an indication of how out of joint with our time the work may be, or we with it. At the beginning of a new century, MacDiarmid's 1955 book gives one the impression the prose poems of Rimbaud may have given in the interwar period, or which much of Marina Tsvetayeva's later work (in particular the more inscrutable of her long poems) continues to give today, of poetry still waiting for competent readers to appear. And until they do, to offer praise of such a poetry will always be in the nature of a wager, of a gamble against time.

To a superficial gaze, MacCaig's poetic practice could hardly be more different from MacDiarmid's.[12] He has an overwhelming predilection for the short lyric, often running to as few as two or three stanzas, having no more than four lines each. His work is characterised by firm, brief, elegant gestures, so elusive as to be over almost before the reader has had a chance to grasp them. While MacDiarmid moves along a trajectory which takes him between languages and, eventually, into territories where only a minority of readers have so far been willing to follow him, it can be argued that MacCaig's poetics emerged fully formed in the first volume he subsequently chose to recognise, *Riding Lights* (1955), and did not undergo significant alteration in the course of an enviably long and protracted maturity. The last collection to be published in his lifetime dates from 1988 (*Voice Over*). MacCaig (1910–96) has, moreover, gained a certain reputation as a poet for the schoolroom, one whose deft, witty cameos of the natural world provide excellent material for teaching children and adolescents.

Such estimations are profoundly mistaken. If MacDiarmid, in *In Memoriam James Joyce*, goes about upsetting hierarchies and reversing priorities with a ludic energy and excess alien to the tragic undertones that can from time to time be detected in MacCaig's work, both poets undermine the notion that language merely denotes, encapsulates or represents the world. MacDiarmid's formulation is characteristically (for this epoch in his career) wordy:

> Concerned, I repeat, with the shrewd analysis
>   of the space-time network
> As the distinctive character of human consciousness
> And of language as the instrument
> For the progressive articulation of the world
> In spatial and temporal terms. Not retaining
> The naive or 'copy' theory of language and creating
> An artificial difficulty about space . . .
> The answer takes us beyond the theory that language
> Reduplicates or reconstructs a pre-existently given world

> And leads in the direction of the theory outlined
> In Cassirer's masterly discussion of speech
> In his *Philosophie der Symbolischen Formen*
> In which the temporal as well as the spatial functions
> Are exhibited as underived, or properly creative, functions
> Through which speech actually shapes and extends
>   our experience . . . (p. 794)

MacCaig exhibits a feeling of frustration, of being imprisoned in language, which is absent from MacDiarmid's poem. If he would like language to be a tool, a set of ultimately self-effacing labels offering direct access to the material world, he is forced to acknowledge that it is instead both dynamic and opaque, a material so all-embracing and impenetrable it may in the end prove impossible to get beyond it, to escape from its toils into a world that is 'real'. That he perceives this frustration as related to gender emerges from these half-serious lines, in a poem from the 1977 volume *Tree of Strings*:

> I groan, and think, If only I were Adam
> To whom everything was exactly its own name –
> Until one day the other appeared, the shameless
> Demander of similes, the destroyer of Eden. (p. 322)

Where MacDiarmid is concerned to revise a poetics of basically Romantic ascendancy, MacCaig's lyrics struggle in vain to bolster up a subject position which dates back to the eighteenth century, to the Enlightenment and, beyond that, the formulations of Descartes. The crisis MacCaig registers has implications in terms of both gender and race, given that the subject position then envisaged, despite its claims to universality, was unmistakably connoted in terms of gender, language and skin pigmentation. His determination to identify with the use of reason and with empirical deduction ('I, an adult man,/ Am reason functioning' (p. 47)) cannot but sound forlorn in a world marked by the aftermath of the Second World War and the collapse of the British imperial enterprise.

MacDiarmid, it has to be said, with his love of the obscure, the quirky and the irrational, had less difficulty in coming to terms with an epoch offering minimal certainties to those who live in it. This loss of certainty and even mastery (the word has an appropriately masculine ring) accounts for the elegiac tone which pervades the poetry of MacCaig. It is his reaction to a forced renegotiation of the position of the speaking subject, which Derrida renders as follows in the lecture 'La différance', first delivered in 1968, which has already been quoted:

> the subject (in its identity with itself, or eventually in its conscious-ness of its identity with itself, its self-consciousness) is inscribed in language, is a 'function' of language, becomes a *speaking* subject only by making its speech conform – even in so-called creation, or in so-called transgression – to the system of rules of language as a system of differences, or at the very least by conforming to the general law of *différance* . . .[13]

Instead of treating words like Lewis Carroll's Humpty Dumpty (as an authoritarian employer might a subservient workforce), the subject becomes such by submitting to rules, by accepting the dictates of lan-guage rather than dictating to it, or dictating it.

MacCaig's lyrics are unambitious in terms of scale. They exhibit a wry playfulness which can effectively mask their preoccupation with major questions of philosophy and epistemology, of how we can know and conceive our manner of being. By carefully restricting one's choice of poems, it is feasible to pass him off as a talented descriptive writer with a gift for striking metaphors. Yet even in the popular 'Summer Farm' he cannot resist the temptation to hint at the problematics of the subject, hungry for a place at the centre of things, yet denied self-identity:

> Self under self, a pile of selves I stand
> Threaded on time, and with metaphysic hand
> Lift the farm like a lid and see
> Farm within farm, and in the centre, me. (p. 7)

A line such as 'A hen stares at nothing with one eye' pinpoints the ambiguous status of language, conveying meaning by stating the impossible.

'Instrument and Agent' (p. 3) evokes the attitude of a primary school teacher, confronted each year with a new class, who is determined to be impartial and fair-minded. The real issue at stake, however, is the extent to which the mind can apprehend external objects without turning them into something very different from their original selves. This is what separates the star that has 'come a million miles' from the star which has 'gone those inches farther' to be lodged in the perceiver's brain. In *Tree of Strings*, again, we come upon the lines 'And all the time/ we won't let them alone –/ eyes change what they look at,/ ears never stop making their multiple translations' (p. 325).

'Double Life' (pp. 10–11) is a stunning evocation of Edinburgh on a chill October day and a probing examination of the enigma of perception, the impossibility of being a detached observer. It displays MacCaig's talent for descriptions based on simile or metaphor and the suspicion with which he regards that talent ('I am growing, as I get older, to hate metaphors – their exactness/ and their inadequacy' (p. 197)) as well as indicating the grammatical prejudices that arise from his longing for things to be themselves and only themselves, for self-identity:

> If these cold stones
> Could be stones only, and this watery gleam
> Within the chasms of tenements and the pretty
> Boskage of Dean could echo the groans
> Of cart-wheeled bridges with only water's voice,
> October would be just October.

Such bald equivalences are, however, impossible. The trams edging their way down the steep, crooked slope between Edinburgh's Old Town and its New cannot be reduced to a fact of geometry. They immediately become something other, both alien and related:

> When the trams
> Lower themselves like bugs on a branch down
> The elbow of the Mound, they'd point the diagrams
> Buckled between the New Town and the range
> Of the craggy Old: that's all.

But such a state of affairs remains a pipe dream. Now the poem adopts the language of a teacher, explaining the behaviour of different parts of speech to his class:

> A noun
> Would so usurp all grammar no doing word
> Could rob his money-bags or clap a crown
> On his turned head, and all at last would be
> Existence without category – free
> From demonstration except as hill or bird.

The prejudice in favour of nouns, and moreover in favour of nouns which are straightforward monosyllables, is easily explained, because nouns bring language closest to the desired function of a system of labels, an adjunct to a world which is already parcelled up, divided into discrete entities. Verbs, on the other hand ('doing words'), like similes or metaphors, build bridges between nouns and objects, make them interrelate, blur the boundaries between them, bringing them together into categories. Characteristically a smaller lexical group than nouns, they are also, generally, more difficult to translate, more quintessentially 'linguistic'.

Language is dynamic in nature. It cannot 'leave the world alone' or avoid being implicated in the entities it alludes to, the processes it picks out. Therefore, in the fourth and final stanza, the poet acknowledges the impossibility of any clear distinction between subject and object, between self and other, because he is always already caught up in, present in the phenomena he aspires only to observe:

> But now, look around, my history's everywhere
> And I'm my own environment. I cling
> Like a cold limpet underneath
> Each sinking stone and am the changing sea.
> I die each dying minute and bequeath
> Myself to all October and to this
> Damned flinty wind that with a scraping kiss
> Howls that I'm winter, coming home to me.

This uncomfortable realisation that observer and observed cannot be disentangled from one another, that they are mutually implicated, constantly contaminating each other, again brings Derrida to mind (in a passage relevant to the conclusion of 'Growing Down', the 'love poem which is not a love poem' analysed below):

> It is because of *différance* that the movement of signification is possible only if each so-called present element, each element appearing on the scene of presence, is related to something other than itself, thereby keeping within itself the mark of the past element, and already letting itself be vitiated by the mark of its relation to the future element, this trace being related no less to what is called the future than to what is called the past . . .[14]

Simile and metaphor, and engagement with the 'linguistic' qualities of language are unavoidable in poetry. MacCaig's interrogation of them, and their inevitable reinstatement, hint at a Postmodernist aesthetic, which relinquishes Modernism's aim to break with the past and is paradoxically content to highlight what has always been there, what has always been the case.

(An alternative way to tease out this dynamic in 'Double Life' could simply be to draw attention to the exquisite craftsmanship of its four eleven-line stanzas, each reproducing the same intricate scheme of rhymes and half-rhymes with a careful interplay of six and five (*abcbacdceed*). Why does the poem 'need' this backbone? Why does the poet need to set himself such technical challenges, and bring them off with such panache?)

If the Edinburgh of 'Double Life' is more Victorian than either medieval or eighteenth-century, there is something very Victorian, too, in the way 'Birds All Singing' (pp. 19–20) bemoans an idealisation of nature that is no longer possible in the wake of Darwinism. At times MacCaig's lyrics put up a hopeless fight against their own status as poetry, against what is considered to be poetic. At the simplest level, the poem is a debunking of pastoral. The word 'pastoral' occurs in emphatic position, at the end of a sentence and a stanza, precisely halfway through. (Male) birds sing (the masculine bias of the poem is both unthinking and instinctive for MacCaig) not as a form of courtship but to mark out territory. The aim they have in mind is 'Not passion but possession'. The man annotating the song, however accurately he takes down the sounds (the signifier) misinterprets the meaning (the signified). If the (male) bird is sustained by an illusion of physical terri-tory, the human subject is sustained by an illusion of metaphysical space – his own, unrepeatably individual thinking processes:

> The man,
> Caught up in the lie the bird began,
> Feigns a false acre that the world can't hold
> Where all is for his sake . . .
> Territories of existence, private states
> Of being where trespassers are shot at sight . . .

The ornithologist is 'as false as a machine'. He is an emblem for the scientific observer who imagines he can function as a detached recorder of external realities. But his attempt at interpretation is doomed to mis-interpretation. The closer he believes himself to his ideal, the further away from it he is. MacCaig beautifully exploits the highlighted position of a word at a line ending and the ambiguity of the English verb 'to lie', which means both 'to be situated' and 'to state that which is not true', creating at the same time a telling oxymoron: 'Nothing *truly lies/* In its own lucidity' (my italics).

One feels justified in detecting echoes of the Edinburgh poet Robert Fergusson (1750–74), who died in the city's madhouse, in the bleak closing stanza, which reiterates the idea that self-identity is impossible for human beings, against an atheistic background that denies any hope of transcendence:

> And man, with straws of singing in his hair,
> Strolls in his Bedlam transfiguring every fact,
> In full possession of what he never lacked,
> The power of being not himself – till with
> A twitch of the morning air
> Time topples bird and man out of their myth.

By the very fact of listening and transcribing, the man in this poem wished to differentiate himself from the bird, to be subject to its object. And instead he engages in an illusion no less preposterous than the bird's attempt at owning real estate.

His predicament is, however, also the poet's. A poem which aims to replace soppy pastoral with something more nitty-gritty has merely abandoned one interpretation in favour of another, which could be equally mistaken. A poem which scorns anthropomorphism, the attribution of human feelings to animals and things, has adopted as its only conceivable structure a parallel where men's actions are analogous to those of birds. They are in the same predicament, making the same mistakes. The bird functions as a kind of parable. We are once more in the presence of the dynamic of interrogation and reinstatement highlighted by Linda Hutcheon.

'Growing Down' (pp. 46–7, from the 1957 volume *The Sinai Sort*) is both one of MacCaig's most powerful love poems and a protest against the very notion of writing a love poem. It offers, if not a way out or a way forward, then at any rate a different way of viewing his predicament. The subject, forced to abandon the illusion of self-identity, of occupying a fixed position at the centre of the world from which it would be feasible to chart the whereabouts of that which it is not, finds consolation in a notion of mutual definition, of intersubjectivity. (There is an interesting counterpart in the object relations approach to human psychology propounded by Winnicott.)

A note appended to the poem's title indicates that, as well as being addressed to the beloved, it is concerned with the nature of language, associating the use of metaphor with primitivism, as if making comparisons were something language should have grown out of. The title, however, hints that the poem will turn ideas of maturity and immaturity, of adulthood and childishness, on their heads. What matters is not so much 'growing up' as 'growing down'.

The opening stanza reads like a shocked reaction to a request for a love poem. How can he be expected to reverse evolutionary development, to descend to the level of an ape, to exhibit the woman he loves publicly within 'A cage of pictures'? What the speaker aspires to is detachment, and wholesale identification with his reason. Part of that identification is a denial of the body, which the poem caustically undermines by comparing the speaker's intellect, the location of his thinking faculties, to the bedpan used to relieve incontinent or unmovable hospital patients ('my cold brainpan'). Writing poetry is a subhuman, apelike activity, condemned to imprecision: 'with a *simian* hand I pin some phrase/ Upon your *seeming*' (my italics). The beautiful phonetic echoing should not go unnoticed.

As with 'Birds All Singing', the halfway stage of this poem marks a turning point. His brain contains pigeon-holes, carefully prepared for a world of discrete entities that can be labelled. And instead, the effect of loving her is to catapult him into a poetic reality of images:

> – But back to the little room inside the skull:
> A place you don't inhabit, though you visit there.
> I search its pigeon-holes for something dull
> That might mean you, but even its cold air
> Is so transfigured by you that I gaze
> At glittering row on row of images.

The stanza that follows is highly humorous in its depiction of the speaker caught (presumably) in the act of having a surreptitious shit, and deeply moving in the acceptance of being human encapsulated in its closing couplet:

> So I stand here, a guilty primitive,
> My education down about my knees,
> Caught in the act of living, if to live
> Is to be all one's possibilities,
> A sum of generations six foot high,
> Learning to live and practising to die.

This is a poem which ends in a very different place from that where it began. The difference is evident in the way 'images', from a term of abuse, becomes positive; in the redefinition of what it means to be adult; and in the enthusiastic espousal of mutuality.

Being adult means being 'image among images,/ Phenomenon among phenomena'. The only way of finding out where you are is by reaching out to another and allowing that other to reach out to you. The impossibility of self-identity ('Accumulations of ourselves') is what makes communication possible. The speaker asks the woman he loves also to be his teacher as, at the culmination of a kind of emotional orienteering expedition, the acceptance of mutuality allows each to locate the other:

> – Make even me an image to understand,
> Till from my shadow or advancing star
> You can discover where I am and prove
> The everlastingness of common love.

Such mutuality is very alien to the arrant egocentrism which appears to dominate the poetry of Sydney Goodsir Smith. First published in 1948, his *Under the Eildon Tree*, a sequence of twenty-four elegies, appeared in a revised edition in 1954.[15] If using this fact to locate him in the 1950s reeks of sleight of hand, such significant collections as *So Late Into the Night* (1952) or *Figs and Thistles* (1959) help to justify placing him here, rather than alongside poets whose work was more profoundly marked by the war and its aftermath. The volumes by MacDiarmid and MacCaig examined above highlight the extent to which, by the 1950s, the initiative in Scotland had passed to poetry written in English. This was the reverse of the situation between the wars, when the work of Muir, or the English poems of Soutar, appeared to mark time, inhabiting a world untouched by Modernism, still redolent of the English Romantics and of Georgian poetry. For Goodsir Smith, and even more for Robert Garioch, the choice of Scots threatened to impose major limitations. This is why they found themselves defiantly espousing anachronism, while at the same time engaging in complex manoeuvres aimed at broadening the language's field of applicability, and thus regaining for their work at least a semblance of modernity.

Born in New Zealand, and educated at Marlborough, Goodsir Smith (1915–75) could never lay claim to a 'natural' or 'instinctive' grasp of Scots. His particular idiolect is aggressively bookish and anachronistic, right down to the spelling. If MacDiarmid quarried published sources in order to enrich his vocabulary, these were not exclusively of a literary nature, and gave the Scots he employed a quality of surprise upon the page. It is part of Goodsir Smith's aggressive, self-consciously decadent stance that his elegies should read as a mosaic of references and half-quotations, put together by one who willingly casts himself as an epigone.

Among the more salutary consequences of this strategy is a consistent, playful intertextuality, one of the principal pleasures the *Under the Eildon Tree* sequence has to offer.

Early on in his career, Goodsir Smith rubbished the notion that poetry should reproduce everyday speech, in an 'Epistle to John Guthrie' from *Skail Wind* (1941):

> We've come intil a gey queer time   *very*
> Whan scrievin Scots is near a crime,   *writing*
> 'There's no one speaks like that', they fleer,   *mock*
> – But wha the deil spoke like King Lear?

It was crucial to alert his readers to the chasm separating the English of poetry from English in colloquial usage:

> Did Johnnie Keats whan he was drouth   *thirsty*
> Ask 'A beaker full o' the warm South'?
> Fegs no, he leaned across the bar   *[imprecation]*
> An called for 'A point o' bitter, Ma!' (p. 13)

That it should still have been necessary, two decades after MacDiarmid had burst upon the scene, to make the point that literary use of Scots need not reflect its status in present day society, is eloquent of the relatively beleaguered position of Scots language poetry at this time. Battling against such prejudices provided a rationale for the whole corpus of Goodsir Smith's work, for his extensive and provocative use of eclectic vocabulary and wilful archaisms. He tried to turn to his advantage his chosen language's major weakness: its limited range of uses and the absence of an official standard, or a variety of class registers. Reinventing the language in his own terms and for his own ends brought with it a danger of solipsism; of talking, and being comprehensible, primarily to himself. Goodsir Smith circumvents this danger by deploying a corrosive, deflating and well nigh ubiquitous irony. His projected persona is its principal victim.

The fifth elegy, simply entitled 'Slugabed' (pp. 154–5), is a good example of his characteristic mixture of self-aggrandisement and self-deprecation. It is anything but an edifying self-portrait:

> Liggan my lane in bed at nune   *alone*
> Gantan at gray December haar,   *yawning; sea mist*
> A cauld, scummie, hauf-drunk cup o' tea
>   At my bed-side,

> Luntan Virginian fags . . .   *puffing on*
> Wi ase on the sheets, ase on the cod   *ash*; *pillow*
> And crumbs of toast under my bum . . .

There follows an apostrophe to Stalin, in which the poet casts himself as a representative of a capitalist society in the closing stages of moral and physical collapse. Indeed, with its mixture of Russian references and fragments of French, German and garbled school Latin, the elegy mimics the kind of cosmopolitanism so execrated by Soviet Russia's cultural bureaucracy. The irony does not stop there, however.

> Losh, what a sermon yon wad be!   *[imprecation]*
> For Knox has nocht on Uncle Joe
> And Oblomov has nocht on Smith
>   And sae we come by a route maist devious
>   Til the far-famed Aist–West Synthesis!
>   Beluved by Hugh that's beluved by me
> And the baith o' us loe the barley-bree –   *whisky*

Stalinism and radical Calvinism are equally obnoxious orthodoxies. This poet is as out of place in postwar Scotland as the hero of Goncharov's novel, the 'superfluous man' *par excellence*, was in Russia, even prior to the Bolshevik revolution. The establishment of a Scottish–Russian axis, with a revived Gaelic culture providing a counterweight to the triumphs of communism, had been MacDiarmid's ideal in the early 1930s. Goodsir Smith subjects it to merciless ridicule, as any notion of ideological commitment evaporates in an alcoholic haze.

> Thus are the michtie faaen,
> Thus the end o' a michtie line,
> Dunbar til Smith the Slugabed
> Whas luve burns brichter nor tham aa   *than*
> And whas dounfaain is nae less,
>   Deid for a ducat deid
> By the crueltie o' his ain maistress.

With his slogan of 'Not Burns, Dunbar!' MacDiarmid had proposed replacing populist adulation of Robert Burns with a cult of the sixteenth-century poet's abstruse and sophisticated verse. This ideal, too, has failed. Smith offers himself as evidence of its decay.

It is hard not to conclude that the *Dàin do Eimhir* of Sorley Mac-Lean are a significant intertext for *Under the Eildon Tree*, given the exacerbating self-laceration of MacLean's protagonist, torn between personal fulfilment in love and his political allegiances. The two poets were close friends at the time Goodsir Smith's elegies were written. In the second, the speaker addresses the issue of a fitting subject for his verse:

> Forbye, there's ither subjecks for a makar's pen   *poet's*
>   Maist wechtie and profund indeed,
> Maitters o' war and peace and dour debate   *grim*
> Of foreign levie and domestic malice,
> As the preachers say
>   – But no for me!
> As weill gie me the wale o' skillie or drambuie   *choice*; *gruel*
> As scrieve a leid o' politics or thee! (p. 150)   *write: song*

The opening lines of Ovid's *Amores*, and recurrent passages in Propertius's *Elegies*, confront head on the then prevailing attitudes, which saw amorous poetry as intrinsically inferior to the epic themes of war, not least because of its female audience. Goodsir Smith's approach is in line with the central European tradition of male-authored love lyric, while at the same time reinforcing his chosen role of epigone, an echoer of previous styles, one who stubbornly goes against his own best interests in both love and poetry.

Pound's controversial versions from the Latin, published in 1933 as *Homage to Sextus Propertius*, were a significant influence on the book of elegies. Goodsir Smith concludes *Figs and Thistles* with two substantial translations, and it is likely that Pound was influential in his choice of Tristan Corbière's 'The Gangrel Rymour and the Pairdon of Sanct Anne' rather than another work by the poet from Brittany. A Scots version of Alexander Blok's 'The Twal' precedes it, like a wistful homage to MacDiarmid's pro-Russian sympathies and to his practice, while the Corbière translation (which is extremely faithful) suggests a model both nearer at hand and closer to Goodsir Smith's heart, the poetry of the French Decadents who followed upon Baudelaire. 'Paria', placed at the end of the 'Raccrocs' section of Corbière's *Les Amours Jaunes* (1873), has intriguing similarities to the fifth elegy from *Under the Eildon Tree*:

> – Moi, – coeur eunuque, dératé
> De ce qui mouille et ce qui vibre . . .
> Que me chante leur Liberté,

À moi? toujours seul. Toujours libre. . . .
– Quand je suis couché: ma patrie
C'est la couche seule et meurtrie
Où je vais forcer dans mes bras
Ma moitié, comme moi sans âme;
Et ma moitié: c'est une femme . . .
Une femme que je n'ai pas.[16]

Corbière's speaker shamelessly advertises his solitude, his lack of success in love and his scornful indifference to any form of political commitment.

The *nostalgie de la boue*, an attraction for figures who are marginalised and pushed to the edge of society (as is the poet, after his own fashion), and for abnormal physical sensations, whether the product of alcohol or drugs, those from which a 'normal' sensibility would shrink, offers a further link between Goodsir Smith and Baudelaire, Corbière and Laforgue, most notably in 'The Grace of God and the Meth-Drinker' (pp. 94–5). The subject is a homeless alcoholic, fallen on such hard times that all he can afford is methylated spirits. Goodsir Smith describes him with fascinated revulsion, and with a perverse, provocative attention to olfactory detail:

Hidderie-hetterie stouteran in a dozie dwaum   *hither and thither; staggering; trance*

O' ramsh reid-biddie – Christ!   *coarse; mixture of cheap red wine and methylated spirits*

      The stink
O' jake ahint him, a mephitic   *toilet*
Rouk o miserie, like some unco exotic   *smell; extremely*
Perfume o the Orient no juist sae easilie tholit   *tolerated*
By the bleak barbarians o the Wast
But subtil, acrid, jaggan the nebstrous   *probing; nostrils*
Wi 'n owrehailan ugsome guff, maist delicat,   *overwhelming; repugnant; stench*

Like in scent til the streel o' a randie gib . . .   *urine; tomcat*

The lines claim that the smell of the man, far from being disgusting, is over-refined for the unsophisticated speaker, operating a telling reversal of the beautiful and the ugly, the attractive and the repellent. At the end of the poem, the speaker recognises himself in the drunkard, were it not for the unfathomable operations of grace, at the hands of 'a mercifu' omnipotent majestic God', who is referred to with undisguised scorn ('You –/ God there'). The slighting acknowledgement of Calvinist theology should not go unnoticed.

This same attraction for what revolts bourgeois sensibilities, for extremes of sensual experience, underpins what is arguably the high-point of the elegies, the thirteenth, entitled 'The Black Bull o' Norroway' (pp. 167–71). This is the name, with its ironic aura of outstanding sexual potency, of the pub where the speaker picks up a prostitute aged not more than 17, just next to the 'Fun Fair and Museum o' Monstrosities'. She is described as:

> A wee bit piece
>   O' what our faithers maist unaptlie
>   But romanticallie designatit 'Fluff'.
> My certie! Nae muckle o' Fluff   *much*
>   About the hures o' Reekie!
> Dour as stane, the like stane
> As biggit the unconquerable citie   *built*
> Whar they pullulate . . .

The speaker reminds one of a drunkard met in a pub whose penchant for eloquence risks getting the upper hand, so that he has to struggle to return to the point, and is constantly in danger of losing the thread of his argument. Propertius's Cynthia is thought to have been a prostitute, and Ovid penned an elegy encouraging slaves to turn a deaf ear to the antics of their mistresses. In the best tradition of the Latin poems, young Sandra, too, has an old woman in tow:

> Her mither in attendance, *comme il faut*
> *Pour les jeunes filles bien élevées,*
>   Drinking like a bluidie whaul tae!

The narrator, one presumes, is footing the bill. That French aside indicates Goodsir Smith's fondness for juxtaposing opposite tonalities within a single poem, the local and the cosmopolitan, the erudite and the vulgar. The fourth section offers an apocalyptic vision of the capital sunk in an orgy of unbridled intercourse:

> The yalla squares o' winnocks   *windows*
> Lit ilkane by a nakit yalla sterne   *each one; star*
> Blenkan, aff, syne on again,
> As the thrang mercat throve,   *busy*

The haill toun at it
Aa the lichts pip-poppan
  In and out and in again
   I' the buts and bens   *two-roomed cottages*
   And single ends . . .   *one-roomed flats*
Hech, sirs, whatna feck of fockerie!   *abundance; fornication*
Shades o' Knox, the hochmagandie!   *exual intercourse*
  My bonie Edinburrie,
  Auld Skulduggerie!
Flat on her back sevin nichts o' the week,
Earnan her breid wi her hurdies' sweit.   *buttocks*

The aptest personification of the city, it would seem, is a prostitute who cannot afford to take even Sunday off. Then, without any hint of a transition, the poem shifts to the courtly Scotland of Mary Stuart, 'Whar Bothwell rade and Huntly/ And fair Montrose and aa the lave/ Wi' silken leddies doun til the grave.' The speaker himself, dressed in crimson, is of their company. In the paragraph that follows Sandra's sleeping body becomes an archipelago the speaker's gaze can wander through, in a fashion richly reminiscent of earlier love poets (not least John Donne). It culminates, nonetheless in a ruthless plunge in tone:

     – My Helen douce as aipple-jack   *sweet*
     That cack't the bed in exstasie!
     Ah, belle nostalgie de la boue!

The detail of the sheets stained with excrement is as crucial to Goodsir Smith's effect as the haunting vision of a moonlit Renaissance Edinburgh, carrying associations with the virgin goddess. Although anthologists may be drawn to excerpt an elegy like the eighth, uniform in tone and conforming to more traditional expectations of a love sequence, it is such effects of undercutting, sarcasm, brusque changes of level, and sudden descents into vulgarity that typify Goodsir Smith's practice as a poet.

    He is a renegade, not just in a moral and political but in a literary sense. At its best, his work is resolutely cosmopolitan. The French models he draws upon so richly are contacted, not by means of MacDiarmid, nor thanks to some revamped version of the Auld Alliance, but via Pound and, less directly, Eliot. His debt is to the Modernist revolution in English poetry. None of his contemporaries took comparable risks in satirising the left-wing affiliations which had become more or less *de rigueur* for a Scottish poet at this time. Goodsir

Smith's impressive deployment of free verse most likely has similar sources, in Eliot and ultimately in Laforgue, whose influence Eliot acknowledged where his own prosodic innovations were concerned. Goodsir Smith's is the very opposite of cut up prose. His prosody sets the reader on his or her mettle, as competing metrical patterns supplant one another with dizzying speed. Such verse, rather than depoeticising poetry, draws our attention to the crucial role of metrical organisation in distorting language, in emphasising sound as against sense. In the process, the poet creates an effect of 'remembered harmonies' which is crucial to his chosen stance as epigone.

Among these remembered harmonies those of the courtly poets in Scots of the early sixteenth century are fundamental. Goodsir Smith's achievement would have been unthinkable had he not had the Scots tradition, and in particular that of cultivated or aureate Scots, to draw upon. The elegy immediately preceding 'The Black Bull o' Norroway' is a brilliantly executed pastiche on the theme of Orpheus and Eurydice (pp. 163–6). It closes with a Latin tag, and uses a refrain drawn from a poem by Robert Henryson, a near contemporary of Dunbar, on the same topic: '*Quhar art thou gane, my luf Euridices?*' The speaker's self-deprecation ('Anerlie [*only*] my ain sel I couldna bend./ "He was his ain worst enemie,"/ As the auld untentit [*untempted*] bodachs [*old men*] say') strengthens, rather than undermines, a pervasive sincerity of tone. Occasionally the Scottish colouring has an awkward ring ('The howff sees me nocht/ Nor the lassies i' the glen'), but the poem rises effectively to emotional heights of rigid rhetorical patterning:

She stummelt on a bourach, outcried 'Orpheus!'	*pile of stones*
– Een, what wey were ye no blind?	
– Lugs, what wey were ye no deif?	*ears*
– Hert, what wey were ye no cauld as ice?	
– Limbs, what wey were ye no pouerless?	
– Hairns, what wey did ye no haud the owerance?	*Brains; retain control*

As might be anticipated, undercutting and bathos have their role to play here too. But such passages deal predominantly with the enemy, '*The sycophantic gods, ulyied and curlit/ Reclynan in the bar on bricht Olympus*' and especially with Jupiter, '*The Wide Boy – ex officio!/ – The Charlatan*'. They do not corrode Orpheus's plangent narration.

The Orpheus elegy is not just an impassioned outpouring but also a deeply felt homage from an 'after' to a much lamented 'before', no longer accessible in any terms except those of stylisation and pastiche.

It is symptomatic of the precarious nature of the solutions Goodsir Smith found for his own predicament, struggling with the Scots language in an environment where the dreams and promises of the 1920s had failed to achieve realisation. They worked for him, but there is little evidence that they could have been extended to a school of followers or proselytes. As will transpire in the following chapter, Robert Garioch honed rather different tools to deal with a similar predicament, hinting at solutions which were, potentially, applicable on a broader scale.

Notes

1. The poem is quoted from the two volume *Complete Poems* ed. M. Grieve and W. R. Aitken (London, Martin, Brian and O'Keeffe 1978). Specifically on the later poetry, see Riach's monograph *Hugh MacDiarmid's Epic Poetry* (Edinburgh, Edinburgh University Press 1991), Robert Crawford '"The Glow-Worm's 96 per cent Efficiency": Hugh MacDiarmid's Poetry of Knowledge' in *Proceedings of the British Academy* 87 (1995) pp. 169–87, Carl Freedman 'Beyond the Dialect of the Tribe: James Joyce, Hugh MacDiarmid and World Language' in Nancy K. Gish ed. *Hugh MacDiarmid: Man and Poet* (Edinburgh, Edinburgh University Press 1993) pp. 253–73, Philip Pacey '*In Memoriam James Joyce*' in *Akros* 34–5 (1977) pp. 99–108, Alan Riach 'The Later MacDiarmid' in Cairns Craig ed. *The History of Scottish Literature vol. 4: the Twentieth Century* (Aberdeen, Aberdeen University Press 1987) pp. 217–27 and Roderick Watson 'Hugh MacDiarmid and the "Poetry of Fact"' in *Stand* 9 (4) (1968), as well as the articles by Buthlay, Herbert, Morgan and Perrie mentioned below.
2. Regarding MacDiarmid and Jamieson, see inter alia Kenneth Buthlay 'Adventuring in Dictionaries' in Nancy K. Gish ed. *Hugh MacDiarmid: Man and Poet* (Edinburgh, Edinburgh University Press 1993) pp. 147–69.
3. See Hugh MacDiarmid *A Drunk Man Looks at the Thistle* annotated edition by Kenneth Buthlay (Edinburgh, Association for Scottish Literary Studies 1987) p. 175.
4. Kenneth Buthlay 'The Ablach in the Gold Pavilion' in *Scottish Literary Journal* 15 (2) (November 1988) pp. 39–57.
5. Walter Perrie 'Prosody and Politics in *In Memoriam James Joyce*' in *Out of Conflict* (Dunfermline, Borderline 1982) pp. 29–52.
6. See W. N. Herbert 'MacDiarmid: Mature Art' in *Scottish Literary Journal* 15 (2) (November 1988) pp. 24–37.
7. Roland Barthes 'The Death of the Author' in *The Rustle of Language* translated by Richard Howard (Oxford, Blackwell 1986) pp. 49–55, here p. 50. The 'radical reversal' by which Proust, 'instead of putting his life into his novel . . . made his life itself a work of which his own book was the model' (p. 51) is of course analogous to the reversal of hierarchies between language and the world here attributed to MacDiarmid.
8. Linda Hutcheon *A Poetics of Postmodernism: History, Theory, Fiction* (New York and London, Routledge 1988) p. 42.
9. Edwin Morgan 'Jujitsu for the Educated' in *Twentieth Century* 160 (September 1956) p. 955; 'James Joyce and Hugh MacDiarmid' and 'MacDiarmid's Later Poetry against an International Background' in *Crossing the Border: Essays on*

Scottish Literature (Manchester, Carcanet 1990) pp. 169–204; and 'Recycling, Mosaic and Collage' in *Edinburgh Review* 93 (Spring 1995) pp. 149–66.

10. Peggy Kamuf *A Derrida Reader: Between the Blinds* (Hemel Hampstead, Harvester Wheatsheaf 1991) p. 73.

11. From the essay 'Au sujet du "Cimetière Marin"', English translation in Graham Dunstan Martin *Paul Valéry: Le Cimetière Marin* (Edinburgh, Edinburgh University Press 1971) pp. 75–93, here pp. 83, 85.

12. Poems are quoted from Norman MacCaig *Collected Poems: a New Edition* (London, Chatto and Windus 1990). Marjory McNeill is the author of a cautious biography, *Norman MacCaig: a Study of his Life and Work* (Edinburgh, Mercat Press 1996) while Joy Hendry and R. J. Ross have edited *Norman MacCaig: Critical Essays* (Edinburgh, Edinburgh University Press 1990). See further Anette Degott-Reinhardt *Norman MacCaig's Lyrisches Werk: eine formanalytische Untersuchung* (Frankfurt am Main and New York, Peter Lang 1994); Douglas Dunn '"As a Man Sees –": on Norman MacCaig's Poetry' in *Verse* 7 (2) (Summer 1990) pp. 55–67; Marco Fazzini 'The Language of Alterity: MacCaig the Equilibrist' in his *Crossings: Essays on Contemporary Scottish Poetry and Hybridity* (Venice, Supernova 2000) pp. 39–61; Erik Frykman *Unemphatic Marvels: a Study of Norman MacCaig's Poetry* (*Gothenburg Studies in English* 35) (Gotenborg 1977); Edwin Morgan 'The Poetry of Norman MacCaig' in *Crossing the Border: Essays on Scottish Literature* (Manchester, Carcanet 1990) pp. 240–7; Robin Fulton 'Norman MacCaig' in *Contemporary Scottish Verse* (Loanhead, Macdonald 1974) pp. 69–87; Colin Nicholson '"Such Clarity of Seeming": Norman MacCaig and his Writing' in *Studies in Scottish Literature* 24 (1989) pp. 30–48 and Mary Jane W. Scott 'Neoclassical MacCaig' *Studies in Scottish Literature* 10 (1972–3) pp. 135–44. *Chapman* 45 (1986) carried a special Norman MacCaig feature with articles by Thomas Crawford and Iain Crichton Smith.

13. *A Derrida Reader*, p. 67.

14. Ibid., p. 66.

15. Despite the not entirely satisfactory nature of the edition, poems are quoted from Sydney Goodsir Smith *Collected Poems* with an introduction by John Calder (London, John Calder 1975). An autobiographical letter to Maurice Lindsay has usefully been printed as a *Saltire Self-Portrait* (Edinburgh, Saltire Society 1988). Alongside essays by various hands, *For Sydney Goodsir Smith* (Loanhead, Macdonald 1975), contains 'A Checklist of the Books and Pamphlets' by W. R. Aitken. See also Thomas Crawford 'The Poetry of Sydney Goodsir Smith' in *Studies in Scottish Literature* VII (1969) pp. 40–59; Robert Garioch 'Under the Eildon Tree' (in Scots!) in *Akros* 10 (May 1969) pp. 41–7; Eric Gold *Sydney Goodsir Smith's 'Under the Eildon Tree'* (Preston, Akros 1975); Thom Nairn 'A Route Maist Devious: Sydney Goodsir Smith and Edinburgh' in *Cencrastus* 33 (Spring 1989) pp. 6–9; Alexander Scott *The MacDiarmid Makars 1923–1972* (Preston, Akros 1972) pp. 14–19 and Christopher Whyte 'Slugabed and Godless: Functions of Humour in Sydney Goodsir Smith' in Carla Marengo Vaglio, Paolo Bertinetti, Giuseppina Cortese eds *Le Forme del Comico* (Alessandria, Edizioni della Orso) pp. 579–90 and (in French) 'Corbière, Laforgue and Goodsir Smith' in David Kinloch and Richard Price eds *La Nouvelle Alliance: Influences Francophones sur la Littérature Écossaise Moderne* (Grenoble, Université Stendhal 2000) pp. 61–90.

16. See *The Centenary Corbière: Poems and Prose of Tristan Corbière* translated and

with an introduction by Val Warner (Cheadle Hulme, Carcanet 1975) pp. 72–3, where these lines are translated '– A eunuch heart, robbed/ Of what casts your moorings and throbs . . ./ What does their Liberty mean to me?/ Always alone. Always free. [. . .] – My country, when I lie down to rest/ Is the bruised mattress for my soul/ Repose, where I shall force to my breast/ My other half, like me without a soul;/ And my other half; is a lady . . ./ A lady not possessed by me.'

6
The 1960s
(Robert Garioch, Tom Leonard, Edwin Morgan)

Robert Garioch's solutions to the problems posed by writing poetry in Scots differed as much from those of Sydney Goodsir Smith as the backgrounds of the two poets differed from one another. Garioch (1909–81) came from the skilled working class in Edinburgh and so had access to spoken forms of Lothian Scots from an early age. His father and grandfather were both painters, while his mother was a music teacher before her marriage. Garioch was himself 'one of the last picture-house pianists' in the early 1930s, working at the Lyric in Nelson Square.[1] This helps to explain his enduring interest, not just in music, but in those elements of poetry whose means of signification is most alien to everyday language, metre and rhyme. Throughout his poetic career Garioch was a craftsman first and foremost. While it would be an exaggeration to say that he is absent from his poetry, he shows little interest in exploring the torments of a self-questioning or self-deriding subjectivity, after the fashion of Goodsir Smith or MacCaig. For Garioch, the poet as ordinary human being, with a day to day biography, changing surroundings and shiftingly unpredictable intuitions or perceptions, cannot furnish the primary material of his own craft. He is not interested in constructing or reconstructing an image of himself through the medium of poetry.

This, along with the problematic status of the language in which he wrote, explains why translation came to play such a crucial role within his output. It is more than likely that his major achievement, in its way no less of an open, cumulatively borrowed text than MacDiarmid's *In Memoriam James Joyce*, is the selection of sonnets translated from the Roman dialect of nineteenth-century poet Giuseppe Belli.[2] Translation is something still chronically devalued by our culture, when set against original composition. This prejudice is largely responsible for

Garioch's failure to attain the kind of recognition he so amply deserves. Had he lived in the epoch of Chaucer, or of Gavin Douglas, his fate would have been a very different one.

Between February 1958, when a commission from Donald Carne-Ross brought the Roman poet to Garioch's attention, and his death in 1981, he translated a total of 120 sonnets from Roman dialect into Scots, sometimes beginning, in the fashion of a music student harmonising a Bach chorale, with the cadences or rhyme words. Garioch himself appears to have believed his inspiration was running dry, and to have been somewhat shamefaced about such extensive recurrence to another man's work, given his remarks to Antonia Stott that 'it is frantic kind of fun, and keeps my hand in, now that my invention is showing signs of wear' or that work on the sonnets 'cheers me up especially as I have been so dull lately in the matter of any sort of writing'.[3] Nonetheless his Belli translations are a stunning performance, a testament to his exhilarating technical invention and mastery, his sympathy for the not infrequently bawdy humour of his *romanesco* originals and his ability effortlessly to cross the relevant cultural barriers.[4] Perhaps Rome in the decades immediately preceding Italian unification, a theocracy where power was invested overwhelmingly in the Catholic clergy, had more in common than one might think with the Edinburgh Garioch grew up in, a city whose deep-seated Calvinism still exerted a powerful grip on the day-to-day existence of its religious and social élites. The sonnets can be looked upon as a logical development of the depersonalisation which had always been an aim of Garioch, one he paradoxically shared with MacDiarmid.

Extended poetic translation, where the translated text comes close to matching the power and conviction of its original, is like opera, in the sense that it sets up such a degree of semantic richness that even the most astute critical intelligence is hard pressed to come up with a theoretical model which will make discussion of it feasible. One could fairly argue that translation, and the study of translation, are indispensable to the understanding of poetry, since it is really only through the juxtaposition of different languages that a reader reaches the necessary degree of defamiliarisation, restoring to words their quality of 'thingness'. The implication that people with access to only a single language must be severely restricted in their perception of how poetry operates seems inescapable. The issue, however, is a complex and controversial one.

An inkling of Garioch's achievement may be gained by looking at the sonnet entitled 'Ritual Questions'. The material from which the sonnet is built is deliberately banal, phatic language conveying no useful information but merely establishing, or expressing once more, to the point of redundance, the relationship between the speakers. Dribs and drabs of conventional utterance, formulae repeated every day until they threaten to lose all their meaning, are transformed by a quality of acute attention (and the point is highly relevant to Tom Leonard's work), evidenced in their unobtrusive casting into sonnet form. It is worth adding that the aggressive and virtuosic overstepping of line-breaks is Garioch's idea, and not copied from Belli's original, where each line had been end-stopped. The effect is to highlight the form into which the material has been cast. Such a comment may risk falling into the old mechanistic contrasting of form and content almost as separate and distinguishable items. Yet what happens here is that the form renders the content meaningful. The two, then, are indeed interdependent and defy separation:

> Says he: 'Some sneeshin?' – 'Thanks,' he says, 'I'll try   *snuff*
> ae pinch. Hou're ye?' – 'Braw, and yirsel?' – 'Gey weill,
> thank ye.' – And syne he says: 'Hou dae ye feel,
> this weather'" – 'Garrs me cheenge ma   *makes*;
>   sarks, och aye.'   *shirts*
> Says he: 'And hou's yir health?' – 'Soun as a bell,
> and yours?' – 'Thank Gode, I'm's weill as maist of men.' –
> 'Yir fowk?' – 'Graund; yours?' – 'The same,
>   faur's I can tell.' –

If the Belli sonnets are Garioch's crowning achievement, the fact that he was still engaged with them in the years immediately preceding his death gives what he managed to complete a provisory feeling. This can, in retrospect, be extended to his whole output, as if that itself were an open text. Robin Fulton points out that Garioch's last single collection of 1973 contained items predating the 1966 volume, and argues that in putting together his *Collected Poems* Garioch 'treated all of his poems as, in a sense, contemporaneous, feeling free to arrange them in groups which largely cut across any chronological lines.'[5] The implication is of a body of work all of whose significant aspects are constantly in *in fieri*, in a state of becoming. Because successive collections do not chart the journey of a soul or, in any explicit manner, the development of a talent, they tend not to have a strongly defined individual character, being more in the nature of selections from work in progress, making it hard to pinpoint any single book as crucial.

As time went on, Garioch made no secret of his growing antipathy towards MacDiarmid and the cultural and political options which MacDiarmid stood for. How could a self-effacing figure like Garioch have tolerated as mentor a man with such an overweening public ego, to the extent that those who knew MacDiarmid in his private manifestation had difficulty in reconciling one with the other? In a letter of 1 December 1980 to J. B. Caird, Garioch notes that:

> MacCaig... *does seem* to be impressed by attributes of MacD[iarmid] that are not there at all, so far as I can see, or by his behaviour, that looks very like antics to me. In fact, I weary of that deflated windbag... in a major poet, I should expect to find a love and mastery of the sounds, meanings and influential/co-operative properties of words...

He may again have had MacDiarmid in mind when observing, in a letter to Alastair Mackie from the end of the following month, that 'more and more I see the value of the "mediocre", so much despised by certain great people whose value declines in my judgement by several degrees every year or even month.'[6] MacDiarmid had sought to cancel out, at one fell swoop, the history of Scottish poetry from the Union of the Crowns in 1603 until the end of the First World War, giving Dunbar the place hitherto allocated to Burns. Garioch, on the other hand, identified strongly with the eighteenth century, in particular with the most brilliant, and tragic, figure in the movement known as the Vernacular Revival, Robert Fergusson, who died in the Edinburgh madhouse at the age of 23. His extended verse epistle to Fergusson will be discussed later in this chapter.

If one were to single out one trait as marking Garioch's output, it would be a sense of the covert, a fondness for alibis. Alibis are crucial to the functioning of one of his best known and most dissembling lyrics, 'Sisyphus'. The metrics of the poem are what Russian Formalist critic Jurij Tynyanov would have called 'motivated'.[7] In other words, the rhythm presents itself first and foremost in mimetic terms, a convincing reproduction of the movement and sound of a heavy boulder rolling down a hillside and coming to a halt at the bottom of it. Garioch has selected one of the better known torments assigned to the inmates of Hades by classical legend, a man condemned eternally to push a boulder to the top of a hill and have it slip from his grasp at the very last moment, so that he has to begin his work all over again.

The story has a classical origin and the metre works carefully to conceal its own classical ascendancy. It is a scrupulous, even pedantic attempt to recreate, in a stigmatised vernacular idiom lacking a codified spelling or grammar, the standard metre of Greek and Latin heroic poetry. The alternation of long and short vowels in the model is here replaced by a patterning of stressed and unstressed syllables. Garioch finds a single realisation for the fluidities of the classical metre, which had admitted the substitution of two short syllables for one long in certain cases. His line is a hexameter, with five dactyls followed by a spondee (||+—|+—|+—|+—|++ or +-||): 'Bumpity| doun in the| corrie [*circular depression*] gaed| whuddran [*rebounding*] the| pitiless| whun stane [*lump of hard rock*].'

Garioch has also disguised his myth in modern day dress. The mention of a 'cheque' paid monthly, rather than of a wage-packet handed over weekly, suggests that this is one of several ironic meditations to be found in Garioch's work on his own plight as a secondary school English teacher. One of the most hilarious is 'The Humanists' Trauchles [*travails*] in Paris', a translation, or adaptation, of a Latin elegy by another alter ego of the poet, Scottish Latinist, Presbyterian reformer and tutor to the future King James VI of Scotland and I of Great Britain, George Buchanan (1506–82). The lexical range exhibited in 'Sisyphus' is aggressively impure, moving from terms like 'disjaskit' or 'forfeuchan' [both meaning, roughly, *worn out*], through others shared with modern day English but given a Scots realisation, such as 'hannlit' or 'feenisht', to items like 'the boss' or 'a cheese-piece', rooted in the everyday and without a prior claim to belong to either language.

There is no reason to imagine that Garioch had not read Camus, or was not familiar with the French writer's *The Myth of Sisyphus*, first published in 1942. For Camus, 'there is no more dreadful punishment than futile and hopeless labour' and Sisyphus is 'the absurd hero', 'proletarian of the gods', his fate emblematic of the modern factory worker: 'The workman of today works every day in his life at the same tasks . . .' He is incapable of tragedy until he becomes aware, and that awareness is identified with 'that return, that pause', the moment in which Sisyphus, motionless, watches the rock roll away from him, before descending to begin his task once more. The possibility of being conscious, being aware, is what can transform the worker and, indeed, all men, bringing together ancient wisdom and modern heroism. No fate is so terrible that it cannot be overcome by scorn, and in a conclusion which is appropriately upbeat, given Camus's political commitment, he insists that we conceive of Sisyphus as happy, given that 'The struggle itself towards the heights is enough to fill a man's heart.'[8] The hero of Garioch's poem, which can be read as an ironical comment on Camus's formulation, is not, in the end, a victim of circumstances, but a collaborator in meaninglessness:

Eftir an hour and a quarter he warslit   *wrestled*
  his wey to the brae's heid,

hystit his boulder richt up on the tap of the
    cairn – and it stude there!
streikit his length on the chuckie-stanes,   *stretched; small pebbles*
    houpan the Boss wadna spy him,
had a wee look at the scenery, feenisht a
    pie and a cheese-piece.

It is he who gives 'the boulder a wee shove' in the interests of dull, unvarying security. The poem offers an image of how Garioch understood alienated existence and alienated labour. This may well be a coded self-accusation, based on his own frustrating professional life, and the extent to which it limited the time and energy he was able to devote to making poetry. If this is true, the covert, self-effacing manner of its execution is thoroughly characteristic of his work.

Sonnets and, indeed, any fixed metrical form fascinated Garioch. This is not just a question of unmitigated traditionalism, though that may have been an element in the attraction. Using inherited forms allowed him to distil, as it were, his own personal voice, to purify it and blend it with other tonalities possessed of a different resonance. By speaking through the forms of other poets, he both allowed his voice to merge with theirs and gained their authority for his. Garioch's contribution to a memorial volume Sydney Goodsir Smith edited to mark the two hundredth anniversary of the earlier poet's birthday was the epistle 'To Robert Fergusson'. It begins with an explicit disavowal of the contemporary:

> Fergusson, tho twa-hunder year
> awa, your image is mair clear
> nor monie things that nou appear   *than*
>   in braid daylicht.
> What gars perspective turn sae queer?   *makes*
>   What ails my sicht? (lines 1–6)

For it Garioch chose the stanza christened 'Standard Habbie', after the elegy on the Kilbarchan piper Habbie Simson composed by Robert Sempill of Beltrees, probably in the 1640s. At the time Fergusson made use of it, it had yet to be rechristened the 'Burns stanza'. If MacDiarmid's determination to break with the past and make things new was shown by his decided avoidance of this form, Garioch's taking it up suggests in turn how different the position he assumed was from MacDiarmid's.

An address to, even a dialogue with Fergusson, allows Garioch to outline his own stance regarding language choice and the contemporary world. The poem is scattered with references to Fergusson's work. These include the popular festival poem 'Leith Races'; a pastoral elegy in memory of a minor poet and former professor at Fergusson's university St Andrews, William Wilkie; an eclogue set in Greyfriars churchyard and embracing a fierce polemic against the Union; and the eighteenth-century poet's most ambitious undertaking, an account of the capital city conceived as running to several cantos and named simply 'Auld Reikie'. Garioch looks back with envy, and not without a discernible debt to Edwin Muir's theses in *Scott and Scotland*, at an Edinburgh where people spoke and poets wrote in the same language:

> For ye had at your fingernebbs   *fingertips*
> real levan words to weave your webs
> of sound and sense, of smiles and slebs,   *pouts*
>   whilst Embro callants   *youths*
> ne'er thocht to runkle up their nebs   *noses*
>   at guid braid Lallans. (lines 79–84)

Since then, the language used in Edinburgh has curdled, and there are now two tongues, 'ane coorse and grittie', the other 'copied . . . frae Wast of Newgate'. Without claiming objective superiority for either, Garioch declares his loyalty to 'the corrupt twang/ of Cougait', not least because it is 'nearer tae/ the leid [*language*] ye sang.'

Though the poem begins with a flight from the contemporary, what Garioch actually does is to recast Fergusson's collapse into religious obsession and madness, in strikingly contemporary terms, as the modern poet's predicament when faced with the aftermath of the Second World War and the onset of the Cold War:

> What gart ye break thro reason's ice?   *made*
> Compared wi ye, we're no sae wyce.
> Maybe we're yaised wi madness; vice
>   and lust for pouer
> bring furth some hellish new device
>   ilk ither hour. (lines 163–9)   *every*

The nearly two centuries separating Garioch from Fergusson do not prevent the earlier poet from functioning as a suitable mentor, a focus for both self-projection and identification. The remainder of the poem sets out to abolish the gap between them:

My ain toun's makar, monie an airt	*poet; place*
formed us in common, faur apairt	
in time, but fell alike in hert;	*very*
I whiles forget	
that ye ligg there ablow the clart	*lie; dirt*
of Canogait. (lines 199–204)	

A deft transition from the 'would' form of verbs, which blends the imperfect and the conditional, and is therefore ambiguous as to whether it denotes what used to happen frequently, or what one would wish to happen, to the narrative simple past, beginning with line 247, six stanzas before the poem's close, encourages the illusion that Garioch and Fergusson have indeed, at an unspecified point in both their lives, accompanied one another in turn to the doors of their homes ('scotch-convoy'), at the end of a drunken spree.

The epistle to Fergusson indicates that Garioch's deployment of Scots could never be taken as axiomatic, but must be argued for poem by poem and would indeed frequently constitute the subject-matter of his work. What attracted him about the eighteenth century was the contrast between the stigmatised situation of Scots in twentieth-century society and its status two hundred years before. At that period the phenomenon known as 'vernacular humanism' meant that university educated men well versed in Latin, having frequently received instruction through that medium, might use a rich and broad form of vernacular Scots in their day-to-day existence, without any trace of self-consciousness. Such an option was not available to Garioch. The perceived link between speaking Scots, lack of higher education and lower social status continues to influence social interchange in Scotland today. Consequent indignation provides the fuel for much of Tom Leonard's poetry, establishing an important link between him and Garioch.

Vernacular humanism is not a phenomenon that can be limited to the eighteenth century. It goes back at least as far as pre-Reformation Scotland, with the translation into Scots of Virgil's *Aeneid* by Bishop Gavin Douglas of Dunkeld alongside which Fergusson had planned to set his own versions of the *Eclogues* and the *Georgics*.[9] It embraces the Scots prose version of Boece's Latin history commissioned by King James VI and the work of Scottish Latin poets gathered in a celebrated volume published in Amsterdam in 1637, the *Delitiae Poetarum Scotorum*. Garioch produced Scots versions of two plays by George Buchanan, in which the young Montaigne may well have acted when Buchanan was his tutor in Bordeaux.[10] His finest achievement in this area is, however, a version of a piscatorial eclogue by Buchanan's successor and rival as

Latin translator of the psalms, Arthur Johnston. 'A Fisher's Apology' is a delightful performance, a monologue placed on the lips of a salmon fisherman from Aberdeenshire, where Johnston had returned after leaving his teaching post at the University of Sedan.[11] The fisherman rakes together every argument he can think of against the Presbyterian ban on fishing on the Sabbath:

> Whit fir duis Sunday offer sic hauls if it winnae let ye
>   Spreid nets? This kinna temptation jist maks
>   gowks of folk . . .   *fools*
> Naethin comes of my craft binna the purest pleisor;   *except*
>   Whit the mandment bans is naethin mair nor wark.

The playful intermixing of pagan elements takes place on the level of the writer's and the reader's consciousness rather than the speaker's. Despite its precise local significance, this poem will not allow us to overlook its cultivated and internationalist pretensions. The Scots version shows Garioch following, with a notable degree of success, in the footsteps, not just of the Catalan poet Carles Riba in his versions of Homer and the celebrated *Bierville Elegies*, but also of Hölderlin, Goethe and Rilke, as he tries to come up with an acceptable equivalent, in a modern European vernacular, for the elegiac distich or couplet of classical authors. The uncodified and stigmatised status of Scots makes the enterprise all the more meaningful and poignant.

Translation mattered so much to Garioch because it was a strategy he could use to oppose the use of Scots as a so-called 'reductive idiom'. Neither MacDiarmid nor Garioch aimed to produce dialect poetry. Yet there can be little argument that, in social terms, Scots was restricted to dialectal use throughout the lives of both poets. Dialect writing implies careful transcription of actual, non-standard speech, bringing with it an expectation that such poetry will be restricted to what speakers of dialect can reasonably be expected to say in actual social situations. Neither of these restrictions applies to poetry written in an idiom conceived of as standard. Translation freed Garioch's poetry in Scots from restrictions of subject matter, allowing him to experiment with and hopefully expand his medium against a range of subject matters. The latter were all the more attractive the more arbitrary the choice of Scots in dealing with them might seem. Garioch's spelling works for a high degree of phonetical precision, with minimal use of the apostrophe. Moreover, his metrical precision brought him face to face with questions such as the correct syllable count for items like 'trauchlit' (three or two?) or 'warld' (two or one?). Not since MacDiarmid's rhyming of 'bairn' with 'sparin'' in his 'The Bonnie Broukit Bairn' from *Sangschaw* had an ear of similar acuteness been brought to bear on the linguistic material of Scots. Such collaboration between poet and philologist is far from uncommon. During the 1920s and the 1930s, the prince of Catalan poets Josep Carner engaged in an ongoing dialogue with Pompeu Fabra, largely responsible for standardising the language, about precisely such points of conventional interpretation.[12]

As far back as 1961, David Craig had argued that a 'sceptical, ironic downrightness' had become 'the standard idiom of Scottish poetry', gesturing predictably in the direction of nationalist essentialism when he specified that 'the peculiar Presbyterian frame of mind got an impulse from, and in turn singled out and reinforced, an existing national bent'. Burns, in his view, wrote like someone for whom 'a sense of being "on the outside" was inevitable', someone 'without a share in the full resources of wealth, goods, power, opportunity, or range of job available in his country'.[13] Scots would therefore be peculiarly adapted to cutting pretension down to size, in rapidly returning to the ranks of the ordinary anyone who showed signs of getting above his station.

Garioch can be seen to struggle determinedly in his work against this casting of Scots in the role of a 'reductive idiom'. Careful concealment of his own erudition and metrical skill in 'Sisyphus' even suggests a degree of anger associated with the struggle. And if pretension was the one failing his opponents would have shown no mercy to, this would explain his tendency to clothe his polemics in unassuming garb. 'The Percipient Swan' is an extraordinarily angry poem, pronounced by a swan whose movements in the pond of a corporation park where he is trapped are no less restricted than the two-stressed, monotonously curtailed lines of the poem itself. The creature, its imprisonment, and its bored audience who 'hae my wings clippit' can be taken to stand for Garioch, the Scots language poet, rebelling against the straitjacket of the reading public's projections. The bird is rescued by sheer malevolence:

> I'm gey-near ready
> to gie a wee *chanson*;
> there'll be a flap
> whan ye hear my swan-song.
>
> For my sang sall foretell
> no my ain destruction;
> I sall rhyme the end
> of your hale stupid faction.

'Perfect', though similarly covert or camouflaged, takes a broader view of the poet's predicament. In its careful characterisation of alienated and unalienated labour it can be seen to develop the argument implicit in 'Sispyhus'.[14] A carpenter, a skilled craftsman now reduced to pushing buttons on a machine, inveighs against the depersonalisation of his work, given that he believes himself to be 'daft' ('crazed, possessed, inspired') rather than 'donnart' ('dehumanised, moronic'). With its implicit conservatism about methods of production, the poem risks further associating Garioch's practice, and by implication his choice of Scots, with a disappearing world, branding both as obsolete. But if one takes its eloquent description of the resistance of the material, of how the wood fights back, as a way of talking about how language resists the poet, then 'Perfect' opens up and liberates itself from any specific national or linguistic setting:

> Wuid is sweirt. It's no willin.   *stubborn*
> Its naitur is to haud up a lot of leaves
> and swee about in the wind.

> Wuid doesnae want to be flat.
> It wants to rax itsel and twist about.   *stretch*
> I choose timmer, that auld and seasont,
> that muckle droukit and dried and blaffert about,   *drenched; blown*
> it has lost aa ambition to dae as it likes.

The perfection adumbrated in the title constantly eludes this craftsman, who would never let a piece of work out of his hands if the customer could be persuaded to develop 'perfect patience'. The making of poetry, like any artistic fashioning, is a model of unalienated labour, in which what matters is the dynamism of the process, the relationship established between the maker and the material resisting him. Such labour can never really reach closure. The releasing of any single artefact for use by others merely marks one further stage in the craftsman's continuing development.

Garioch claims to have been inspired in his most ambitious, if not his most successful, undertaking, the extended Scots poem 'The Muir', which runs to 511 lines, by hearing the 1953 Reith Lectures on 'Science and the Common Understanding', though Fulton reminds us that the first manuscript sketches of this poem are dated 1952, while the major part of it was written in autumn 1955.[15] Here is an attempt to think the unthinkable, to embody in a poem the speculations and implications of quantum physics. It is hardly surprising to find Garioch referring in his opening paragraph to an earlier, yet more familiar and traditional 'unthinkable', the Christian Hell, and to Dante's attempt to apprehend it in his 'Inferno'. The poem's intellectual pyrotechnics make for stressful reading, so that Garioch's choice of form all too easily escapes our notice. His pentameter lines are grouped in quatrains rhyming alternately (*abab*). The fact that the first rhyme of each successive quatrain echoes the last rhyme of the preceding one sets up a teasing and energising play of four against five (*ababbcbcc . . .*) When a rhyme is repeated in the line immediately following, one is uncertain whether to read this as completing a sequence of five (*ababb*) or initiating a new sequence of four (*bcbc*). Presumably the answer is that it should be interpreted as both. The inspiration may well come from the Scots abridgement of Ariosto, *Roland Furious* by John Stewart of Baldynneis (?1550–?1605). Garioch's determination to bridge the gap between science and the humanities would have encountered the sympathy, not just of his near contemporary Edwin Morgan, but of William Wordsworth. It was an enterprise Robert Crawford would return to some decades later. Unfortunately, the poem's taxing subject matter has attracted few readers. But then, Garioch's production as a whole continues to languish under such neglect.

The parallels between Garioch's praxis and Tom Leonard's are obvious if, to a certain extent, surprising.[16] Both worked with stigmatised forms of language, demonstrating an extraordinary acuteness of ear, and aimed to counteract suppression and marginalisation by exhibiting specimens of that language for our perusal, with a deliberate emphasis on their potential for aesthetic appreciation. Leonard's chosen idiom was doubly stigmatised, as Scots rather than standard English and as a deviant or substandard form of Scots without any known historical tradition. The two men worked in opposite directions. Garioch aims at standardisation in terms of both spelling and phonetics, helped in this by the phonological precision of inherited metrical forms. Leonard (1944–) works to defamiliarise, using the written form to alienate and disorient his reader so that, once it has been deciphered, and the connection with known habits of speech established, the effect is of a flash of recognition.

It is argued in the third chapter of this study that, until more or less the last three decades of the twentieth century, Glasgow tended to be excluded from representations of Scotland and 'Scottishness'. The city had little to offer traditional nationalist thinkers, bent on unearthing a transhistorical 'national character'. The trend has since been dramatically reversed. The dominant representations of Scottishness today are urban rather than rural, drawing overwhelmingly on life in the industrial central belt. Rather than idealisation, we find an emphasis on social dysfunction, on oppressed and marginalised figures, ultimately traceable to French naturalism and the socially committed art of Émile Zola. Though more evident in prose than poetry, this 'hegemonic shift' in representation is relevant to both the poets examined in the remainder of this chapter. Indeed, their contribution to it, in the more delicate medium of verse, should not be underestimated.

Tom Leonard can hardly be described as prolific poet. His 'Six Glasgow Poems', however, first published in 1969, miniatures to all intents and purposes, have exerted an influence out of all proportion to their size. Though Leonard has continued to write and publish in both English and in Scots, he has not repeated this amazing feat. Nothing from his later work pulls such a punch, compressing an immense power for change in the space of six pages. Intense compression is, of course, a major virtue of his poetry.

Are these poems written in Scots? An untitled poem from 'Ghostie Men' points to the stigmatisation within a stigmatisation which characterises Leonard's medium:

> right inuff
> ma language is disgraceful
>
> ma maw tellt mi
> ma teacher tellt mi
> thi doactir tellt mi
> thi priest tellt mi

Not just authority figures, but also members of his own family insist that his language is of a kind nobody ought write in. Behind them and giving weight to their views are the members of the Scottish literary establishment and even the ten volume dictionary which represents the treasury of national speech:

> po-faced literati grimly kerryin thi burden a thi past tellt mi
> po-faced literati grimly kerryin thi burden a thi future tellt mi
> ma wife tellt mi jist-tay-get-inty-this-poem tellt mi
> ma wainz came hame fray school an tellt mi
> jist aboot ivry book ah oapnd tellt mi
> even thi introduction tay thi Scottish National Dictionary
>   tellt mi

The poem ends with a stubborn refusal to give any of them heed:

> ach well
> all livin language is sacred
> fuck thi lohta thim

Leonard's defence of his choice of idiom is not local or particularised. He is not interested in setting up a Glasgow or West Coast nationalism to combat the brands of Scottish nationalism which marginalise him. His position is a perfectly simple one. Any kind of language, any linguistic expression, demands to be held up to the light, to be the focus of attention and to be manipulated to aesthetic ends, by the very fact of its existing.

He is unashamedly intellectual in his approach to his craft. An essay from his collected volume *Intimate Voices* (pp. 95–9) explains in detail the background to his work with non-standard forms of Scots. Insisting that 'All modes of speech are valid – upper-class, middle-class, working-class, from whatever region: linguistic chauvinism is a drag', he questions the effect on literature in Britain of the consecration of one particular form of English, whose superiority is rooted in economic power, as desirable and correct. He particularly resents the implication 'that the language of the economically superior classes is *aesthetically* superior' betraying again the fact that his own concerns are primarily of an aesthetic and not a demagogic or even democratic nature. He shares with Edwin Morgan a willingness to celebrate MacDiarmid's achievement from an *other* position, one not determined by either sympathy with, or hostility towards his aims. Yet if, on the one hand, Leonard praises MacDiarmid's 'life-long advocacy of, and concentration on, lexis itself', he shows admirable perspicacity when he remarks that in 'his insistence on the primacy of name and category' MacDiarmid 'is still fundamentally using language as an instrument of appropriation, as a means of "possessing" reality'. Leonard's remark provides a basis, rather chillingly, for reading *In Memoriam James Joyce* in terms of aggressive, colonialist appropriation, thus casting a rather different light on the poem's exhilarating ransacking of different lexes and cultures.

William Carlos Williams is Leonard's hero in this theoretical excursus, a Williams who once famously remarked at a British Council event in New York, when challenged by a member of the audience about the right he and those like him had to use the language of Milton and Shakespeare, that his right came 'from the mouths of Polish mothers'.[17]

So the 'Six Glasgow Poems' do rather more than giving the oppressed

a voice, or creating a space for the speech of socially marginalised subjects. While conforming to the norms of dialect poetry in their apparent
status as transcribed speech, an impartial record of the kind of things
people who use this form of language might be expected to say, the way
this speech is transcribed is creative and even anarchic in its own right.
Leonard's eschewal of capitalised words and apostrophes, his playful, at
times arbitrary placing of word boundaries and an allusive spelling like
'insane', turn the first item in the sequence, 'The Good Thief', into a
sophisticated visual game:

> heh jimmy
> yawright ih
> stull wayiz urryi
> ih
>
> heh jimmy
> ma right insane yirra pape
> ma right insane yirwanny us jimmy
> see it nyir eyes
> wanny uz
>
> heh
>
> heh jimmy
> lookslik wirgonny miss thi gemm
> gonny miss thi GEMM jimmy
> nearly three a cloke thinoo
>
> dork init
> good jobe theyve gote thi lights

The title is in English, like those of all the poems in the sequence (with
the exception of one single word), and respects conventional spelling
and word boundaries. The implication is that it does not belong with
the utterance, but comes from outside. Leonard treats these fragments
of Glasgow speech as found poems, objects whose aesthetic potential
will be revealed once they are objectified, distanced, and rendered
strange. The speaker here is clearly male, a football supporter, a working-
class Glaswegian fully aware of the city's longstanding Protestant and
Catholic divide and of how this colours spectator sports in Western
Scotland. The title, however, asks us also to read his words as those of
one of the two thieves crucified on either side of Jesus. The mention of

'three a cloke', both the traditional time for starting a football match and the supposed time at which Christ yielded up the spirit, with the accompanying arrival of darkness, is a sly allusion to the Biblical story.

The maleness of this poem's world is balanced in the fourth item of the sequence. Its title, 'The Scream', plays on the meanings of a single lexical item in standard English and in Glasgow speech, as an expression of horror or alarm and an enormously enjoyable or entertaining incident. The gaggle of schoolgirls who have managed to jump off the bus at the traffic lights, without paying for the ride, have a Maenad-like and manic quality, reinforced by their use of invective ('rose shoutit shi widny puhllit furra penshin') and the degendered use of the designation 'daft kunt' for the frustrated bus-conductor.

In Leonard's poetry, the Catholic immigration to Glasgow and its descendants at last enter the stage of Scottish representation, as much as or more than a century after their physical arrival. Whether this is one aspect of Leonard's willingness to portray sexual practices a conventional heterosexual couple would be less than likely to avow their interest in ('treat me izza sexual object', but see also 'The Performance') or to explore the gendering and sexual identity of the male speakers encapsulated in his poems, must remain an open question. They include the autodidact, the self-educated working-class or lower middle-class man who crops up again and again in the literature about Glasgow. One example could be the character of Don John in Catherine Carswell's novel *The Camomile* (1922). 'The Hardmen', on the other hand, constitute a stereotype which Leonard in turn quotes and impersonates, satirises and destabilises, as in the poem of this title, ending with a warning which tellingly highlights the potential transition from the homosocial to the homoerotic:

> geeyi a tip sun
> fyirivir stucknthi dezirt
> stuckwia Glasweejin
> a *hard*man
>
> noa sumhn
> wotchyir bawz

Leonard's mischievous attribution of an underlying, barely controlled bisexuality to such icons of central Scottish urban masculinity has a particular relevance to the life and work of the man who would be named his city's first poet laureate, Edwin Morgan.

Morgan (1920–) came from a securely middle-class background in a leafy suburb south-east of Glasgow's city centre.[18] His otherness has none of the aggressive, insecure, slightly hectoring tone associated with the speakers in Leonard's poems. His academic career culminated in appointment to a chair in the English Department of Glasgow University. To a solid, deeply rooted literary background, Morgan added familiarity with poetry in a range of European languages, from several of which he produced English versions of such merit that they would eventually form a collected volume to set aside his original work. Both Garioch and Leonard found it necessary to deal with explicit social stigmas, finding strategies which might allow them to weaken, or at the very least denounce, the restrictions that these placed upon them. Morgan's inexhaustible experimentation, his prosodic innovations and the easeful manner in which he draws on the English and the American traditions, as well as those of mainland Europe and of Anglo-Saxon literature, give his work a self-assured quality which sets it apart from that of the other two. If he seemed to arrive from somewhere else, with respect to as much of a Scottish tradition as had managed to establish itself in the years between the wars, he brought with him no sense of disenfranchisement or injustice.

Morgan's strength comes in part from a chosen, conscious identification with his city. Glasgow, as a centre for trade, has always tended to look westwards towards the New World, and the grid plan of the city's streets north of the river has a distinctively American feel about it. In cultural terms, too, writers from Glasgow showed throughout the twentieth century an interest in American models, of which Leonard's essay on William Carlos Williams is just one example. *No Mean City*, the novel which would dictate during decades the modes of fictional representation for Glasgow, and beyond it for urban Scotland as a whole, a combined effort by writer H. MacArthur and journalist Kingsley Long first published in 1936, is heavily indebted to American gangster movies.

It therefore feels perfectly natural that, at the opening of 'The Second Life', the poem which gives its title to the 1968 collection marking Morgan's maturity, and which celebrates the poet's entering his fifth decade, he should refer to 'Thomas Wolfe's New York'.[19] The pastoral preoccupations of the Scottish Renaissance Movement might never have existed. Here as more generally in Morgan's work the modern, the technically innovative, is wholeheartedly embraced. It is no accident that Scots versions of the Futurist influenced Russian poet Mayakovsky mark a highlight in his career as a translator. Glasgow's cityscape, like that of New York, has its 'stunning plunging canyons', its 'skyscrapers' and 'foghorns' as 'aircraft roar/ over building sites'.

Morgan's 40th birthday is not just a coming of age but a rebirth. His city, too, is being reborn, as phalanx upon phalanx of the slum tenements which had for so long rendered the city notorious fall to the demolition workers, while tower blocks take their place,

> the slow great blocks rising
> under yellow tower cranes, concrete and glass and steel
> out of a dour rubble it was and barefoot children gone

The subsequent fate of those tower blocks and of the families rehoused in them will give readers in the twenty-first century pause for thought. But we are in the 1960s and Morgan's optimism knows no limits. The yellow of the tower cranes reflects that of 'the daffodil banks that were never so crowded and lavish'. The same urge of nature, whose irresistible cycle sets the daffodils flowering, powers the city's transformation, as if the new constructions were equally organic and no less timely.

The poet looks back to the winter months preceding when, from the windows of the flat in a 1960s high-rise block which was his home during much of his life, he watched the skaters on the frozen pond beyond the busy highway separating him from them. A renewal is occurring inside him too and, as the poem proceeds, its second, more covert agenda gestures towards explicitness. Seven lines from the beginning, 'a looming mastery' has laid 'its hand' on a young man's ambiguously, perhaps euphemistically designated 'bowels'. After 'aspiring', the word 'rise' occurs three times, then 'stir' four times within three lines, until 'desire' and 'strength' are imaged as 'an arm saluting a sun'. To put it a touch mischievously, it is beyond doubt that new blocks of housing are not the only erections being celebrated.

Here, as typically in his work until the 1990s, Morgan limits himself to half-statements, allusions and displacements. In the third extended paragraph of 'The Second Life' a 'seed in darkness' introduces the notion of a 'snake', immediately replaced by an 'eye' which sloughs off its film rather than a skin. And though it is this 'eye' which concludes the paragraph, echoing the ending of the first as it 'salutes the sun', it is hard to overlook the persistently phallic imagery, the slipping back of the foreskin through which 'we come alive/ not once, but many times'.

While accepting the need to be covert, Morgan also gestures towards what he is concealing. 'Many things are unspoken/ in the life of a man', and his 'unspoken love' for his native city is only one of at least two kinds of love. The isolated injunction to 'Slip out of darkness, it is time' can be read as addressed to himself and to his phallus, as well as to his city in the throes of rebirth. And when, in the last paragraph but one, he announces that he has no other children than 'the children of my heart', the meaning of the last lines, with orgasm achieved and ejaculation following, seems unmistakable:

> On the generations,
> on the packed cells and dreaming shoots,
> the untried hopes, the waiting good
> I send this drop to melt.

The poem's debt to Walt Whitman, then, cannot be restricted to its effortless deployment of a free verse so natural in its inflections as to seem inseparable from the utterance, to its generous embracing and affirming of a modern, urban community in all its varied manifestations. Whitman was Morgan's master, too, in manipulating, even contaminating a poetic medium to accommodate contents of a literally criminal nature in the society of the time. This tension between saying and not saying, between coming out and staying in, which Eve Kosofsky Sedgwick would quite rightly identify as a tension of the closet, is fundamental to Morgan's poetry.

Any temptation to categorise, ghettoise or essentialise Morgan's work should be avoided. Kosofsky Sedgwick herself was unwilling to posit a rigid homosexual subject, constrained by his or her sexuality to write in a particular way. What fascinated her was the realisation

> that many of the major nodes of thought and knowledge in twentieth-century Western culture as a whole are structured – indeed, fractured – by a chronic, now endemic crisis of homo/heterosexual definition, indicatively male, dating from the end of the nineteenth century.[20]

She claims that the tension between speaking and not speaking a sexual orientation, the status of a secret, came to be emblematic for the very possibility of knowing, to function as a symbol for epistemology. Reading Morgan's work of the 1960s and 1970s today, what strikes one most is its explicitness. It is difficult to recreate imaginatively, at this distance, an audience and an environment so repressive, or so innocent, that a poem like 'Glasgow Green' was taught in secondary schools without either teachers or pupils appearing to notice what was 'also' happening in it.

To say that the poem deals with a 'homosexual rape' is not quite accurate. Everything taking place behind the bushes, on the cruising ground into which Glasgow Green is transformed after midnight, is subject to not only a moral prohibition but the threat of prosecution and imprisonment. It is outside the law, and 'ought to be' outside the speakable. And indeed, Morgan operates a film-like cut only moments in advance of anal penetration. Here, as often in his love poetry, absences and elisions are not dictated so much by the nature of his subject matter as by the need for censorship and, crucially, self-censorship, if what he wrote was to be publishable. This is one sense in which not just Scottish, but most Western readers come unprepared to his work. Were we to become skilled readers of Russian Soviet poetry, or of most poetry published in European countries beyond the Iron Curtain between the Second World War and the collapse of the Berlin Wall, we would learn constantly to be aware of the possibility of censorship and the manner in which it forms, or deforms, a specific text. To confront significantly censored texts from Glasgow of the 1960s and 1970s, in a state whose uninterrupted democratic tradition and respect for the right to free speech continue to be a source of pride, is disconcerting at the very least. Yet this is an appropriate description for Morgan's poetry of love and sexuality at this time. Not until 1968, in England, and 1980, in Scotland, would significant areas of male homosexual activity be removed from the criminal sphere. The notion of self-censorship, not as a means of suppression, but as a means of communicating effectively an otherwise taboo message, can help us understand the fascination with codes, with alien languages and forms of life, with impersonation and ventriloquism, that is a constant throughout Morgan's work.

The second half of 'Glasgow Green' deploys, with breathtaking audacity, the language and imagery of the King James Bible in an impassioned sermon, a challenging and even hectoring defence of criminal love. Procreation is no longer a priority here. At the same time, Morgan does not conceal the intimate pain, the dysfunctional behaviour caused by social marginalisation and exclusion:

How shall the race be served?
It shall be served by anguish
as well as by children at play.
It shall be served by loneliness
as well as by family love.
It shall be served by hunter and hunted in their endless chain
as well as by those who turn back the sheets in peace.

Though this may be a love of thorns rather than one of roses, the thorn, too, has its seed and demands a harvest. When the poem's close describes 'beds of married love' as 'islands in a sea of desire', it is easy to miss the deftness and the subversive nature of Morgan's gambit. Sexuality and love within the legalised institution of heterosexual marriage are defined as other than, raised above desire, as if desire were unknowable within the marriage bed. Corrosive as it may be of family values, such an assertion might have evoked a degree of sympathy in a Provençal troubadour.

The hypothesis, then, is that the Protean nature of Morgan's poetry, its love of disguises, disconcerting codes and borrowed voices, was a means of dealing with a very specific prohibition, an injunction to silence which he circumvents in a myriad different ways. Behind this Protean nature there may lie a real difficulty in attaining a coherent subject position, if one's sexual practice locates one, not only beyond the law, but beyond the speakable. Absolute freedom, however, is a notion as useless, and as disempowering, for the poet as for any individual. What matters is to discover the limits on one's freedom and push repeatedly at them. Otherness in Morgan's poetry can never relapse into a tired binary of what is the same and what is different, an impoverishment to merely two positions for describing the multifariousness of the experienced world. Since from the start he is defined as, experiences himself as, different, what results is a protracted dance through 'other' 'others', giving rise to a delight both aesthetic and human, a dance which, in theory at least, need never conclude. Morgan's poetry, then, is neither dictated nor constrained by his sexual orientation. His recourse to gesturing, to substitution and codification merely brings him closer to the very condition of language. Language can never install a presence of that which it denotes. Were it to do so, it would cease to be language. In this sense, language was always on Morgan's side.

The bardic, sermonising tone in the second half of 'Glasgow Green' was ripe for broader use, as can be seen from a diatribe against his country first published in *Penguin Modern Poets* 15, 'The Flowers of Scotland'. Here free verse expands beyond versicles and verses into entire paragraphs.

The love poems in *The Second Life* and *From Glasgow to Saturn* are more intimate in tone, often teasingly and deliberately ambiguous. In 'One Cigarette', inattentive readers can fail to detect the lack of indication of the loved one's gender, a missing sign which is itself a sign. So the best definition of such poems could well be as 'double texts', inviting both a 'heterosexual' and a 'homosexual' reading, though in this case the opening line's gesture to what is hidden ('No smoke without you, my fire') and the prevailing phallic imagery would seem to tip the balance. 'Without It' and 'The Unspoken' undisguisedly set out to make a poem from what is missing, or beyond speech, and in doing so exemplify Morgan's strategy for undermining censorship. For once what cannot be said, and is not said, has nevertheless been evoked (as in 'One Cigarette'), that presence begins to hover over and infiltrate a whole range of texts (not just by Morgan). Discourse never consciously censored is irrevocably contaminated. The relatively few explicit poems, such as 'Christmas Eve', where the speaker turns down a soldier's come-on on the upper deck of a double-decker bus ('It was not/ the jerking of the bus, it was a proposition') then bitterly regrets it, function as levers or wedges, hitching more equivocal poems up beyond the level where an inattentive reading might have left them.

What might have become a failure of entitlement, as a gay man writing in a heterosexist literature, as a Glaswegian contributing to mainstream Scottish literature, turned into the pretext for endless experimentation. Morgan's interest in concrete poetry derived from a characteristic willingness to look far afield, beyond Scotland, beyond Britain, beyond Europe which led him into contact with a group of Brazilian poets who were experimenting in this very direction. Coming back to Scotland, his tribute 'To Ian Hamilton Finlay' from *The Second Life* shows Morgan's affection for an eminent practitioner of concrete poetry:

> You give the pleasure
> of made things,
> the construction holds
> like a net; or it
> unfolds in waves
> a certain measure . . .

Morgan's concrete poems are neither a surprising nor a disconnected element in his work, given that they are coded texts highlighting their status as such. Codes can bind together members of secret societies or of stigmatised groups, allowing them forms of communication impermeable to outsiders. But language is itself a code, a system of agreed conventions which render communication possible. The constructive principles of Morgan's free verse have yet to be elucidated. Indeed, the lack of any serious consideration of his innovative prosody is something of a critical scandal. It is far from formless. The use of iambic pentameters to provide pungency or closure should not mislead us as to its effective novelty. If Morgan's writing skilfully dissimulates its 'formfulness' (should such a term be permitted) it makes sense to have it balanced by concrete poetry which appears to dispense with 'content' in any accepted sense, confronting us with a kind of kit, a text that foregrounds its own constructive principles.

'Message Clear' works on the same basis as the *Emergent Poems* published one year earlier in 1967. An utterance, given in full at the end, is conceived of as a series of letters, any number of which may be left out, so allowing new words or utterances to 'emerge', as long as their order in the 'master' or 'concluding' utterance is rigidly respected. In theory, once one understands how such a text is made, it would be possible to produce more of them, though clearly no two individuals would be likely to come up with exactly the same realisation on the basis of any single statement. 'Canedolia' takes as its raw material place names from a gazetteer of Scotland. Words of Gaelic origin are pre-ferred. Opaque to a contemporary audience, they come unequivocally from beyond, from outside 'ordinary language'. Answers to the poem's first question ('*who saw?*') are all monosyllables, beginning and/or end-ing in a consonant. Answers to the second ('*how far?*') are disyllables ending in a vowel. The next two sets of answers play with what look like adjective and verb endings respectively, while the last but one (after the question '*who was there?*') treats four-syllable place names (over-whelmingly of Gaelic origin), all stressed on the first and third syllables, as if they broke up quite naturally into a first name and a surname:

> petermoidart and craigenkenneth and cambusputtock and ecclemuchty and corriehulish and balladolly and altnacanny and clauchanvrechan and stronachlochan and auchenlachar and tigh-nacrankie and tilliebruaich and killieharra and invervannach and achnatudlem and machrishellach and inchtamurchan and auchter-fechan and kinlochculter and ardnawhallie and invershuggle

One could argue, then, that 'Canedolia', though it may look like an anti-poem, is in fact thoroughly traditional. What is does is bring us face to face with the nature of language in poetry by the simple device of putting new rules in place of the conventionally accepted ones.

'Canedolia' would appear not to 'mean'. Sándor Weöres, a contem-porary Hungarian poet Morgan has translated extensively, produced samples of poems in an unknown language, pure signs (though the des-ignation indicates that we have to suppose a meaning behind them, inaccessible to us).[21] In 'The First Men on Mercury' the planet's native inhabitants respond to perfectly intelligible questions with a language of their own. But as the poem goes on, the positions of 'self' and 'other' are mutually contaminated. Identifiable elements crop up more and more in the Mercurians' discourse, while the visitors from earth become infected by 'Mercurian'. This is a kind of dance, a dialogue of chronic instability where roles and voices are exchanged in what is nonetheless an orderly progression. The implication is that contact with what is different, with the 'other' must inevitably undermine self-identity, the ability to remain faithful to a stable idea of the self, to continue to be what one was an hour or half an hour ago:

> Of course, but nothing is ever the same,
> now is it? You'll remember Mercury.

The concrete poem 'Pomander' exemplifies constant, unceasing linguistic transformation in a less explicitly alien context, and there are grounds for assigning it to the category of science fiction. 'In Sobieski's Shield' engages more profoundly with this category. This poem is suffused with deep, tremulous emotion, nonetheless mastered and articulated with a very masculine courage. Morgan no doubt took delight in the link between this distant 'minor planet in a sun' and the shield which defended the Polish hero and breaker of the 1683 Siege of Vienna. All lines, with the exception of those concluding the first, third and fourth paragraphs, are longer than a pentameter. Morgan dispenses with full stops and following capital letters, at the same time using rigorous enjambment. Readers must make a conscious effort to decide where sentences end and begin, rather as the speaker, 'dematerialised' from a dying world and 'rematerialised' light years away, struggles to come to terms with what has happened and where he finds himself. The poem deals with a liminal moment. One state of being has ended and another just begun. Though 'the effects/ of violent change are still slightly present' the speaker is 'very nearly who I was'. His wife 'has those streaks of fiery red in her/ hair that is expected in women' and his son's voice has broken ('at thirteen he is a man/ what a limbo to lose childhood in where has/ it gone'). The boy has also lost a nipple. Nobody can cross such a threshold without undergoing some kind of irreversible alteration.

The words 'second life' occur twice in the poem (though the speaker wonders 'what made me use that phrase who are we/ if we are not who we were we have only/ one life'). So there is a clear link to the title poem of the collection, with which 'In Sobieski's Shield' shares a solemnity, a barely controlled exhilaration that sets it apart from the playfulness of 'The First Men on Mercury'. Particularly moving in this poem is the idea that human bonds and human solidarity survive even these most radical of transformations. The words 'who are we/ if we are not who we were', left hanging, without a clear answer or a resolution, can fittingly serve to sum up Morgan's creativity as a whole. We are indeed no longer what we were, though our continuing to be, and the connection between what was and what is, are not put into question.

Besides offering pictures of imagined worlds, Morgan records the life of his own city, which the prejudices of the Scottish Renaissance Movement had subjected to its very own ban of silence and invisibility. 'Glasgow 5 March 1971', from *Instamatic Poems*, despite offering grounds for facile moralising in the 'two drivers' who 'keep their eyes on the road', disturbs by its turning of a horrifically violent act into an object of aesthetic contemplation. (Such aestheticisation of violence is a trait Morgan shares with George Mackay Brown, whose work is examined in the following chapter.) 'Trio', on the other hand, is a wonderfully exuberant celebration of three Christmas shoppers striding down a central Glasgow thoroughfare. They are almost but not quite a family. The girl in the middle holds 'a very young baby' while the man and the girl on either side carry respectively a guitar and a Chihuahua. Each of the transported objects gets a long, deliciously detailed line to itself, as if they were held up as equivalents. The dog wears a mockery of human clothing and the guitar expands like a living thing, while the baby is compared to inorganic trinkets:

> The chihuahua has a tiny Royal Stewart tartan coat like a
>   teapot-holder,
> the baby in its white shawl is all bright eyes and mouth like
>   favours in a fresh sweet cake,
> the guitar swells out under its milky plastic cover, tied at
>   the neck with silver tinsel tape and a brisk sprig of
>   mistletoe.

The threesome is explicitly offered as a transcendence of Christmas conceived in orthodox, Christian terms:

> The vale of tears is powerless before you.
> Whether Christ is born, or is not born, you
> put paid to fate . . .

Here as in 'Glasgow Green' the imagery and rhetoric of institutionalised religion are turned to different, humanist or even atheist ends. The poem erupts in its central line, emotion brimming over into incoherence in a threefold apostrophe.

'In a Snack-Bar' offers a grimmer side of the city for our contemplation. A blind hunchback needs help to negotiate the stairs down to the toilet, where he must be positioned in front of the urinal, then guided to clasp his hands around the soap. The speaker identifies with his condition, trying to imagine what sightless perception of one's surroundings must be like. The peculiar intimacy the two men contract so briefly issues in compassion rather than repulsion:

> His brooding reflection darkens the mirror
> but the trickle of his water is thin and slow,
> an old man's apology for living.
> Painful ages to close his trousers and coat –
> I do up the last buttons for him.

The old man's few utterances have almost the strangeness of the inhabitants of Mercury. It is not hard, finding the poem in the same collection as 'Glasgow Green', to detect a gay subtext, especially in lines like:

> Wherever he could go it would be dark
> and yet he must trust men.
> Without embarrassment or shame
> he must announce his most pitiful needs
> in a public place. No one sees his face.

The concluding exclamation is the weakest part of the poem. The lines at its core, however, linger in one's mind, their tone not dissimilar from the exhortations of 'Glasgow Green', though their emotion comes closer to 'In Sobieski's Shield':

> He climbs, we climb. He climbs
> with many pauses but with that one
> persisting patience of the undefeated
> which is the nature of man when all is said.

For one who, by his own proclamation, would have no children of his own, Morgan's poetry has been astonishingly generative. The best word to sum up his gift is *fertile*. Not only does he constantly enrich and enlarge his own possibilities of expression. His poems function as spurs and prompts, offering challenges and opportunities to those who will come after. Till he was well into middle-age, the choice to live in Glasgow and celebrate the city, at a time when something resembling a school of Glasgow writing was in the tentative process of taking shape beneath the nurturing hands of Philip Hobsbaum, confirmed his status as outsider. There were grounds for wondering whether circumstances had dealt with him unfairly. But Morgan's skilful playing, however, turned the card he had been dealt into a joker, then a trump card. There can be little doubt that, at the turn of a new century, the crucial point of reference for younger poets, both men and women, the most stimulating and enabling influence on them, had long ceased to be MacDiarmid's, and was Morgan's.

Notes

1. See Garioch's 'Early Days in Edinburgh' in Maurice Lindsay ed. *As I Remember: Ten Scottish Authors Recall how Writing Began for Them* (London, Robert Hale 1979) pp. 45–58.

2. All poems are quoted from Robert Garioch *Complete Poetical Works* ed. Robin Fulton (Edinburgh, Macdonald 1983), where the Belli sonnets can be found on pp. 215–80. See further Robin Fulton sel. and ed. *A Garioch Miscellany* (Edinburgh, Macdonald 1986), D. M. Black 'Poets of the Sixties III: Robert Garioch' in *Lines Review* 23 (Spring 1967) pp. 8–15, J. B. Caird 'Robert Garioch: a Personal Appreciation' in *Scottish Literary Journal* 10 (2) (1983) pp. 68–78, Donald Campbell 'Another Side to Robert Garioch, or, A Glisk of Near-forgotten Hell' in *Akros* 33 (April 1977) pp. 47–52, Douglas Dunn 'Cantraips and Trauchles: Robert Garioch and Scottish Poetry' in *Cencrastus* 43 (Autumn 1992) pp. 37–43, B. Findlay 'Robert Garioch's *Jephthah* and *The Baptist*: Why He Considered it "My Favourite Work"' in *Scottish Literary Journal* 25 (2) (November 1998) pp. 45–66, Robin Fulton 'Linguistic: Robert Garioch and Others' in his *Contemporary Scottish Verse* (Loanhead, Macdonald 1974) pp. 153–83, R. D. S. Jack *Scottish Literature's Debt to Italy* (Edinburgh, Istituto Italiano di Cultura 1986) pp. 54–9, J. Derrick McClure *Language, Poetry and Nationhood: Scots as a Poetic Language from 1878 to the Present* (East Linton, Tuckwell Press 2000) pp. 132–41, Margery Palmer McCulloch '"Fell Alike in Hert": Robert Fergusson and Robert Garioch' in *Cencrastus* 75 (2003) pp. 38–44, Andrew Macintosh 'Robert Garioch and Fergusson: Under the Influence?' in Robert Crawford ed. *Heaven-taught Fergusson: Robert Burns's Favourite Scottish Poet* (East Linton, Tuckwell Press 2003) pp. 181–97, Edwin Morgan 'Garioch Revisited' and 'Garioch's Translations' in *Crossing the Border: Essays on Scottish Literature* (Manchester, Carcanet 1990) pp. 222–39, Mario Reilich 'Scottish Tradition and Robert Garioch's Individual Talent' in *Lines Review* 136 (March 1996) pp. 5–17, Graham Tulloch 'Garioch's Different Styles of Scots' in *Scottish Literary Journal* 12 (1) (May 1985) pp. 53–69, Roderick Watson 'The Speaker in the Gairdens: the Poetry of Robert Garioch' in *Akros* 6 (16) (April 1971) pp. 69–76 and Christopher Whyte 'Robert Garioch and Giuseppe Belli' in Bill Findlay ed. *Frae Ither Tongues: Essays on Modern Translations into Scots* (Clevedon, Multilingual Matters 2004) (*Topics in Translation* 24, forthcoming).

3. See his letters to Stott of 1 June 1976 and 16 December 1980 in *A Garioch Miscellany* pp. 155, 165.

4. Garioch even went one better than Belli by inserting 'St Peter's cock' among the relics listed in 'The Relicschaw' (*Complete Poetical Works*, p. 242).

5. *Complete Poetical Works*, p. vii.

6. See *A Garioch Miscellany*, pp. 96, 98–9.

7. For Tynyanov, 'motivated' effects were those such as schoolchildren are so often taught to seek out, in which the sound of the words imitates what is being talked about (cf. Tennyson's (in)famous 'murmuring of bees in immemorial elms'). He saw such effects as negative indices, the exception rather than the rule, and insisted that phonetic patterning and organisation in verse are not normally imitative in nature. See *Readings in Russian Poetics: Formalist and Structuralist Views* edited and prefaced by Ladislav Matejka and Krystyna Pomorska, with introduction by Gerald L. Bruns (Chicago and Illinois, Dalkey Archive 2002) pp. 130–2 (an excerpt from Tynyanov's *The Problem of Poetic Language* of 1924).

8. Albert Camus *The Myth of Sisyphus* translated by Justin O'Brien (London, Penguin 1955) pp. 107–10.

9. See the letter of 1 December 1774 from George Paton to Bishop Percy quoted in Matthew P. McDiarmid ed. *The Poems of Robert Fergusson* vol. 1 (Edinburgh and London, William Blackwood 1954) p. 34.

10. See George Buchanan *Jephthah* and *The Baptist* translatit frae Latin in Scots by Robert Garioch Sutherland (Edinburgh, Oliver and Boyd 1959).

11. For Arthur Johnston, see James W. L. Adams 'The Renaissance Poets (2): Latin' in James Kinsley ed. *Scottish Poetry: a Critical Survey* (London, Cassell 1955) pp. 89–94; Leicester Bradner *Musae Anglicanae: a History of Anglo-Latin Poetry 1500–1925* (New York, Modern Language Association of America 1940) pp. 172–83; and T. D. Robb 'Arthur Johnston in his Poems' in *Scottish Historical Review* X (1913) pp. 287–98.

12. See Albert Manent *Josep Carner i el Noucentisme* 2nd edn (Barcelona, Edicions 62 1982) pp. 138–40.

13. David Craig *Scottish Literature and the Scottish People 1680–1830* (London, Chatto and Windus 1961) pp. 76–7, 80.

14. Fulton gives 29 May 1963 as the date of the composition of 'Sispyhus' and 21 October 1970 for 'Perfect'.

15. *Complete Poetical Works*, p. 298.

16. Poems are quoted from Tom Leonard *Intimate Voices 1965–1984* (London, Vintage 1995). *Edinburgh Review* 77 (May 1987) contains a bibliography of Leonard's work to date and interviews with Kasia Boddy and Barry Wood, along with two essays by Leonard, 'On Reclaiming the Local' and 'The Theory of the Magic Thing', which are reprinted in Murdo Macdonald ed. *Nothing is Altogether Trivial: an Anthology of Writing from the Edinburgh Review* (Edinburgh, Edinburgh University Press 1995) pp. 212–20. See further Ken Cockburn 'Towards this Particular Place: Tom Leonard's *Places of the Mind* and its Relationship to his Earlier Works' in *Verse* 11(1) (Spring 1994) pp. 120–6, Keith Dixon 'Notes from the Underground: a Discussion of Cultural Politics in Contemporary Scotland' in *Études Écossaises* 3 (1996) pp. 117–28, Ronald K. S. Macaulay 'Urbanity in an Urban Dialect: the Poetry of Tom Leonard' in *Studies in Scottish Literature* XXIII (1988) pp. 150–63, Patrick Reilly 'The Mirror of Literature: the Development of Catholicism in Scotland since 1845' in *Scottish Affairs* 8 (Summer 1988) pp. 86–95 and 'You are the People, Who are We? Some Reflections on the Irish Catholic Contribution to Scottish Society' in Raymond Boyle and Peter Lynch eds *Out of the Ghetto: the Catholic Community in*

Modern Scotland (Edinburgh, John Donald 1998) pp. 142–62, and Roderick Watson 'The Rage of Caliban: the "Unacceptable" Face and the "Unspeakable" Voice in Contemporary Scottish Writing' in Horst W. Drescher and Susanne Hagemann eds *Scotland to Slovenia* (Frankfurt am Main, Peter Lang 1996) pp. 53–69 and 'Postcolonial Subjects? Language, Narrative Authority and Class in Contemporary Scottish Culture' in *European English Messenger* 7 (1) (Spring 1998) pp. 21–31.

17. See *The Autobiography of William Carlos Williams* (New York, Random House 1967) p. 311.

18. Poems are quoted from *Collected Poems* (Manchester, Carcanet 1990), further to which Morgan has published *Hold Hands Among the Atoms* (Glasgow, Mariscat Press 1991), *Sweeping Out the Dark* (Manchester, Carcanet 1994), *Collected Translations* (Manchester, Carcanet 1996), *Virtual and Other Realities* (Manchester, Carcanet 1997), *Demon* (Glasgow, Mariscat Press 1999), *Cathures: New Poems 1997–2001* (Manchester, Carcanet 2002) and *Love and a Life: 50 Poems* (Glasgow, Mariscat Press 2003). See also *Nothing Not Giving Messages: Reflections on Work and Life* ed. Hamish Whyte (Edinburgh, Polygon 1990), 'Edwin Morgan Talking with Robert Crawford' in *Talking Verse* ed. Robert Crawford, Henry Hart, David Kinloch, Richard Price (St Andrews and Williamsburg, Verse 1995) pp. 146–61, Robert Crawford and Hamish Whyte eds *About Edwin Morgan* (Edinburgh, Edinburgh University Press 1990), Colin Nicholson *Edwin Morgan: Inventions of Modernity* (Manchester, Manchester University Press 2002) and further Kasia Boddy 'Edwin Morgan's Adventures in Calamerica' in *Yale Journal of Criticism* 13 (1) (Spring 2000) pp. 177–94, Rodney Stenning Edgecombe 'Some Early Vision Poems by Edwin Morgan' in *Studies in Scottish Literature* XXXII (2001) pp. 13–25, Marco Fazzini 'Playing Translation with Morgan and MacCaig' in *Forum for Modern Language Studies* 33 (1) (1997) pp. 27–36, and 'From Glasgow to Outer Space: Edwin Morgan's (Un)realities' in his *Crossings: Essays on Contemporary Scottish Poetry* (Venice, Supernova 2000) pp. 63–91, Ian Gregson 'Edwin Morgan's Metamorphoses' in *English* 39 (164) (1990) pp. 149–64, Roderick Watson 'Edwin Morgan's Urban Poetry' in *Chapman* 64 (Spring/Summer 1991) pp. 12–22 and 'Edwin Morgan: Messages and Transformations' in Gary Day and Brian Docherty eds *British Poetry from the 1950s to the 1990s: Politics and Art* (Macmillan, Basingstoke and St Martin's Press, New York 1997) pp. 170–92 and Christopher Whyte '"Now You See It, Now You Don't": Revelation and Concealment in the Love Poetry of Edwin Morgan' in *The Glasgow Review* 2 (Gender) (Autumn 1993) pp. 82–93.

19. American novelist Thomas Wolfe (1900–38), from North Carolina, like Morgan taught English at university, before publishing four novels which together constitute a huge autobiographical canvas on an epic scale.

20. Eve Kosofsky Sedgwick *Epistemology of the Closet* (New York and London, Harvester Wheatsheaf 1991) p. 1.

21. See Sándor Weöres *Selected Poems* ed. Miklós Vajda and trans. Edwin Morgan, William Jay Smith et al. (London, Anvil Press 1988) pp. 44, 131.

7

The 1970s
(W. S. Graham, Derick Thomson, George Mackay Brown)

Edwin Morgan's decision to remain in Glasgow, pursuing an acade-mic career in his native city and making it a major focus of his poetry, while at the same time taking full advantage of the opportuni-ties offered by its very particular sexual culture, ran very much against the grain in the Scotland of the immediate postwar years. W. S. Graham and, in the generation immediately following, Kenneth White, took a more conventional path, abandoning the central industrial belt (indeed, the country itself) and seeking a home for themselves and their poetry in very different contexts which did not, however, exclude the possibility of backward glances at childhood, and at an environment which had been grown both from and out of. Though Graham and White acted in accordance with the prevailing pressures at the time, paradoxically it was Morgan who, in the end, achieved a stabler collocation, and a stronger reputation than either of the others.

Attempting to find a placing for the work of W. S. Graham (1918–86), in a Scottish or a British context, continues to be problematic. Asked where he can be found, one would be tempted to answer that he set out from base a long time ago, on a wilful and perhaps wrong-headed trajectory, and has not been heard of since.[1] *Malcolm Mooney's Land* (1970) opens with a sequence about a lone explorer in an icy polar landscape. There is no certainty that the messages this man formulates, addressed to Elizabeth, the mother of his child, and possibly to a broader range of recipients, will ever reach their destination. Provocative use of enjambment, when he laments how 'Footprint on foot/ Print, word on word' appears to be 'on a fool's errand', together with the implication that the snow stands for a page in a published book ('Better to move/ Than have them at my heels, poor friends/ I buried earlier under the printed snow') implies that we are intended to view the expedition as a metaphor. The speaker's determination to 'put down something to take back' is kept alive by the niggling attentions of 'the word-louse', a parasitical creature reassuringly beyond conscious control. The immense spaces beyond the narrow confines of the tent imperil his chances of keeping a fitting record in diary form. The dawning day, Friday, 'holds the white/ Paper up too close to see/ Me here in a white-out'. Rather than functioning obediently as the medium in which a preconceived and prearranged content can be transcribed, language resists the lone explorer's efforts. It becomes an impediment, bent upon a mortal fixity where any kind of utterance will be impossible: 'Have I not been trying to use the obstacle/ Of language well? It freezes round us all.' Such single-minded dedication to a lonely and perhaps doomed task cannot but raise ethical issues and, in a thinly veiled reference to the fate of Europe's Jews in the Second World War, the speaker wonders whether it is 'right to stay here/ While, outside the tent/ The bearded blinded go/ Calming their children/ Into the ovens of frost'. The assimilation of heat and cold in that last metaphor is particularly powerful.

The outcome is an isolation which the speaker acknowledges as of his own making ('I have made myself alone now') and which may even constitute, perversely, the purpose of his expedition. Though he aches for reciprocity, for the 'benign creature with the small ear-hole' or 'the unblubbered monster' who 'goes listening', it seems beyond his reach. A fox which left its 'prints/ All round the tent and not a sound' failed to articulate his name. He is accompanied, inhabited or even obsessed by voices, 'more the further I go', perhaps demanding expression from and through him as they recall 'old summers/ When to speak was easy'. To do so is not easy now, and they are drowned out when a blizzard arrives 'filled with other voices/ High and desperate'. He longs for posthumous embodiment in a heroic narrative, thanks to which Elizabeth can explain the absent father to his child: 'Tell him a story./ Tell him I came across/ An old sulphur bear...' But what finally triumphs is lack of differentiation, between the page and the words printed upon it, between the image and what it stands for. Only 'Words drifting on words. The real unabstract snow' will be left.

The sequence skilfully mirrors the path Graham, with a stubbornness which must have characterised the man himself, chose for his own poetry. He would have realised that the Modernist base camp from which he set out was becoming increasingly outmoded, if only he had taken a sincere interest in what was happening around him in either literary or political terms. In important respects Graham is a throwback, one who acknowledges the almost mortuary nature of his enterprise when he insists, in the seventh section of 'Approaches to How They Behave' (p. 169), that he looks 'fashionable enough wearing/ The grave-clothes of my generous masters'. One is reminded of the fleeing prisoners said to have lurked in hiding in the forests of south-east Asia, long after the defeat of Japan at the end of the Second World War had removed any reason for their actions. If Graham counted Rimbaud and, to a lesser extent, Corbière among his heroes (and celebrating such a debt to the Decadent poets of mainland Europe was well nigh obligatory from a British Modernist standpoint), he stands in a mirror relation to them, as powerfully linked to the past as they were harbingers of the future. Corbière's fondness for writing about sailors no doubt evoked a fellow feeling in Graham. The Breton poet's identification with a similar land's end mirrored Graham's chosen residence in Cornwall. But where Rimbaud pushed ahead of contemporary poetry, eventually leaving it so far behind that his own trajectory risked being bereft of meaning (even among poets, there is a limit to the possibilities of autism) Graham erects a perverse monument to classic Modernism. At times one has the impression of seeing the wheel laboriously reinvented before one's very eyes. The energy and sheer determination Graham brought to his chosen task cannot fail, however, to inspire a degree of rueful admiration.

What makes him into a Modernist out of his time? The difficulty of his poetry, which forges a personal idiom by destabilising and redefining grammatical functions, demanding a special effort of any readers who wish to follow him. Graham is both an outsider and an effortless élitist, committed to a sense of the self as forged in the struggle against overwhelming forces, and nonetheless determined to wrest from the situation utterances whose value will ensure them permanence. This subjectivity is gendered as masculine and, in its relation to a feminine muse figure, draws strength from a series of binary oppositions clung to all the more rigidly the more they threaten to dissolve. Finally, a link to Romanticism makes childhood a privileged locus of self-definition, bringing echoes of Coleridge to the fore, prompting the formation of the heroic narrative of a self whose efforts are all the more ennobled the more they prove to be doomed to failure. Though a mellowed and even benign irony comes to the fore in Graham's last collection, *Implements in Their Places* (1977), the undertakings chronicled in the previous volumes are viewed with a deadly seriousness.

In returning to Greenock and to images of his parents or of his childhood, Graham shows no interest for what they may have become in the meantime. Here once more, he resembles the explorer for whom the known places he has left behind, the base camp he may never see again, are fixed elements, incapable of change unless through their elaboration as personal memory. Seen from this perspective, his birth becomes a mythic event:

> When I fell down into this place,
> My father drew his whole day's pay,
> My mother lay in a set-in bed,
> The midwife threw my bundle away. (p. 93)

This is from 'The Nightfishing', in whose final section the evocation of Coleridge's Ancient Mariner, becalmed in the Sargasso Sea and surrounded by the bodies of his dead comrades, is unmistakable:

> My dead in the crew
> Have mixed all qualities
> That I have been and,
> Though ghosted behind
> My sides spurred by the spray,
> Endure by a further gaze
> Pearled behind my eyes.
> Far out faintly calls
> The mingling sea. (pp. 106–7)

We encounter here a speaker whose subjectivity does not enter into crisis and is not questioned; a wished for message or text, set out in a medium which can rarely be trusted; and, somewhere beyond, the potential receiver and decoder of that message. Binary oppositions are as fundamental to Graham's aesthetics as the grid of lines drawn on the map where the explorer of the frozen north hopes to chart the unknown territories he is lost in. This sense of the uncharted, of course, recalls in a very literary way Rimbaud's biography, his relinquishing of France and poetry for Africa. It also explains the preoccupation in Graham's poetry with finding a place, somewhere that can be known, where one can stop, a defined position from which to speak. Such definition depends, however, on reciprocity, since the charted place is also somewhere you can be found, a point on the map to which others can trace you. This may be why the speaker in 'Malcolm Mooney's Land' demands, in a tone of frustration, why 'there has to be/ Some place to find, however momentarily/ To speak from, some distance to listen to?' (p. 145).

Graham's poetry is resolutely masculine. The muse figure it posits is also a sexual partner who can be physically possessed. The associated chauvinistic nonchalance makes Graham's relationship to her very different from that of a timorous and reverent Hesiod, surprised while tending sheep on the slopes of Mount Helicon so many centuries before. The dimensions of his sexual organ ensure that he will satisfy her. 'For her I have/ The length and breadth of Love/ That it shall lusty keep/ Her mind and body good./ Her bent is mine', and the poet adds that 'Always surely your bent/ Is mine. Always surely/ My thoroughfare is you' (pp. 126–7, from the last of 'Seven Letters' in his collection *The Nightfishing*). In making love to her, he is able to direct both of them, as when 'like a belly sledge' he 'steered us on the run/ Mounting the curves to almost/ The high verge' until they go 'down/ Into the little village/ Of a new language' ('The Lying Dear', p. 149). This figure is viewed more dismissively in Graham's later poetry, where she becomes a 'monster muse old bag', looking in 'between the mad/ Night astragals' while he is on the verge, or in the very act of composition ('Five Visitors to Madron', p. 181). There may be an intentional reframing of the person from Porlock, who so famously interrupted the composition of Coleridge's 'Kubla Khan', when Graham degrades her to a mere ancillary, 'only here as agent', unable to 'carry a message to you either/ Written or dreamed by word of her perfect mouth', someone who 'comes on Wednesdays, just on Wednesdays/ And today I make a Wednesday' ('Clusters Travelling Out', p. 187).

If his gendered stance is indeed an inheritance from Modernist forebears, then it would be fair to say that a certain stagnation of the relevant coordinates makes Graham's poetry possible, marking out the limits within which it will move. He resists pressures to compress the opposing poles of giver and receiver of a message, or of he who dictates the message and the message itself. During decades when the concept of textuality was being expanded to embrace any possible perception of reality, when, indeed, Postmodernism implied that experience could only be accessed in so far as it became a text, Graham, rather than blending into language or seeing himself as formed by it, viewed it as an obstacle, a suspect medium to the extent that it failed to mould itself according to his wishes. Such suspicion is evident in titles like 'What is the Language Using Us For?' (p. 191) or 'Language Ah Now You Have Me' (p. 200), the former, in particular, deriving its power from the implication that something has gone wrong, that a relationship has been reversed in a manner that demands consternation rather than cele-bration. Convention, the 'caught habits of language' threatens reliable communication. Poetic utterance is 'a public place/ Achieved against subjective odds', 'an obstacle to what I mean', and the multiple possi-bilities of interpretation are a kind of nemesis. Poets can 'never know/

What we have said, what lonely meanings are read/ Into the space we make' ('The Constructed Space' p. 152). 'Dear Who I Mean' (p. 51) envisages the poem as a kite in the form of a dragon, a 'letter let out/ On the end of its fine string' which risks damage from the 'cunning god' who will 'pretend/ To carry in spittled jaws/ The crashed message'. Yet the hope persists that from its fragments there may be reassembled a 'dragon to live your life with'.

Malcolm Mooney's Land represents a point of arrival in Graham's poetic trajectory, of coagulation and definition, even if this has the fixity of a lone explorer frozen in ice. 'The Nightfishing', on the other hand, the title poem of his 1955 collection, offers a moment of transcendence, almost a privileged myth. The sequence of seven sections, of which the third is the longest and most crucial, has a musical structure. Significant lexical items recur with an incantatory regularity: 'place', 'changing', 'grace', 'still', 'haul', 'white'. Detecting the shoal of herring, then letting down the nets and pulling in the catch, offers a splendid metaphor for that negotiation with the barely conscious or the uncontrolled which makes poetic composition possible. The moment between the lowering of the nets and their raising is also the moment of becoming of the poem, in which 'These words take place' with a 'sudden perfection' which 'speaks us thoroughly to the bone'. Graham perceives himself as both 'chosen and given' and is 'named upon/ The space which I continually move across'. Agency gives way to receptivity. The idea of grace (so fundamental to Calvinist theology) implies that what occurs has been enabled from elsewhere, and the speaker experiences repeatedly a death which may, in Elizabethan terms, have an association with sexual climax and male orgasm, but which is also a constant relinquishing and recreation of the self in utterance. The poet 'uttered that place/ And left each word I was', realising that 'he who takes my place continually anew/ Speaks me thoroughly perished into another.' For once, the notion of a poem as a laboriously formulated message with limited chances of finding an audience or communicating the desired meaning dissolves, and the speaker becomes his own 'fruitful share'. Interestingly, discussion of the pliability of language, of its potentially treacherous nature, is absent from the sequence.

Can one validly argue that a poet's main achievement is untypical of him? That it violates the premises underpinning much of his work? Since the basic dynamic of 'The Nightfishing' is one of grace, of being given to, it does exclude the reciprocity hankered after throughout his poetry, though one of Graham's most welcome and distinctive notes, of a full and tender sexuality, a secondary rather than a dominant theme in his work, resounds again and again throughout the sequence. Rather than reciprocity, what he achieves in 'Joachim Quantz's Five Lessons' (pp. 222–6) from *Implements in Their Places* is the more muted fulfilment of transmission, of a satisfying relation between teacher and pupil. The flute is naturally a phallic symbol, and Quantz's pupil is another man being encouraged to 'speak and make the cylinder delight us'. Karl is 'not only an interpreter', he is 'a little creator/ after the big creator' and, in his small way, as necessary. Although he must not 'intrude too much/ Into the message you carry and put out', a degree of self-consistency is possible. He will remain 'faithful to who you are speaking from' and, even if the sounds he produces are separate from him and will always be 'something else', nonetheless his audiences 'will hear you simultaneously with/ The Art you have been given to read'.

The sequence reads like a poetic testament. The young flautist functions as another self, an extension of both his teacher and Graham. The blurring of boundaries between interpretation and original composition implies that an accommodation with Postmodernism might have been feasible, had Graham chosen to pursue this line of argument. But there is an unmistakable sense of closure. Quantz has no intention of either writing or performing any more, and this renunciation makes his monologue possible. Elsewhere in the volume, as in 'Implements in Their Places', which reads like an almost Ovidian annotation of a mature love affair, Graham is satisfied with reminiscence, with echoing his earlier efforts in a very minor kind of poetry:

> When I was a buoy it seemed
> Craft of rare tonnage
> Moored to me. Now
> Occasionally a skiff
> Is tied to me and tugs
> At the end of his tether. (p. 237)

Certain things remain unchanged, as in the address quoted below, which formulates all Graham's hostility towards his chosen medium. The imagery is unequivocally sexual, and the frustration at a necessary relinquishment of control as real as ever:

> Language, you terrible surrounder
> Of everything, what is the good
> Of me isolating my few words
> In a certain order to send them
> Out in a suicide torpedo to hit?
> I ride it. I will never know. (p. 244)

The year in which *Malcolm Mooney's Land* appeared also saw the publication of a pivotal collection by a Gaelic poet whose achievement has
too long languished in the shadow of Sorley MacLean's. His influence
on the younger generation of writers in the language has been pervasive
and more crucial than MacLean's, if not entirely beneficial. But then,
what influence ever is? The collection proved its author's ability, not just
to accommodate changing currents and fashions, but to forge ahead of
them, continually redefining himself in a protean manner, in defiance of
the restrictions and fixity the choice of Gaelic might seem to condemn
him to. With *An Rathad Cian* (1970) (an English version appeared the
following year as *The Far Road*) Derick Thomson (Ruaraidh
MacThòmais) (1921–) bid farewell at one and the same time to the
island where he had been born and grown up, and to the earlier poetic
manner with which he is still too often identified, thus preparing the
ground for the impressive plunge into the multicultural realities of a
post industrial Glasgow, which informs his more recent production.[2]

It is worth dwelling on that earlier manner, because it constitutes such
a satisfying achievement in itself, and because it has been so productive
in the work of younger Gaelic poets, whose at times formulaic
appropriation of it has risked turning it into something of a rut they can
get stuck in. Thomson's first collection *An Dealbh Briste* (*The Broken
Picture*) appeared in 1951. The variety of approaches and voices to be
encountered in it shows the poet still to some extent in the process of
formation, of defining clearly a personality of his own. Thomson grew
up in the same Lewis village as Iain Crichton Smith, who was seven
years his junior, yet their experiences of the place could hardly have
been more different. In part this can be attributed to the fact that
Thomson grew up in a bilingual household, using both English and
Gaelic from an early age, that he attended the services of the established
Church of Scotland rather than one of the more radical forms of
Presbyterianism which flourished in Gaelic-speaking Scotland after the
disruption of 1843, and that his father, James, was both a schoolmaster
and a poet, the author of a Gaelic collection entitled *Fasgnadh* and a
man with a wide range of cultural interests. It is evident that Thomson
has read MacLean's work and admires it. The lines 'Bidh eagal orm
roimh do bhòidhchead/ is tusa pòsda mus d' fhuair mi/ aithne air do
chliù' ('I shall be afraid of your beauty – you were married before I had
knowledge of your maidenly virtue') (from ''Nam dhachaigh eadar dhà
dhùthaich') ('In my House between Two Countries')) can read like an
echo of the older poet's love cycle. Generally, though, Thomson's use of
rhyme and his metrical patterning are more conservative than
MacLean's, and show a clear debt to the traditions of nineteenth-century

song still very much alive in Lewis. 'A' snìomh cainnte' ('Weaving Words') can be useful in helping us to clarify what makes the two poets different. Thomson is more plangent, more inward-turning. If one were to speak in terms of dynamic range, then Thomson moves between a *pianissimo* and a *mezzo piano*, very occasionally rising to a *mezzo forte*, while MacLean not infrequently pulls out all the stops to attain a *fortissimo* or even further. MacLean's utterance has a public, bardic strain, where Thomson is more introspective, exhibiting a richer and more highly developed sensuality and an almost Proustian awareness of earliest impressions, with the associated ability to achieve regeneration by recalling them.

'Dà là' ('Changed Days', from *An Dealbh Briste*) lays the groundwork for much of what Thomson was to write in the period leading up to *An Rathad Cian*. One is reminded of Eliot's notion of the 'objective correlative' as Thomson discusses the appropriate choice of images to represent emotion. He does not shrink from citing the English Romantic Wordsworth's use of a withered bush as his symbol for grief, while the rising moon stood for joy. Thomson's own choices are rather different:

> Ceud gu leith blianna 'na dhèidh sin
> fhuair mise samhla air lèireadh,
> 's ged dh'fhaodadh nach tuig thu mo chàs-sa,
> 'se th' ann *kiosk* air ceann stràide.
>
> 'S mur b' e gum bheil aogas na brèig air
> bheirinn dhut samhla air èibhneas –
> gach *neon* tha 'n taighean nam fionnsgeul
> air leth-taobh Stràide a' Phrionnsa.
>
> *A hundred and fifty years later*
> *I found a symbol for grieving,*
> *and though you may not understand my trouble*
> *it is a kiosk at a street end.*
>
> *And but for the fact that it looks false*
> *I would give you a symbol for joy –*
> *the neon lights on the cinemas*
> *along one side of Princes Street.*

Since at least the end of the eighteenth century, a serious problem facing poets who wrote in Gaelic had been that, while they themselves had increasingly to come to terms with a society transformed by the

Industrial Revolution and its aftermath, the language was not expanding, in day to day use, in a way that would automatically allow them to portray that world. The two images Thomson chooses are not only unequivocally modern and therefore alien to 'natural', 'ecological' sentimentalisations of Gaelic culture. They are also quite literally outside the language. Neither word, indeed, is strictly speaking English either, 'kiosk' having a Turkish origin and 'neon' being based on the Greek word for 'new'. The effect is to jolt the reader, foregrounding the choice of poetic imagery and the specific problems of making such choices in Gaelic (since in poetry the choice of an object is always also the choice of a word). At the same time, the perceived awkwardness of Thomson's choices beautifully mimics the speaker's own difficulty in integrating and coming to terms with the feelings for which he seeks a correlative.

The splendid 'An Tobar' ('The Well') from the same collection works more unobtrusively thanks to its more 'organic' imagery. Differently from MacLean, whose poetry is so extraordinarily personal (one could even add ego-centred) or else, in 'An Cuilthionn', espouses political positions which could never appeal to a majority of his readers, Thomson returns again and again to meditate on the community he grew up in and the fate of its language and the associated culture. An old woman begs a boy to fetch her water from a nearly forgotten spring, with the implication that both the woman and the water represent a culture on its last legs, incapable of renewal. 'Achadh-bhuana' ('Harvest Field'), on the other hand, is an infinitely delicate treatment of the loss of a girl's virginity, not to the speaker, but to another man, because the speaker has held back. The half-harvested field ('pàirt gun a' bhuain') where some of the crop is still green evokes the situation the speaker and the girl had shared, suspended between adolescence and maturity, while the fact that the wound she receives from a hidden blade cannot be healed ('dhiùlt e slànadh') shows the irrevocable nature of her loss, and of the consequences it will bring.

Thomson's range, however, is broad, and a poem already referred to, ''Nam dhachaigh eadar dhà dhùthaich' ('In My House between Two Countries') explains how he is trapped between two languages, between images of the seashore and rural purity and others like that of a prostitute on the corner of a city street. There is something of the Yeats of 'The Circus Animals' Desertion' in the 'daoimein/ cladhaicht á mèin an aoibhneis,/ 's a' ghrùid 's am morghan làmh riuth'' ('diamonds dug from the mine of ecstasy,/ with the scum and the gravel by them') which constitutes his poetry, as if beauty must necessarily be plucked from amidst such ugliness. No beauty, however, is capable of ridding the poet's house of its reek of death.

This theme returns again and again in his next volume, *Eadar Samhradh is Foghar* (*Between Summer and Autumn*) (1967). 'Cainnt nan oghaichean' ('Grandchildren's Talk') is a wry celebration of the arrival of electricity in island communities. Though lights can now be switched on, failure to pass on the language to the next generation ensures that a very different, if no less important light will be switched off. While there is no explicit reference, the context leads one to read the wounded lark on the threshold of death in 'Uiseag' ('The Lark') as one more image for the plight of Gaelic:

> tha do latha dheth seachad,
> is dè math bhith gad iargain?
>
> Ach ged a theireadh mo reusan sin rium,
> 's ged tha 'n fhuil tha mu mo chridhe a' reodhadh
> brag air bhrag, is bliann' air bhlianna,
> cluinnidh mi i ag èigheachd ris a' chuimhne
> 'O! na faiceadh tu i air iteig
> cha sguireadh tu ga h-ionndrain gu sìorraidh.'

> *it's all over with you,*
> *and what's the good of mourning?*

> *But though my reason might say that to me,*
> *And though the blood around my heart is freezing –*
> *year upon year I hear its sharp reports –*
> *yet still it shouts to the memory*
> *'O! could you but have seen her on the wing*
> *you would go on longing for her for ever.'*

While to speak of photograph and caption would be an undue simplification, it is clear what type of poem is emerging. An image is presented to us, affecting, sensually developed, and we are expected to interpret it in a nearly allegorical way, to work out what the poet is using it to tell us about a rather different subject. This is one reason why Thomson's poetry translates into English with unusual effectiveness.

The strategy remains alive in Thomson's writing because he not only experiments with it but also makes its operation part of what he writes about, as in the grim 'Cisteachan-laighe' ('Coffins'), surely the crowning achievement of his second volume, placed, significantly, at its close. Here not only the imagery itself but the attribution of meaning is drawn into the working of the poem and offered for our consideration. As it opens, the speaker, now an adult, passes a joiner's shop in the city and remembers how, as a child, he had watched his grandfather making coffins. Then he had no idea about what death meant. Even when standing at his grandfather's grave, he had failed to reflect that the coffin maker was now coffined himself. All that the child longed for was warmth, tea and sociability. Up to this point in the poem, lack of knowledge and the failure to attribute meaning, to move from object to symbol, have been foregrounded. In the concluding section, however, the coffin comes closer and closer until the speaker, with the reader, becomes claustrophobically imprisoned inside it. At school, the speaker failed to realise that the children sitting around him were effectively coffins within which something crucial had died or was dying ('cha tug mi 'n aire do na cisteachan-laighe,/ ged a bha iad 'nan suidhe mun cuairt orm'), notwithstanding the English and Lowland ornamentation used to adorn them. The realisation comes, the crucial link is made, at the very moment when he perceives nails penetrating him and experiences a pain to which neither tea nor company will bring relief (''s cha shlànaich tea no còmhradh an cràdh'). As the poem proceeds, its speaker fails to carry out, or postpones carrying out, the task assigned its readers, of noticing analogues and establishing connections. What makes this poem such a perfectly crafted object is the way it submits, along with its message, its method for the reader's consideration and perusal.

'Mu chrìochan Hòil' ('In the Vicinity of Hol') (again from his second collection) is a generous revisiting of the scenarios of Thomson's child-hood, to which he returns, with thinly veiled bitterness, in 'Hòl, air atharrachadh' ('Hol, Changed') from *Smeur an Dòchais* (*Bramble of Hope*) (1991). The earlier poem's extended lines constitute a convincing and flexible naturalisation into Gaelic of the English iambic pentameter. Wordsworth is clearly present as an influence, though Thomson's incisive intellect and his uncomfortable clarity of vision produce a distinctly modern idiom, with Proustian echoes:

> As aonais sùgh an taiseachaidh bha sin
> bha 'n diugh mo chrìdh air crìonadh, 's cha bu lèir
> dhomh, air taobh thall nan duilleag, madainn mhoch
> a' sgaoileadh brat na fionnarachd roimh 'n là,
> 's an iarmailt fhuar ga failceadh leis a' chuan . . .

> *Without that moistening juice*
> *my heart had withered by now,*
> *I would not see, through the leaves, early morning*
> *spreading a cloak of freshness in front of day,*
> *and the cold air being washed by the sea . . .*

An Rathad Cian was a milestone in both poetic and personal terms. Thomson's attitude to Lewis has none of the virulence that characterises Iain Crichton Smith's. The cycle marks his definitive acceptance of exile, because his childhood is now a considerable distance in years away, and he is never going to reinhabit its physical setting. The fifty-six items comprising it make up an elegy, almost a funeral oration, though what has died is neither Lewis nor Thomson, but the bond between them. The earlier ambiguity arising from Thomson's being poised between two languages is replaced by a different and more complex kind of ambivalence:

> chuimhnich mi air Bean Lot,
> 's an dèidh sin, an dèidh sin,
> tha mi gu bhith 'na mo charragh-cuimhne. (poem 53)

> *I remembered Lot's wife,*
> *and yet, and yet,*
> *I am going to be a memorial-pillar.*

Aware as he is of the dangers involved, Thomson nevertheless determines to build his own memorial, or rather, to become it. There follows the haunting image of an oarsman, 'Mo chùl ri mo cheann-uidhe/ m' aghaidh ris na th'air mo chùl' ('My back turned to my destination,/ facing what lies behind me', poem 54). He is able to contemplate without flinching that which he is leaving behind. Readers, too, are drawn in as the boat itself becomes a kind of coffin, the coffin of a bond relinquished: 'grèim againn air an eileatrom/ 's i tulgadh 's a' tulgadh air bàrr cuimhne' ('we grasp the bier-poles,/ rocking and plunging on the surface of memory', poem 55).

The death of Thomson's mother was among the triggers for the cycle. While it is easy to connect poems like 34 'Na canadh duine' ('Let No One Say') or 49 'An galar' ('The Disease') with such an event, second person address throughout the cycle is too rich to be pinned down in this way. Lines such as these could be addressed as much to the island as to the poet's mother:

> Chaidh mi mach á tarraing do phlanaid,
> chan eil mo cheum trom, ged is trom am meadhon-latha,
> air na ròidean eòlach sin,
> tha mi seòladh ann a fànas leam fhìn. (poem 49)

I escaped the pull of your planet,
my step is weightless, heavy though middle age may be,
on these well-known roads,
I float alone in space.

   That sense of being in free fall was introduced at the very start of the cycle in poem 3, where a young cormorant announces 'tha mi saor anns an speur,/ 's mi tuiteam' ('I am free in the sky,/ falling'). Frightening as the loss is, it offers its own brand of liberation. There is a high degree of echoing and consistent cross-reference linking poem to poem, often across a considerable distance. One way of describing the cycle, and the experiences it evokes, is as a handful of peats which can keep the fire burning just a little bit longer. This image, from poem 51 'Nuair a thig an dorch' ('When the Dark Comes'), sends the reader right back to poem 7, the marvellously sensual 'Dh'fhairich mi thu le mo chasan' ('I got the feel of you with my feet'). Lewis is of course the addressee, and what is being celebrated is getting permission to ditch shoes and walk around barefoot with the arrival of summer. But the tone is like that of a love poem: 'Dh'fhairich mi taobh an ascaoin dhìot 's an taobh caoin/ 's cha bu mhisde' ('I felt the rough side of you and the smooth/ and was none the worse of it'). As a boy, when his bare feet got cold, the poet would warm them on a peat sod next to the hearth. The middle-aged man still has mud between his toes, the mud of memory and sensual recollection he feels no need to wash away. The imagery echoing from here to poem 51 is delicate yet profoundly powerful in effect.
   A noteworthy strength of the cycle is its refusal to collude in the fantasy of a pristine, unadulteratedly Gaelic world, as adumbrated by MacLean in the elegy for his brother Calum:

> Ghabh thu an ratreuta,
> fhir bhig a' chridhe mhóir,
> ghabh thu do dhìon air cùl a' ghàrraidh
> far 'm mìlse muran na Gàidhlig . . .

> *You took the retreat,*
> *little one of the big heart,*
> *you took your refuge behind the wall*
> *where the bent grass of Gaelic is sweetest . . .*[3]

This appears to be precisely what MacLean is doing, given the elegy's significant position toward the close of his life's work. *An Rathad Cian* is filled with impurities. Among the figures it portrays, Donald Matheson (poem 20) claims to have known Hoover and Roosevelt and reads the *Spectator*, while another returned emigrant speaks to his dog in Spanish, remembering 'coilltean Chile' ('the woods of Chile'), Punta Arenas and Santiago (poem 17). The little girl in poem 19 has a plastic toy from Hong Kong ''s bidh a' chreathail a' breothadh anns an t-sabhal ùr le mullach zinc air' ('and the cradle will rot in the new barn with its zinc roof'). The imagery the poet himself introduces refuses to be consistently Gaelic. The addressee of poem 10 is 'sgìth le coiseachd ròidean Ruisia,/ rocach mar chaillich Thibetich' ('tired with walking the roads of Russia,/ wrinkled like an old Tibetan woman'), her hands 'an-fhoiseil/ air cuibhle na h-ùrnaigh' ('restless/ on the prayer-wheel'). At the cycle's conclusion, the poet himself speaks in terms of different religious traditions: 'thàinig mi mach ás do theampall,/ ás a' cheò chùbhraidh ... chuir mi orm mo bhrògan ... chuir mi a' chuibhle/ air falbh fon chuibhrig' ('I have come out of your temple,/ out of the fragrant smoke ... I have put on my shoes ... put the prayer-wheel/ beneath the cover').

Thomson, as revealed in the cycle is, of course, a moderate in terms of creed. If he is a sceptic, that scepticism is expressed as a gentle ecumenism that embraces different forms of Christianity, along with other belief systems. This is why he is able to joke about 'Playing football with a prophet' (''A cluich air football le fàidh') in poem 11, and to assert with gentle humour that

> thuig mi, gu math tràth,
> gu robh fàidhean anns an Eaglais Shaoir cuideachd,
> fàidhean ann am Barraigh
> agus eadhon anns an Eilean Sgitheanach ...

> [I] *understood, quite young,*
> *that there were prophets in the Free Church too,*
> *prophets in Barra, and even in Skye ...*

The leap forward in technique is rooted in the fact that, with *An Rathad Cian*, it is no longer possible to distinguish vehicle from tenor, the image from that which it is intended to represent. Thomson leaves allegory far behind, given that Lewis is what the cycle is about in every sense, both its subject matter and the imagery that pervades it. If what can be termed the caption technique of earlier volumes pushed us towards specific interpretation, to a point of arrival, with *An Rathad Cian* an unstable oscillation sets in, so that we are constantly driven back to the perceptible realities of the island, as if these can never be exhausted through any attribution of meaning. It is Thomson's delicate sensuality, continued access to the store of sensations from his distant childhood, that makes this oscillation feasible.

Thomson has published three more books of verse since 1970, not to mention the 'Dàin ás ùr' section of new poems in his collected volume *Creachadh na Clàrsaich*. He claims to have as much unpublished and uncollected verse as would fill three more, so that any assessment of the latter part of his career has to remain highly provisional. *Meall Garbh* (*The Rugged Mountain*) (1995) can be seen as a backward step, its central sequence, written in 1988, returning to the Perthshire landscape of Thomson's adolescence and envisioning a new kind of clearance, aimed at restoring what had once been:

> chuirinn na coigrich dhan an fhàsach –
> gu Glaschu 's Dun Dèagh is Bradford,
> Bognor Regis is Hull is Southport,
> Comar nan Allt is Milton Keynes is Surbiton –
> is chuirinn na Gàidheil 'nan àite . . . (poem 11)

> *I would send the strangers to the wilderness –*
> *to Glasgow and Dundee and Bradford,*
> *Bognor Regis and Hull and Southport,*
> *Cumbernauld and Milton Keynes and Surbiton –*
> *and I would put Gaels in their place . . .*

The sequence 'Air stràidean Ghlaschu' ('On Glasgow Streets'), which opens *Smeur an Dòchais*, marks a clear advance. Subdued as the tone is, Thomson here stakes out an unequivocal claim as a poet of urban realities. His attitude to Glasgow is a disenchanted one and, given that the sequence focuses on street life, it is no surprise that he is drawn to depict the disturbed, the marginalised and the deprived rather than those for whom the city has meant success and integration. Deft as these cameos are, they prompt uneasy reflections on immigration, emigration and the juxtaposition of different cultures. How much irony is there in the statement, closing poem 7, that the spectacle of Burmese girls in a café helps the poet understand why educational authorities refuse to take Gaelic education seriously? Visiting Tradestown Street (poem 13) brings to mind the erratically epic poetry of Uilleam MacDhunlèibhe (William Livingston 1808–70), a fiery Gaelic patriot of the Victorian period. Though Thomson can see the parallels between this immigrant from Islay and 'Innseanaich len taighean-badhair,/ turban an àite a' bhonaid Ghaidhealaich' ('Indians with their emporia,/ the turban instead of the Highland bonnet') his assessment of the situation is far from hopeful, with 'eachdraidh air a cur an dìmeas/ 's an là ùr fad air falbh' ('history depreciated,/ and the new day far distant'). Elsewhere, he manages to contemplate the fading of Gaelic with something resembling equanimity. Indeed, mature and conscious reflection on the vicissitudes of cultural displacement and replacement constitutes a precious strand in these later volumes. 'Feòrag ghlas, tuath air Braco' ('Grey Squirrel, North of Braco') from *Meall Garbh* compares the ousting of the red squirrel by the grey to the Gaels' assimilation of the Picts. The poet imagines the squirrel he has glimpsed arguing its right to be in Perthshire on the basis of Scottish emigration to the New World. A not dissimilar line of argument about the mutuality of population exchange and the longterm consequences of colonialisation could indeed be deployed by the Indian shopowners of Tradestown. Interestingly, in this case Thomson lays the blame for the eradication of Gaelic firmly at the feet of Gaels themselves.

Thomson's productive journey is a long one, extending across more than half a century, and it is not yet complete. Insufficient critical attention has been paid to his work after 1970 for a definitive balance yet to be hazarded. Rather than being confined by his choice of language, he has pushed the boundaries of his poetry outwards, achieving a meditation on cultural change and interchange and on the possibility of cultural death which never becomes cold or cerebral because he never loses touch with individual meanings, with how such phenomena feel and taste, and how they inscribe themselves within the fated limits of one single human existence. And everywhere one encounters his saving humour, at times rising to the savage invective of an Alasdair Mac Mhaighstir Alasdair, but more generally understated, delicate, bringing with it a needed sense of balance and proportion.

A sonnet from *Loaves and Fishes* (1959) offers a useful and remarkably concise introduction to the world of George Mackay Brown's poetry.[4] The title, 'Chapel between Cornfield and Shore, Stromness', places it firmly in an Orkney setting, announces that religion will be a major preoccupation, and cites the two means by which the communities Brown (1921–96) depicts sustain themselves, fishing and agriculture. The poem itself sets in motion at least three lexical series, concerning church architecture and the connected ideology ('arch', 'chancel', 'choir', 'sanctuary', 'ritual', 'ceremonies'), agriculture ('uprooted', 'acre', 'corn',

'sun', 'rain', 'dust') and the sea ('ebb', 'wave', 'rockpool'). Their inter-
linking comes about through paradoxical application of the pathetic
fallacy, and is intended to stress their fundamental relation to one
another. The ruined chapel has an 'uprooted' wall, though walls are not
organic, neither grow, nor have roots, and the ruin's stones 'bleed',
though stones have neither a heart nor circulation. With delicate yet
emphatic alliteration, the closing line associates the tools of fisherman
and crofter in 'the hooked hands and harrowed heart' with which each
communicant greets the 'spindrift bread' which is Christ's body. The
purport of the sonnet is, barefacedly and breathtakingly, to predict a
reversal of history. The 'ebb' corresponds to the Scottish Reformation
in the sixteenth century and the associated abandonment or destruction
of the old places of worship, but 'the wave turns round'. The sestet
begins with an imperative which fails to make clear who is com-
manding and who is being commanded, looking forward to the time
when the 'maimed rockpool' that is Orkney, or Scotland, will at last
be reconnected to the larger community of 'flood' and 'ocean', and a
'bronze bell' will preside with its chiming over the combined activities
of 'ploughshare and creel'. The sonnet closes with the image of a
Catholic priest distributing the host to the members of a sinful yet eager
congregation.

The second quatrain describes the turning of the tide and the growth
of the new corn, both inevitable, cyclic reversals of a previous situation.
The cycle can only be completed if there is bloodshed. It requires 'the
crucifixion of the seed'. Religion and agriculture are superimposed. The
seed which breaks open and dies to give new life is identified with the
body of Christ on the cross which, thanks to its willing sacrifice, makes
possible a new life for humanity.

Brown resolutely turns his back upon modernity, confidently pre-
dicting the reversal of those circumstances which have brought into
being the world we know. Against progress and its much vaunted ben-
efits he sets a cyclical pattern with both a religious and an agricultural
aspect, in which he places a faith modernity cannot elicit from him.
The biological aspect of this pattern is explored more fully in 'The
Ballad of John Barleycorn, the Ploughman, and the Furrow' from *An
Orkney Tapestry* (1969). Strictly speaking, the poem is not in ballad
form, all lines being of equal length, but as each stanza ends with
Barleycorn's name, Brown performs the significant technical feat of
devising, without forcing, eleven rhymes for it, one in the second line
of each stanza. This is a dialogue introduced by a male speaker, a
ploughman who answers with another question the question put to him
by a female furrow (the feminine as gap, space, an emptiness waiting

passively to be filled). The main part of the poem, in italics, is taken up with her account of how her beloved has been murdered, his bones broken and ground to dust and, while the latter is burned, his heart drowned in a vat. Winter has arrived, and John Barleycorn is nowhere to be seem. One might read this as merely a poetic account of how bread comes to be baked and whisky brewed. But Barleycorn was 'my priest', caught while 'at his golden prayer', and when the speaker stills the furrow's hunger, at the poem's end, with a bannock, and gives her whisky to drink before bedding her, there is a subtle but undeniable parallel with the taking of communion under the two kinds of wafer and wine. Food and drink have emerged from the furrow thanks to the murder of the harvest. Their ability to sustain further life once they have risen from the dead is offered as a parallel to the sacrifice encapsulated in the Catholic Mass.

Brown, then, synthesises a myth from Catholic doctrine and plant life and sets it at the heart of his poetic world. The myth attributes an essential role to violence, and this aestheticisation of violence is a problem any serious reader of his poetry will have to tussle with at some point. At what price, in human, poetic and ethical terms, can violence be made a thing of beauty, be, to all effects, the focus of celebration? For the poet's attitude is not a neutral one.

The third item in the sequence 'Stations of the Cross', from *Winterfold* (1976), describes, from the point of view of one of the plunderers, how the crew members of a Viking ship massacre a community of defenceless Irish monks and desecrate their church. Here one can say that violence is aestheticised through euphemism: 'Havard flashed his axe in the face of a brother' sounds more like sleight of hand, like a conjuring trick, than a vicious cleaving of bone and flesh. We read of 'a red splash' which might just be altar wine, but is more probably blood, and when we are told that 'Soon that hive was all smoke and stickiness', the stickiness is caused not by honey, but by spilled and quickly drying blood.

The Viking has no previous experience of monastic communities. He is unable to understand the monks' purpose or how they function. This means that he has to translate what he sees into his own terms. And so he speaks of the place they destroy as a hive, its occupants bees, creatures 'like insects' with 'raised hands'. The sign of the cross becomes 'a cross of gray air', pointless and insubstantial, and a boy folding his hands for prayer, no doubt in anticipation of approaching death, 'made a dove of his two hands'. The church is 'a cave of wax and perfumes' while the members of this strange community, where no woman appears to offer hospitality, are 'eunuchs'.

Brown obliges his readers to what is effectively a labour of translation, or rather retranslation. We have to trace a path through these images, these formulas, in order to establish what is actually happening. Things do not appear as themselves, but must become other than themselves. Within Brown's poetic world, violence subsists thanks to a kind of transmutation which brings it into line with his overall imperatives of stylisation and aestheticisation. The consequences for his diction are fundamental to any analysis of his poetry. As much is evident in one of his most accessible pieces, the elegy for his postman father from *Loaves and Fishes* entitled 'Hamnavoe' (Brown's name for Stromness, another example of transmutation). It would be hard to conceive of a more relentlessly poeticised diction than the one we encounter in this poem. Trope after trope is activated, so that the reader is forced to engage in a process of unravelling. The 'closes' to which letters are delivered are personified, 'opening and shutting like legends'. A cart-horse drinking at the fountain is described as dredging, while the striking of its hooves on the cobbles is a kiss of steel eliciting fire. The drinkers in the pub are rendered as 'three blue elbows' falling with the regularity of waves, and the boys with their 'penny wands' are catching not small fry but 'gleams' from water which is 'tangled veins'. Fishing and agriculture are conflated. The herring boats are 'tillers' (a careful pun) trapping 'sudden silver harvests'. The bellman on his rounds who gives the latest local news foretells events, but the past tense allows Brown a further pun on 'fore-tolled'. Oddly, such a tender poem nonetheless demands its sacrifice, its willing bout of pain, as the poet son at the close casts himself in the role of the Roman hero Mucius Scaevola, declaring his readiness to put his hand into 'the fire of images' for his father's sake.

Not violence alone, then, is aestheticised, and in such relentless pursuit of the poetic there is an inevitable danger of falling into kitsch. Cruel as the term may seem, it fits the intermittently lurid nature of Brown's subject matter, as well as the determination his poetry shows to proclaim its status as aesthetic object, deliberately set apart and cut off from the world in which it subsists. It is important that kitsch objects should be useless and out of place, that they should not fit or blend in with their surroundings. Kitsch can be defined as a hypertrophy of the aesthetic function, to the point that, all other conceivable functions having fallen into disuse (and many objects which have become primarily aesthetic in our eyes, such as a Bach cantata or a medieval bishop's jewelled crozier, originally had a range of other meanings which could relegate their beauty to second place), this last remaining function atrophies in turn, reaching excess. For is it not essential that the aesthetic function should subsist in relation to other potential and competing functions? That beauty should bring with it a sense of emergence, of discovery, even of the accidental and unplanned?

If to speak of kitsch may be an overstatement, then at the very least Brown's diction is extremely mannered. A crucial aspect of Mannerist painting was to distort the proportions of the human form so as to deprive the resultant image of any 'natural' quality, advertising the intervention of the painter and lifting his product above the level of mere mirroring or imitation. Brown's diction is mannered as that of the eighteenth-century Augustan poets was mannered, and has its own very specific decorum. *Fishermen with Ploughs* (1971) is concerned with the history of settlement in Rackwick, at the time of writing a deserted crofting township on the island of Hoy, between the Orkney mainland and the Caithness coast. Beginning with a ship which sails from strife-torn Norway in the ninth century, the book's next four sections survey life in Rackwick in the Middle Ages, after the Reformation and the arrival of landlords from Scotland, until the place's desertion when economic progress offers more enticing rewards to its people in other locations. Though the language in these sections is simpler, Brown retains his fondness for epithets. A fishmonger exchanges 'bits of dull silver', his fish, for 'torrents of uncaught silver', the coins he takes from his customers (p. 60), and a cow is 'a lady of butter' (p. 57).

One possible justification (perhaps better described as an alibi, and certainly far from being an explanation) for Brown's peculiar diction is as a homage to the 'kennings' of the medieval sagas which form a crucial stratum in the complex palimpsest of Orkney's cultural history. In the opening section of *Fishermen with Ploughs*, whose characters presumably speak the language of the sagas, diction is so dense that deciphering it can be problematic. Brown in fact offers his readers a kind of key in a summary placed between the contents and the opening of the cycle. Here we learn that 'Dragon' refers to feuding neighbours in Norway, while 'Dove' is the name of the ship which carries the emigrants to Orkney. When their leader, Thorkeld, uses his sword on the village's attackers, we are told that 'the Dragon tasted the bronze fish'. When, in a burnt out stable, he 'coaxed a garnet eye', the eye may belong to his surviving stallion, but this interpretation is not certain. Njal, we read, 'bore his manseed wombfurled waveward'. Again, the dense formulas are euphemistic. It would seem that, in the process of saving Gudrun, carrying her from the women's quarters to the ship, Njal has had time to penetrate her, so that she is already carrying his seed inside her. Brown's formulation of gender relationships deteriorates into the comical when Njal addresses her, in the poem entitled 'Gudrun', as '*Thou sweet grain jar*'. The image of woman as jar, as vessel, pervades the entire poem. Here, as elsewhere in Mackay Brown's work, woman's role as receptacle is so emphasised as to overshadow other possible roles or functions.

The task to which Brown's readers are constrained is not just one of retranslation but of piecing together, thanks to his fondness for ellipsis. And his use of ellipsis brings him, willy nilly, back into contact with modernity, or postmodernity. For what it does is to highlight how discrete events or phenomena can only be strung together in meaningful sequences of cause and effect thanks to the presence of a master narrative. 'Taxman' (p. 27) is a muted protest against the levies on a peasant community which images their labour in 'seven scythes' set aside now the labour is done. The crop being brought home is personified as 'Beard upon golden beard' as if it were a phalanx of marching soldiers. Ale is distributed and dancing begins. Only the arrival of an alien 'horseman' in the last and shortest line allows the reader, by connecting him to the title, to elicit the import of the poem. The presence of ellipsis in 'Witch' (p. 25) is still more striking. Only at the close is the reason for Wilma's victimisation hinted, as the 'bible fishermen' become 'three unlucky fishermen' launching their boat. They must have denounced her for jinxing their expeditions. The ritual of public burning is imaged as a horrific species of couture ('the hangman put his red shirt on Wilma') while the circle of onlookers is a 'cold drunken wheel'. Euphemism and aestheticisation are set to work again. Violence is distanced and turned into something else, made an object for our contemplation. The achieved distancing is a further instance of the poet's skill and thus implicitly held up for our admiration.

In narrative terms, then, Brown's world is offered to us in fragments, like the tesserae of a mosaic we are invited to assemble, or to reassemble. It is unhelpful to read his espousal of Catholicism (the poet was formally received into the Church in 1961) as a genuine desire to convert his readers. The point is perhaps rather that readers will not share his value or belief system, and that this divergence between poet and reader will highlight the role of ideology, and of the associated narratives, in allowing meaning to be conferred upon experience. Fragmentation means that Brown has a fondness for lists and litanies, for twelves, sevens and threes. His poetry is then, intendedly or not, multicultural in a fashion appropriate both to the history of the archipelago he came from and with which he chose to identify, and to the world of the late twentieth century. It is as if Brown re-entered modernity, or postmodernity, in spite of his rejection of it. His weaving of agricultural process and the narrative of the Crucifixion is, of course, heterodox. The Christian narrative does not follow a cyclical pattern, and for

Catholic theology, the sacrifice of the Mass is not a repetition of the sacrifice on Calvary but, mystically, one and the same with it. It takes place not many times but only once.

Brown's offered world of natural cycles and subsistence farming, with its necessary, rhythmically returning violence, is hardly an attractive one for modern readers. Assigning physical labour to the males and identifying the females overwhelmingly with the reproductive function (for what can be the value of a seed that fails to reproduce?) means that the gender ideology of his world is starkly repressive. Brown, like W. S. Graham before him, was a student at Newbattle Abbey, south of Edinburgh, and his time there coincided with the wardenship of Edwin Muir, with whom Brown shared his Orkney background. The closing section of *Fishermen with Ploughs* is in carefully patterned prose instead of poetry, and shows a probably conscious debt to the second of Muir's 'Horses' poem. Though it is presented in real enough terms, the action is so hard to credit that it is better regarded as a fable. A group of adult men and women escape from a nuclear holocaust practically unharmed, one of the women, strangely, suffering blinding but no other injury. By rowing they manage to travel from west central Scotland to Rackwick in Orkney, and there, gradually, the foundations of a new community are laid. The process is again a cyclical one, and Brown's predictions anything but idealised or utopian. No sooner have the first children been born and basic needs been provided for, thanks to the 'brutal stations from winter to the loaf and jar' (p. 95) than an oppressive productive and reproductive hierarchy begins to establish itself. The necessary victim is chosen and publicly flogged, 'still clothed in the tortured flesh of man', because '*Someone must suffer*'. He is to become the outcast, the scapegoat, beachcomber and tinker. The cyclical pattern offers no hint of a possibility of escape from the overall bleakness of Brown's poetic vision, however beautified by language or perceived sacrality.

All three poets in this chapter are concerned with ex-centricity, with the distant and far out, with the decentred. In Graham's case, the expedition into uncharted lands was a condition of his poetry, detaching him from chronology and from the progression and inevitable obsolescence of literary modes. If, in his own life, gravitating to Cornwall meant seeking out a liminal situation, in his poetry increasing isolation allowed him to elude external influences, to pursue doggedly his own poetic itinerary, engaging in a very personal kind of search party no one else chose, or was expected, to join. It would be a foolhardy reader indeed that identified the Orkney depicted in Brown's work with any real environment. If Brown's carefully artificial bodying forth of an island universe offered him a place of retreat from modernity, the growing schematisation that affected it paradoxically brought him back into contact with those very factors he had been determined to evade. If this, in the end, constitutes the strength of his poetry, conferring on it an unexpected and unintentional (post)modernity, this may well have been the very opposite of what the poet strove consciously to achieve. Thomson, with his tenderness, his muted sensuality and his willingness to evolve, to abandon himself to stimuli and circumstances and be changed by them, has the greatest self-awareness, and poetic self-awareness, of the trio. His movement is in the end not one of retreat or distancing but of progression and incorporation, though he manages to give the impression that the island he has bid farewell to, that specific Lewis whose very continuing existence he has come to doubt, can somehow remain alive within him. It is a memory but, like all memories, with the passage of time and in particular the encroaching of old age, it will take on its own contemporaneity, affirming a special grade of presence. And as such it can never be entirely lost.

Notes

1. Poems are quoted from *Collected Poems 1942–1977* (London, Faber 1979). Also of interest are *Uncollected Poems* (Warwick, Greville Press 1990), *Aimed at Nobody: Poems from Notebooks* eds Margaret Blackwood and Robin Skelton (London, Faber 1993) and Michael and Margaret Snow eds *The Nightfisherman: Selected Letters of W. S. Graham* (Carcanet, Manchester 1999). See further Ronnie Duncan and Jonathan Davidson eds *The Constructed Space: a Celebration of W. S. Graham* (Lincoln, Jackson's Arm 1994), and Tony Lopez *The Poetry of W. S. Graham* (Edinburgh, Edinburgh University Press 1989) (with, on pp. 161–4, a listing of secondary literature on the poet), Neil Corcoran 'A New Romanticism: Apocalypse, Dylan Thomas, W. S. Graham, George Barker' in his *English Poetry since 1940* (London, Longman 1993) pp. 39–57, Ruth Grogan 'W. S. Graham: a Dialogical Imagination' in *English Studies in Canada* XV (2) (June 1989) pp. 196–213, Tony Lopez 'T. S. Eliot and W. S. Graham' in *Scottish Literary Journal* 19 (1) (May 1992) pp. 35–46, Edwin Morgan 'Sea, the Desert, the City: Environment and Language in W. S. Graham, Hamish Henderson and Tom Leonard' in *Yearbook of English Studies* 17 (1987) pp. 31–45 and W. S. Milne 'Measuring Watchman: the Poetry of W. S. Graham' in *Agenda* 33 (1) (Spring 1995) pp. 81–8.
2. Poems are quoted from Ruaraidh MacThòmais / Derick Thomson *Creachadh na Clàrsaich: Cruinneachadh de Bhàrdachd 1940–1980 / Plundering the Harp: Collected Poems 1940–1980* (Edinburgh, Macdonald 1982), *Smeur an Dòchais / Bramble of Hope* (Edinburgh, Canongate 1991) and *Meall Garbh / The Rugged Mountain* (Glasgow, Gairm 1995). Thomson is also the editor of *A Companion to Gaelic Scotland* (Oxford, Blackwell 1983). See further his *Introduction to Gaelic Poetry* 2nd edn (Edinburgh, Edinburgh University Press 1990), 'Poetry in

Scottish Gaelic, 1945–1992' in Hans-Werner Ludwig and Lothar Fietz eds *Poetry in the British Isles: Non-metropolitan Perspectives* (Cardiff, University of Wales Press 1995) pp. 157–72 and Christopher Whyte 'Derick Thomson: Reluctant Symbolist' in *Chapman* 38 (Spring 1984) pp. 1–6 and 'Thomson's *An Rathad Cian*' in *Lines Review* 112 (March 1990) pp. 5–11.

3. *O Choille gu Bearradh / From Wood to Ridge* (Manchester, Carcanet and Edinburgh, Birlinn 1999) pp. 272–5.

4. Poems are quoted from *Selected Poems 1954–1992* (London, John Murray 1997) and from *Fishermen with Ploughs: a Poem Cycle* (London, The Hogarth Press 1971). The posthumous volume *Travellers* (London, John Murray 2001) edited by Archie Bevan and Brian Murray brings together hitherto uncollected poems. See further the autobiographical essay in Maurice Lindsay ed. *As I Remember: Ten Scottish Authors Recall How Writing Began for Them* (London, Robert Hale 1979) pp. 9–21 and *For the Islands I Sing: an Autobiography* (London, John Murray 1997), Alan Bold *George Mackay Brown* (London and Edinburgh, Oliver and Boyd 1978), Sabine Schmid '*Keeping the Sources Pure*': the Making of George Mackay Brown (Bern, Peter Lang 2003), Hilda Spear ed. *George Mackay Brown – A Survey of His Work and a Full Bibliography* (The Edwin Mellen Press, Lewiston, Queenston, Lampeter 2000), David Annwn '"The Binding Breath": Island and Community in the Poetry of George Mackay Brown' in Hans-Werner Ludwig and Lothar Fietz eds *Poetry in the British Isles: Non-metropolitan Perspectives* (Cardiff, University of Wales Press 1995) pp. 283–310, Stewart Conn 'Poets of the Sixties – II: George Mackay Brown' in *Lines Review* 22 (Winter 1966) pp. 10–17 and Douglas Dunn '"Finished Fragrance": the Poems of George Mackay Brown' in *Poetry Nation* 2 (1974) pp. 80–92.

8

The 1980s
(Douglas Dunn, Kenneth White, Liz Lochhead, Iain Crichton Smith)

The book of poems with which Douglas Dunn (1942–) marked the death of his first wife, *Elegies* (1985), constitutes a watershed within his work in more than one sense. Its background in the poet's biography brings an especial keenness, not just to the composition of the poems, but to the experience of reading them.[1] Here are no fictitious constructions, no otherworldly engagements with an abstract notion of poetry. It is being brought to bear on one of the keenest instances of grief known to humankind, and the results, in a volume distinguished by its relative shortness, are placed before the broader world, before the public, without ever overstepping the limits of a decorum, a reticence and containment, which denote the irrevocably private nature of that grief. In the closing poem, 'Leaving Dundee', home is redefined. After eight months of oscillating between Hull, where the poet had worked as a university librarian, a colleague of Philip Larkin's, while his wife worked as a curator, he has given in to 'the wild geese cry[ing]/ Fanatic flightpaths up autumnal Tay,/ Instinctive, mad for home', in a possibly unconscious homage to a lyric of Violet Jacob's (see Chapter 3, Note 46). Dunn has chosen to return to his country of origin, though to its North Sea coast rather than to the Renfrewshire where he grew up. And his path will lead him from ordering and cataloguing books to be used by others for academic study to himself occupying a distinguished position within the academy.

With its thirty-nine items, *Elegies* marshals, as it were, and redefines crucial components of Dunn's production until that time, as if in knowing preparation for a new departure. This pivotal status means that it is also, in significant respects, an uncharacteristic collection. Class, a theme of particular importance for Dunn, is present only in a sublimated form. That Scotland is a profoundly democratic society where class distinctions are softened or even elided by broader loyalties can hardly be other than a pious fiction. The numerical restriction of its population and the importance of regional and smaller local allegiances may well bring a particular edge to class distinctions, sharpened in their turn by the awareness of religious or perceived ethnic differences. In 'Washing the Coins' from *St Kilda's Parliament* (1981), the speaker remembers how, as a child labouring at the 'tatty-howking', he would be surrounded by 'muttering strong Irish men and women' who 'worked/ Quicker than local boys' and whom 'you had to watch'. When the time comes to be paid, the farmer's wife, although she knows him, fails to 'tell my face/ From an Irish boy's' and

> she apologized
> And roughed my hair as into my cupped hands
> She poured a dozen pennies of the realm
> And placed two florins there, then cupped her hands
> Around my hands, like praying together.

To have mistaken him for one of the aliens is an insult which demands an apology, and is followed at once by the symbolic act of paying him in coins of a 'realm' which can be none other than the British Empire. The allegiance which woman and boy share, and which excludes the alien Irish, is celebrated in the transformation of recognition and remuneration into prayer, since shared religion is a further element marking the two off and uniting them. One would search most Scottish poetry before Dunn's time in vain for such a compressed, yet moving expression of political, class, religious and ethnic loyalties. The emotion with which the lines are suffused commands respect for the frail con-figurations they embody.

The speaker of Dunn's first collection, *Terry Street* (1969) enjoys a class detachment whose only real analogy would be the immunity enjoyed by diplomatic representatives posted to a foreign capital. The lives he observes around him are described with a clarity and an innocence which presumably derive from Dunn's having left Scotland for England, and experiencing there the more explicit, but no more powerful workings of social class as a system underpinning, not merely economic deprivation and subjugation, but also cultural meanings. The collection cannot be read as an attack on class precisely because class here is productive of meaning, productive of differences which offer themselves as fertile material for the making of poetry. The occlusion or even obliteration of the speaker's own placement within this system confers a note of humility and even piety on his loving recording of what he wonderingly, at times dolefully, perceives. His gaze is, perhaps, the sunlight which catches the trowel of a roof repair man, rendering it precious ('On Roofs of Terry Street'). He is sensitive to distinctions of gender and age, to the woman subjected to domestic violence and who 'buys the darkest rose I ever saw' ('Incident in the Shop') and to the men whose faces are 'too sad or too jovial' to be looked at for long in 'Men of Terry Street'. He is aware, too, of the careful hierarchies obtaining within this world, of those who, 'waiting for the inheritance of the oldest', eventually achieve 'a right to power' and become 'the street patricians' ('The Patricians'). The place he came from is so far off now, so forgotten in the intensity with which he itemises the astonishing reality around him, that the speaker comes close to assuming the functions of a priest. He blesses the people he observes and hopes there will be grass in the home towards which a man is headed, the family possessions displayed for all to see on a squeaking removal cart ('A Removal from Terry Street').

Objects are crucial to Dunn's operation in this collection, because they are eloquent, not just of the past, but of class affiliations, of domestic interiors and of the lives lived within them. They articulate and establish the differences that subsisted in the relationships within which they were used. Whereas those relationships must remain concealed, hidden behind closed doors, and in time be cancelled out by death, the objects live on to tell us about them. The paraphernalia of a home in Terry Street will be other than those of a home in Renfrewshire, or of a middle-class home not far removed, in a different neighbourhood of Hull. This is why such mundane objects as 'television aerials' can become 'Chinese characters' ('On Roofs of Terry Street'). They offer themselves for our deciphering if we will only have the patience to learn the language they are written in.

This status of objects as signs, rather than things to be used, will tend to become apparent when they have gone out of use. It would be fair to say that much of Dunn's earlier poetry resembles a junk shop run by a generous, even an indiscriminate proprietor. If in *Elegies*, the belongings he and his wife have accumulated speak to him of a life that can be no longer, elsewhere objects draw him inevitably back to the previous century, to a Victorian or an Edwardian age where he can trace, perhaps, the origins of the class system which so preoccupies him. There, within the framework of Empire and triumphant industrialism, it could make sense, the bric-à-brac could lose its weight of meaning and become transparent once again. Affectionate, wry threnody for Empire recurs again and again in Dunn's writing in, for example, 'A Poem in Praise of the British' from *Terry Street*, or 'Empires' from *Barbarians*

(1979). The mementoes he so lovingly chronicles, a portrait photograph taken just after the outbreak of the First World War, grandfathers' pocket watches, or the caps which Glasgow schoolboys clutch as they run backwards into the wind, establish a link with this bygone age.

The immunity Dunn briefly enjoyed, and which allowed him to 'guess about' the lives of people 'not one' of whom 'has anything at all to do with me' ('The Hunched' from *The Happier Life* (1972)) was destined not to last, could not have lasted. Some years before the bitter loss of *Elegies* forced Dunn to speak first and foremost of himself, he had begun to put together, as it were, a myth of his own origins. He locates these amongst those whom barriers of accent or education denied access to the closed garden of culture, because they lack 'Possession of land, ownership of work,/ Decency of "standards"' ('The Come-On' from *Barbarians*). 'Gardeners' takes an actual garden as its theme, choosing rather self-consciously the year of the French Revolution as its location. Its speaker has been forced to limit himself to executing, with his 'coarser artistries', the designs of his employers and social superiors. Unfortunately, the poem's prediction that, come the revolution, although 'we hanged you somewhere in its shade', the newly powerful will 'not raze this garden that we made' has rarely been borne out in the history of social upheavals, which have all too often chosen to destroy the aesthetic achievements of a previous age along with the social structures which made those achievements possible. In 'The Student', a poem which, given its populist stance, has an oddly Yeatsian cadence, Dunn chooses as his mouthpiece a tradesman who has faced bayonets and heard the Riot Act read, yet who persists in conning his Latin Tacitus through long, candlelit nights. 'Empires' offers a further backward glance at the age of British greatness. Its resolute espousal of an 'us' and 'them' distinction, claiming some kind of retrospective absolution for the working classes, though impassioned, fails to convince:

> They ruined us. They conquered continents.
> We filled their uniforms. We cruised the seas.
> We worked their mines and made their histories.
> *You work, we rule*, they said. We worked; they ruled.
> They fooled the tenements. All men were fooled.

The poem ends on a note of knowing compassion for the unemployed apprentice involved in an Orange Order march, a singular instance of fixation on the past, of useless identification with the splendours of a vanished empire.

With these precedents, it is no surprise to find Dunn envisaging a grimly paradisiacal democracy, a lost utopia in 'St Kilda's Parliament: 1879–1979' (from the book of the same name). Though not made explicit, the resonances of the title and of the very word 'parliament' were unmistakable in 1979. All the hallmarks of Dunn's characteristic stance are present. The poem celebrates a relict, a photograph taken one hundred years before of 'a remote democracy', one which has a powerfully masculine connotation since, of course, this parliament is composed of males and

> Clear, too, is manhood, and how each man looks
> Secure in the love of a woman who
> Also knows the wisdom of the sun rising,
> Of weather in the eyes like landmarks.

In this minimalist Eden, apples are stray visitors, remembered from being brought by a traveller five years earlier. Though the men stand there available for general appropriation, since they look 'like everybody's ancestors' and therefore offer themselves with seeming willingness to a whole range of possible patterns of identification, the tongue they speak is inaccessible both to the photographer and to Dunn. It marks off this stark Elysium as one neither has any hope of entering, or returning to.

It is clear from *St Kilda's Parliament* that Dunn has progressively abandoned the immunity of *Terry Street* in favour of a collocation in both national and local terms. Rather than an anonymous student, he addresses directly Paisley weaver poet Robert Tannahill ('Tannahill'), whose verses were sung in the local school. Dunn invokes the suicide poet's aid in his own verse writing, casting both men as Calibans to the Ariels of perhaps a different class and country, certainly a different kind of English. The poem shows Dunn engaging with the grimmer aspects of Scottish tradition, in which the demotic is assigned such a multifarious, perverse and elusive role. It uses the Burns stanza and restates the accepted, still indignant commonplaces about Burns's adoption, then betrayal by the capital's intelligentsia. Tannahill's suicide is hardly balanced by the Nirvana he achieves. Is it sufficient compensation to have heard one of his songs on the lips of a farm-girl, turned into a labouring song? Does the essence of a nation's poetry reside with that mysterious entity, 'the people'? Is anonymous absorption into their traditions what every poet hopes to attain? Dunn had already demonstrated in 'The Musician' (from *Barbarians*) his awareness that assumptions of this kind risk imperilling free access to cultural products, where entitlement cannot be justified in local or in national terms. Though the dead MacAuley was familiar with the music of Bach and

Beethoven, he kept this guilty secret from his audience. There was no way he could overcome the barrier between the kind of music he performed, and was expected to perform, and the music he surreptitiously enjoyed:

> It's your carpenter's wrist they remember
> In love with your local tradition.
> Your carpenter's fist could not break through
> To the public of Bach and Beethoven.

'The Apple-Tree' can be read as Dunn's summing up of his connection to his country of origin, before *Elegies* and the reality of physical return. Scotland is still seen as a nineteenth-century conformation of Calvinism and commerce, with its 'Kirk-sanctioned crimes, Kirk-flourished trade, Kirk-coded commerce'. The 'Earth from a kirkyard where the dead remember me' held in one hand, is balanced by the apple the other holds. The apple as a symbol is redolent of the pastoralism that inspired Edwin Muir. But thanks to its link to the Christian myth of the fall, it also hints at a possibility of transcending both Christianity and Calvinism, of redeeming the natural world from the condemnation to which that myth subjected it. Dunn is in south-west Scotland, the land of the Covenanting martyrs from the late seventeenth century, and among the 'lost hollows of the stern conventicles' he seems to seek a new way of keeping faith 'with land and fruit'. He is aware of the dangers which lie in the identification he has gradually edged towards, of too 'quick links forced from character to climate'. The poem's close underlines the problems involved in assigning absolute value to either nation or religion, in a fashion redolent of the agnostic close of MacDiarmid's *A Drunk Man Looks at the Thistle*:

> Forge no false links of man
> To land or creed, the true are good enough. Our lives
> Crave codes of courtesy, ways of describing love,
> And these, in a good-natured land, are ways to weep,
> True comfort as you wipe your eyes and try to live.

Until *Elegies* (and indeed, after it) Dunn's poetry tends to be strongly gendered as male, exhibiting maleness in an unquestioning way as part of its experience and speaking positions. As if to mark the collection's unusual status, Dunn now writes intermittently 'As if I have become a woman hidden in me'. In part this is quite simply the introjection, acceptance and integration of a lost loved one, here an 'other half', a partner, a woman. In the poem in question, 'Dining', the speaker is cooking from his wife's recipes after she has died. 'Thirteen Steps and the Thirteenth of March', on the other hand, sees him in a 'feminine' role, bringing refreshments to the endless train of visitors at his wife's bedside. He admits his 'wept exhaustions over plates and cups', though insisting that these services were carried out 'like a butler', with the degree of impassivity that description implies. The number thirteen pervades the poem, from the date and the steps separating pantry and bedroom to its having thirteen quatrains.

An increasing interest in closed forms is evident in *Elegies*, which includes sonnets, an experiment in *terza rima* with unconventional close ('Land Love'), quatrains rhyming *abba* ('Creatures'), impressively controlled hexameters with alternate rhyme ('Dining'), and a series of shorter items (such as 'Anniversaries'), also in quatrains, but using shorter lines, trimeters and tetrameters. This was an earnest of things to come, notably the extended verse novel *The Donkey's Ears* (2000), though an occasional looseness, a touch of carelessness, prevents Dunn from consistently extracting the added richness of meaning which is the payoff for willingly assumed formal restrictions.

Class and empire are still present. 'The Stories' reviews the options that might have been open to a heartbroken widower in the heady days of Empire:

> I could have died
> On the trails of exploration, under the sun or the arrows.
> And what religion is left now, to serve
> With local Caledonian sainthood, stern, but kind,
> Baptizing the baby Africans, and plodding
> To a discovery of God and waterfalls?
> Nor are there any longer those unvisited isles
> Where a beachcomber might scrounge a boozy salvation.

The objects which senselessly persist in evoking the married life the speaker once enjoyed also testify to an attained level of social wellbeing with its own brand of snobbishness, its memories of continental holidays, of rich, exotic or exquisite food tasted and shopped for in France.

Whether the return to Scotland following his first wife's death, and his entry into the academy, have been of benefit to Dunn as a writer remains a moot point. Many patterns which had so far served to enable his poetry ceased to function, and a certain aimlessness in the choice of subject matter is the result. There are indications that, like many artists and intellectuals at the time, Dunn was caught up in the groundswell of national and nationalistic enthusiasm which marked, in Scotland, the final years of Thatcherism in Britain. Nor does he appear to have been spared the disillusionment that affected, and continues to affect, so many, after Thatcher's demise and the inauguration of a Scottish parliament. In 'Here and There' from *Northlight* (1988), Dunn dialogues with an English friend who argues, concerned, that 'You've literature and a career to lose'. He 'never thought you'd prime a parish pump', or undertake this 'perverse retreat into the safe and small'. The poet replies (not without a certain disingenuousness) that he would be lost without his Scottish accent, insisting that Tayport is precisely the kind of locality where he can build himself afresh and uncover new creative possibilities:

> So spin your globe: Tayport is Trebizond
> As easily as a regenerate
>
> Country in which to reconstruct a self
> From local water, timber, light and earth.

His recent volumes do not quite bear out this boast. Unease and even a certain rootlessness emerge from them. With a powerful sense of poetic fatedness, Dunn imagines himself wearing the ring Pushkin wore at the duel where he found his death, a duel provoked by his determination to defend the honour of a fickle wife with whom he experienced little happiness. The relic was subsequently looted from a museum during the 1917 revolution. The poem in question ('Pushkin's Ring' from *The Year's Afternoon* (2000)) contains a barely disguised reference to the breakdown of Dunn's own marriage, his second, celebrated in a series of poems in *Northlight*:

> Suppose *I* have it. Suppose I'm wearing it
> Right now. For that would be appropriate,
> Having lost another ring, having lost it
> Because of poetry, being married to it.

Memories of his first wife start to flood back. The painted lilies she would so much have loved cry out a message that can be read as a displacement of the poet's own protestation: 'We can survive,/ And darkness is only part of our story!' Are finding a context for that darkness, and ultimately vanquishing it, the tasks which await Dunn's poetic gift today?

The poetry of Kenneth White (1936–) subsists in a relation to translation which is as complex and as significant as that of the work of Sorley

MacLean and other Gaelic poets, though its coordinates are rather different. It is still true today that both White and MacLean have gained a wider reputation, and found an audience, primarily among readers of a language different from the one they actually wrote in. After two relatively slim volumes of poetry published in London in the 1960s, White brought out a series of books in French translation, both poetry and prose, culminating in 1977 with the bilingual volume *Terre du Diamant*, which offered a retrospective anthology of his work up to that date, with the prospect of a series of further texts to come.

The function of translated poetry is normally to make work already firmly established in its place of origin available to the reading public of a different, second language. This was not the case with White. Indeed, when in 1989 Mainstream of Edinburgh brought out *The Bird Path: Collected Longer Poems 1964–1988*, followed the next year by *Handbook for the Diamond Country: Collected Shorter Poems 1960–1990*, they could claim with justification to be 'bringing home' a major poet practically unknown in his native country.[2]

What are the implications of this situation for our reading of White's poetry? From the moment that a body of poetry is read, apparently understood, and becomes the object of journalistic and academic interest, it is given a precise placing, assigned a role within contemporary production which is geographic as well as linguistic. Unless one is prepared to subscribe to notions of absolute autism in the writing of poetry, then this takes place in a situation of dialogue, where the poet, if he has in mind, first and foremost, an imagined audience, will nonetheless be increasingly aware of his actual audience, of its perceptions and expectations. The framework within which White's poetry was assigned meaning was a French, not a British or a Scottish one. That process formed the basis for the attempt to reinsert his work in an English language context, to translate it, as it were, 'back' into the culture from which he had originally come.

A translation is a cusp phenomenon, a pointer to something else, to a beyond which is, at least temporarily, inaccessible. While in simplistic terms many will bewail what has been lost in a translation, this also constitutes its fascination, since it will inevitably point our attention in the direction of an original, the source which it stands in for and represents. This is the 'extra' a translated poem can offer when compared to reading an original, an 'extra' it need not itself contain. Translation of poetry, on at least one level, fulfils a shamanistic function, of mediation between a world which is accessible and another world, one we are cut off from but to which the figure of the shaman, or translator, has privileged access. The issue is worth highlighting because it suggests that the position frequently assumed by the speaker in White's poetry is intimately connected to the circumstances in which a major part of his work has so far won its audience.

White is able to reproduce, with a degree of accuracy verging on the uncanny, the tonalities of MacDiarmid's later poetry. Not just of *In Memoriam James Joyce* but of *The Kind of Poetry I Want*, an extended, aspirational poetics published in book form in 1961, but generously anticipated in MacDiarmid's 1943 autobiography, *Lucky Poet*. The resemblance, however, is deceptive. White's poetry is radically different from MacDiarmid's. MacDiarmid had aspired to write a poetry of fact, a poetry of the apparently unpoetic, faithful to an urge he experienced, more or less since the beginning of his writing career, to move beyond the human and the personal, to annihilate the boundaries between the sentient and the insentient, the animate and the inanimate. In so far as this implied a spiritualised materialism, MacDiarmid was willing lovingly to transcribe scientific, even medical accounts of geological and pathological phenomena. His interest in disease and in the kind of perceptions a diseased organism might be privileged to attain, inherited from Symbolist and Decadent poets at the turn of the century, could then find logical expression in a celebration of the working of bacteria (as with the celebrated *streptococcus* passage from *In Memoriam James Joyce* quoted on p. 100). At the same time (and here again the tendency can be traced throughout his career) MacDiarmid sought to free the reader from any need to create, in order to access his texts, an image of the poet who had made them, a figure with a biography and an experience lodged in time and place which could function as a key to interpretation. One aspect of his quest was a radical alteration in the dimensions of the poem, commitment to a length which could be extended more or less infinitely, yet was suffused with a paradoxical lightness. Underpinning these massive texts was the haunting suggestion that they referred to, functioned as simile for, something else, perhaps more concise and simpler, which could not directly be revealed. Thence the recurring use of the word 'like', found also in White's work.

MacDiarmidian fingerprints are legion in 'Walking the Coast', a sequence of fifty-one poems which appeared in a bilingual edition in Paris in 1980. It incorporates a factual description of a lighthouse (p. 44), an account of the conditions which make possible the flourishing of alpine flora on Ben Lawers (p. 49) direct quotation from the work of 'a physicist/ far out in his field' (p. 59) and takes crystals (p. 60) as a guide to the path thought must follow. A piece of 'rosy quartz' (p. 54) anticipates the 'rosy gull' (p. 67) which is so potent a symbol for White (as in 'In Praise of the Rosy Gull', which opens *The Bird Path* and effectively functions as its epigraph). One cannot help wondering if 'the red branches of the hawthorn' (p. 48) are a reminiscence of the (lifted) passage on the hawthorn tree which offers a lyrical respite during the first section of *In Memoriam James Joyce*. The opening of Rilke's *Duino Elegies*, quoted without attribution but in inverted commas (p. 61) and a litany of Gaelic poets (p. 66, with specific mention of MacDiarmid) recall *To Circumjack Cencrastus*, with its growing enthusiasm for the Gaelic ideal and its erratic pillaging of Rilke's 'Requiem' for the prematurely deceased painter Paula Modersohn-Becker. The penultimate section of 'Walking the Coast' (p. 74) reads like a précis of a major achievement of MacDiarmid's Shetland years, 'On a Raised Beach', and White even slips into Shetland dialect at one point (p. 63), elsewhere echoing MacDiarmid's aggrandised English (p. 66) as well as his fondness for quoting from a range of languages. Such mimicry was not just a phase White would supersede. It returns in the third, fourth and fifth sections of 'The Residence of Solitude and Light' from 'Pyrenean Meditations' (the first part of *Atlantica*, published in Paris in 1986).

What is it then that makes White's poetry so different, in spite of his stated openness to 'placing the accent/ on the union of contraries' (p. 71)? Compared to MacDiarmid, he prefers not just short poems, and sequences composed of a series of short poems, but short lines, too. Avoiding any kind of syntactical complexity, which would in turn correspond to a complexity of perceived relations or of thought, he prefers apposition, each new element taking the place of the previous one, so that only rarely will a poem require an exercise of memory on the part of the reader, the putting together of different sections to arrive at a final effect. He is a man with a message, a teacher, and the urge behind his poetry is fundamentally didactic. 'Are you with me?' he concludes, as if addressing a lecture hall filled with students (p. 229). He cannot afford to alienate his listeners or to undermine their certainties, as MacDiarmid does, by indicating that what really matters is what cannot be articulated or even directly referred to.

Fundamental to the effect of White's poetry is our constructed image of the man behind it. This is another major difference from MacDiarmid. Individual poems often have a diaristic quality, annotations jotted down in a specified geographical location, often an exotic one offering contact with an alien culture. The string that links these isolated beads is White himself, or his projection in the poetry. The result is an edge of self-aggrandisement, along with a persistent vein of not entirely disagreeable charlatanry. The reader notes with a certain unease that the emphasis on whiteness, on a 'white world' and on Scotland as 'Alba', points back to the poet's name and, ultimately, to himself. When he assures us that

'From Strathclyde to Whiteness lies the way', the second capitalisation recalls a surname, and he proclaims elsewhere that 'now I walk in my own image/ follow me who dares' (*Handbook* p. 80).

The image subsists thanks to a consistent process of projection, an offering of *alter egos* who can stand in for the poet in so far as they share qualities with him. 'Ovid's Report' (pp. 34–40) shows the Latin poet 'Divorced from clique and public/ with nobody to clap applause', now 'able/ to move off into the dark and live with it', writing 'at the world's edge', 'with none/ of the old decoration/ none of that foosty rhetoric', bent on discovering 'a new roughness', 'a new clearness'. The poem 'Hölderlin in Bordeaux' (pp. 91–3) arrives at the conclusion that the German Romantic poet 'would have to learn/ how to travel alone', enrolling Martin Heidegger and the hut in Todtnauberg among the self-projections with 'some window overlooking a forest maybe/ a little philosophical light...'. Aquitaine appeals because seen, in its Latin naming ('In Aquitania' pp. 85–91), as an unknown place at the limits of the known world where poetry can be made and remade ('Real writing had deserted Rome', p. 89). White is a new barbarian, proposing to regenerate an effete and tired tradition by drawing on hitherto untapped sources. The Irish abbot and explorer Brandan, in 'Brandan's Last Voyage', aiming 'to write a poem on which/ the minds of men could sail for centuries', situated 'somehow... out beyond the pale... of the literary folk/ lacking their polish, their finesse' (pp. 192–3) is another self-projection, as is the 'silent harpooner' from the Basque country, the 'strange one' (pp. 176–7) who emerges towards the close of 'The Western Gateways'.

There is no doubt that we are meant to construe the figure behind the poetry as at least a version of White's own biography, 'secretly though not unconsciously/ in the cities of Europe/ living my life/ founding and grounding/ a world' (p. 53). But his construction of a heroic past ('I have grown chrysanthemums in the dung of God', p. 31) indicates White's other major debt, to American Beat poets of the days of Kerouac and Ginsberg. This is the source of his undiscriminating New Age optimism. (Brandan makes a surprising detour from Ireland to walk round the 'ancient stones' at Callanish on Lewis (p. 190) before heading towards the New World.) It also explains the awkward colloquialisms peppering his work: 'crow, I tell you is one queer joe' (p. 106), 'the flow doesn't really want/ philosophies or science/ it wants you/ to get into the flow' (p. 144). Many more examples could be found. What makes them awkward is not just the intrusion of an American voice, but a manly tenderness and humour (as in section 11 of 'Brandan's Last Voyage') redolent of the changing room, where women are at last absent, and men can acknowledge a brief solidarity, with its own vein of discomfort because each knows he must prove his manliness alone. The Chinese figure who in 'Eight Eccentrics' decides not to sit his 'civil service exam', and abandons prospects of wife and family, of 'an important post' to 'play the Green Jade Song/ on a seven-stringed lute' and 'grow a magic mushroom or two' (pp. 138–9) is not so different from a university drop-out in 1970s California, strumming his guitar and experimenting with acid. 'Remembering Gourgoumel' (pp. 84–5) shifts significantly from third to first person, its account of one who restores an old house and garden in the Ardèche oddly reminiscent of Yeats's 'The Lake Isle of Innisfree', as are these lines from 'Living in the Hills': 'I look in the fire and think it a dream/ that once I lived in the streets of a city' (*Handbook* p. 30).

White's place of writing is at the edge, making the Atlantic coast of France, and Brittany in particular, an appropriate setting. It is also characterised as a path, liminal too in that it separates the two halves of a landscape, like scissors drawn through cloth. On one level, the path is the search for a new poetics, MacDiarmid again being close because, if the opposition between science and poetry can indeed be collapsed, then poetics can have the validity of a scientific discovery, even of a law which will reveal 'the biological/ aim of art' (p. 47). Appropriation of the physicist's discourse is only one aspect of a more generalised appropriation in White's work. Differently from MacDiarmid, where the expansion of the poem beyond English serves to destabilise that English, to restore to it its quality of language, White merely exhibits passages in Gaelic, or Occitan, or Basque, or French. They do nothing to galvanise his own rather problematic diction. His willingness to draw on Oriental literature and philosophy may be another debt to the Beat Generation. It would be a mistake to assume that White is an expert in the relevant languages. When a foreign word is brought into one's own language, it rarely conserves its original semantic weighting, tending rather to assume a different one within the system of the language which has adopted it. White does not write as someone who has gone deeply into the philology or the specific semantics of the traditions he refers to. Indeed, he has confessed that:

> I do not have the Gaelic, but I've done with Gaelic what I've done with several other languages: I've read everything I could find in translation, and I dip into grammars, dictionaries, and annotated original texts, now and then. The idea is to awaken things latent in myself rather than actually learn the language. (*Handbook* p. 191)

The danger of solipsism rears its head again. Exotic reference serves to access elements already present within the poet. As was argued above, the heroic figures recurring in White's poetry serve primarily as means of self-expansion and projection. His Eastern references act as vehicles for very Western aspirations.

Appropriation for White also has gendered and sexist aspects, no less disturbing because he is evidently unaware of them. To penetrate a woman means appropriating both her country of origin and its culture, as in the second section of 'Mahamudra' ('all that I knew of India/ all that I knew/ centred in your body', p. 147) or the short poems 'Gujarati' ('and when you opened your thighs/ I penetrated India', *Handbook* p. 87) and 'Knowledge Girl' ('the smooth beauty/ of your loving belly/ realizes philosophy', *Handbook* p. 124). Needless to say, the women whose possession offers such rewards are racially 'other' than the speaker. The mind is explicitly gendered in a passage quoted, without a trace of irony, in 'Mahamudra' ('"just as salt is dissolved in water/ so the mind that takes its woman . . ."', p. 150), while in 'Melville at Arrowhead' (pp. 193–5) the novelists' daughters are dismissed as 'pleasant enough young ladies/ but what could they know/ went on back of his blue eyes', while his wife's role is limited to pestering him to take his pills and a concluding '"Herman! supper is ready!"' The counterpart of such chauvinism is the chill male clarity, the aseptic abstraction of the speaker in 'Labrador': 'with every step I took/ I knew a singular health/ mind every day more sharp, more clear' (p. 84).

Walking in White's poetry functions at one and the same time as itself and as an image of his search for a poetics. There are moments when language reveals its uselessness ('I can describe neither the redness of the wine/ nor the whiteness of the mountains', *Handbook* p. 154), since 'no art can touch . . . the summit of contemplation' (*Handbook* p. 77). The poetics which closes *The Bird Path* is actually a list of birds. Tipping the balance in favour of an objective, scientific recording which constitutes its own brand of appropriation, the speaker of 'Late August on the Coast' warns us that 'I don't just mean poetry/ I suppose what I'm after is closer to a kind of cartography' (p. 234). Ultimately, exercise of the body within the landscape may triumph over the exercise of verse: 'Write poems?// rather follow the coast/ line after line' (p. 207).

If White's poetry is characterised by a potentially disarming, but in the last analysis disabling insensitivity to gender questions, Liz Lochhead's in retrospect appears weakened by its commitment to a specific feminist agenda and the sometimes facile oppositions this implies.

'Morning After' (p. 134),[3] from her 1972 collection *Memo for Spring*, exemplifies some of these problems, while at the same time highlighting aspects of Lochhead's style which were to become characteristic. The female speaker has stayed over after a Saturday night of lovemaking and is now on tenterhooks, pretending to read a Sunday newspaper while in fact concentrating all her attention on the otherwise occupied male sitting next to her. She is in a victim position, begging wordlessly that he should focus on her rather than on the news, and the desultory attention he devotes to the pages of the colour section, reading them with 'too passing/ an interest' becomes emblematic of his attitude to her. Lochhead (1947–) makes no attempt to tip over the inherently unstable power relations in this situation, for it is the woman who both narrates and attributes meaning. The latter is done within well-worn stereotypes, with an adroit yet arch play on the newspapers' names. He is the detached *Observer*, concerned with 'larger. . . issues' while she is a *Mirror* which can in the end, only reflect him. The tabloid is associated with the female, the more intellectual broadsheet with the male.

The poem reads as a plea for both sympathy and indignation from the reader, and this aspect of Lochhead's poetry, as the record of a series of unsatisfactory emotional and sexual skirmishes, at times even demeaning for the speaker (in 'Carnival' she 'spin[s] to a mere blur on a wheelspoke/ about your axis' (p. 150)) is the least attractive strand in her work. At a deeper level she is concerned with the search for a speaking position, for a subjectivity connoted as female. On the one hand, that there should have been a need for this, given the historical and cultural context of 1970s Scotland, is understandable. But on the other, the very nature of the search commits her to an ideology of gender oppositions which threatens to undermine any success she might achieve. Are subject positions inevitably gendered? Does gender necessarily constitute their most significant aspect? If a text aspires to be connoted as female in origin, if it seeks to foreground and to problematise femininity, what significance can this have in a situation where the gender of an author can only rarely, in the absence of external or incidental evidence, be deduced from a written text with any certainty?

'What the Pool Said, on Midsummer's Day', placed at the head of *Dreaming Frankenstein*, is both enlightening and chastening in this respect. The poem is impressive for the courage with which it conveys erotic experience, through the dimly veiled image of a dark and sinister pool inviting a man to commit his body to it. There are unmistakable references to fellatio ('I get darker and darker, suck harder'), penetration and orgasm ('clench and come into me'). As one reads, however, one cannot help noticing that the space of the text has somehow been usurped, that the interest effectively lies with the man's experience of the situation, that he, in the end, manages to be at its centre. What reads like the memory of a lesbian encounter ('The woman was easy./ Like to like, I called her, she came') is dismissed, not surprisingly when gender polarities so clearly constitute the focus of concern. Part of the problem is the poem's ambiguous engagement with stereotypes. The female speaker is associated with water, with being dark, still and waiting. She is both 'garrulous' and 'babbling', passive and seductive at one and the same time ('I lie here, inviting, winking you in'). She concedes that the man has good cause to be afraid of her, that his fear is 'reasonable'. Reason is here a male prerogative (as is light), while what is most 'true' within the pool is both 'deeper' and 'older'. 'What's fish/ in me could make flesh of you' signals erection and at the same time hints in passing at misogynistic discourse on the female genitalia. In the end, for all its undoubted power and daring, the poem comes over as a trap, a trap constituted by what may be termed 'projective identification', as a result of which the subject in search of a way to conceive of itself assumes what others tell it that it is, becomes, as it were, their projection. This may be why 'The Mirror', with its vision of a kind of holocaust of all the knick-knacks and trash of attributed femininity, of a woman at last 'giving birth to herself', is placed at the end of the *Dreaming Frankenstein* section, as an aspiration yet to be realised.

Understood in these terms, 'What the Pool Said, on Midsummer's Day' indicates how, at the end of a trajectory of nearly two decades, Lochhead was still struggling to deal with and overcome the implications of her explicitly gendered stance, of seeking to write a poetry that would be women's poetry as well as simply poetry written by a woman. Her assumption of a feminist agenda (and even then feminism was a more complex and articulated phenomenon than her poetry leads one to suspect) proved to be a double-edged sword, though it procured her success and even notoriety. Lochhead risked becoming the kind of woman writer (and the very phrase is problematic) men are not afraid of, one who can all too easily be digested by and absorbed into the literary and academic establishment. She was, indeed, until Carol Ann Duffy made her mark, the only Scottish woman poet ever to have had a book of essays entirely dedicated to her.

If this analysis is not excessively unjust, it would help to explain the importance of clichés and clichéd language for Lochhead's poetry, which eventually led her, as a highly skilled public performer of her own work, in the direction of camp and of a glittering, self-consciously tacky vaudeville, enormously successful with audiences throughout the United Kingdom. Behind the urge to give expression to feminine 'experience', to seek out a gendered speaking position, lay the assumption that somewhere an original, 'genuine' femininity might exist, one which could be articulated in language, even in a language that was seen as occupied by male discourse. Many of the strategies she adopted, such as recourse to the Frankenstein myth originated by Mary Shelley, or the use of fairytale settings to create a more extended and resonant vocabulary for dealing with personality formation and love relationships, can be interpreted in this light. Unfortunately, one of the undoubted strengths of the traditional male speaking position was its disavowal of gender specificity, its aspiration to universality, to speak for an 'everyone' that might even include women. Any attempt to define either language or the imagination in gender terms, to introduce an apartheid of mirroring and corresponding subjectivities, seems vowed to failure. This is why Lochhead, in her quest, repeatedly comes up against stereotypes, often misogynist in origin, which she then impersonates. Her bawd's concluding 'No one will guess it's not my style' (p. 76) could serve here as a motto. The experience of feminine gender as performance, as dressing up, rather than being liberating, is perceived as a source of frustration, as a limitation.

'The Furies' (pp. 74–6) deals with three stereotypes: 'Harridan', 'Spinster' and 'Bawd'. It is interesting to set the middle poem alongside 'Statement by a Responsible Spinster' from Iain Crichton Smith's *The White Noon* (1959). Smith blithely ignores gender boundaries, again and again displaying his willingness to speak of himself as female, to imagine himself in female roles. In the end, his poem is the more compassionate and respectful of the two, an elegy on 'ambiguous love', on one who 'was trapped by pity and the clever/ duplicities of age'. Lochhead's poem patches together commonplaces and set phrases, remaining oddly on the surface in its up-to-date references. It comes over as detached and, ultimately, rather cruel:

> I live and let live. Depend
> on nobody. Accept.
> Go in for self-improvement.
> Keep up with trends.
> I'll cultivate my conversation.
> I'll cultivate my friends.
> I'll grow a herbaceous border.
> By hook by crook I'll get my house in order.

Relations between women in her poems are often mediated, and defined in terms of, the man in whom they share an interest. So 'Box Room' (p. 146) has the boyfriend's mother firmly confining the visiting girlfriend to his childhood room, while he sleeps in the lounge. 'My Rival's House' (p. 77) deals with another potential mother-in-law, who 'thinks she means me well' even though 'what squirms beneath her surface I can tell'. While 'The Other Woman' (p. 92) turns out not to be, as the cliché leads one to expect, a rival in love, but the suppressed side of the speaker's own personality, what matters at the poem's close is nevertheless the danger *he* might be exposed to from her, concern for *his* welfare: 'She's sinister./ She does not mean you well.' 'Poem for my Sister' (p. 98) takes as its starting point the idiom about being in someone else's shoes. The issue here is not so much what may happen between the older and the younger sister as what life, and by implication men, have done to the former and may in due course do to the latter.

Perhaps it was historically inevitable, even essential, that Lochhead should have sought to mark out a space with the ungrateful label 'Scottish woman poet' attached to it, and then to inhabit that space. She must have had a sense of being an utter pioneer, as no real awareness of the work of Violet Jacob or Marion Angus had been preserved, and the work of Janet Little and the song composers of the eighteenth century still awaited rediscovery. Thankless as her task may have been, there can be little doubt about the enabling effect it had on subsequent writers. Once the ground had been cleared, as it were, the work did not need to be repeated. And in terms of discursive space, public perception and publication, Lochhead's success is beyond doubt. This is not, however, where we should look for the strengths of Lochhead's poetry. They lie in a skill, an artfulness carried to a level where it appears entirely artless. Such skill is of an order that merits respect.

What is meant will be clearer if two poems, again separated by rather more than a decade, are set side by side. 'Revelation' (p. 124), which heads the *Memo for Spring* section in Lochhead's collected volume, describes the terror provoked in a small girl by the sight of a bull, and relies on a somewhat facile series of oppositions. The girl is fetching eggs and milk from a neighbouring farm. She is pre-pubertal or at least grappling with the first intimations of puberty, an infant when compared with the 'big boys . . . who pulled the wings from butterflies'. Femininity is associated with delicate growth, fragility and the need for protection, masculinity with needless cruelty and the figure of the bull. The latter embodies a reality the girl has always known to exist but has never needed to confront. 'An Abortion' (p. 9), from the later *Dreaming Frankenstein* section, does indeed depict a female victim at the mercy of insensitive, heartless men. But it reads like the simple delineation of an actual event, seen by the writer as she lifts her head from the desk where

she is at work, a 'shamed voyeur'. The apparent banality and credibility
of the incident, as if it were something any one of us could potentially
have witnessed, gives strength to the poem and even offers it for other
interpretations than the obvious one in gender terms. Does feminism
have meaning for a cow? The question is not a flippant one, and it is
one the poem, if tangentially, offers for our consideration.

It is possible to recreate the kind of excitement readers felt when
confronted with Lochhead's earlier work in poems like 'Obituary'
(p. 132). It conforms to type in chronicling the dwindling stages of a
love relationship, with the woman's guilty confession of how 'sometimes I did not wash your coffee cup for days/ or touched the books
you lent me/ when I did not want to read'. What remains is its detailing
of a walk down Byres Road, and elsewhere in Glasgow's West End, as
if this were the most normal thing in the world, as if any poet need
look no further for his or her material than the simple occurrences of
every day. Given not just the excision of Glasgow from representations
of Scotland through much of the century, but the successful marginalisation of women in the literary tradition Lochhead eventually chose to
identify with, her approach is impressive in its courage and simplicity.
It could imply naivety, the innocence of an outsider coming to poetry
more or less unaware of what is expected or required, what is considered appropriate. The evidence points in another direction. 'That
Summer' (p. 48), in which the speaker, marooned in a cottage somewhere in the Highlands, encounters the decomposing remains of a sheep
as she walks repeatedly to the phone booth in order to call a flat she
knows her boyfriend has abandoned, has the familiar theme of ship-
wrecked, unrequited love. It shares its main motif, however, not only
with 'Sunday Morning Walk' from Crichton Smith's *Thistles and Roses*
(1961), but ultimately with 'Une Charogne' from Baudelaire's *Les
Fleurs du Mal*. Lochhead's apparent artlessness is often very artful
indeed.

She pursues her strategy of reinvigorating or merely highlighting tired
language with an impressive consistency. So 'Laundrette' (p. 116) uses
the clothes which a motley selection of clients grimly watch rotating
behind 'the porthole glass' of the washing machines to evoke their lives,
with a persistent and relentless deployment of clichés, the dog-eared language of everyday exchanges ('not a patch on', 'don't know which way
to turn', 'let out of the bag', 'stew in their juice', 'a weather eye' and so
on). 'The Empty Song' (p. 50) uses an empty shampoo bottle to balance
the advantages of being in love and being alone. She has a remarkably
sensitive ear, which also serves to lift and energise the willed banality
of her material. In 'West Kensington' (p. 49) the speaker wakens in an

ex-lover's flat where, nothing more now than a friend, she has stopped off on her way back from a foreign holiday. Alongside the usual play with set phrases and the familiar tone of self-commiseration ('Shrugging . . . off' the sleeping-bag, and the affair, 'Thanks a bundle', 'manhandled luggage') comes one of the most phonetically poignant lines in all Lochhead's work. Not incidentally it is a perfect iambic pentameter and the repetition of specific vowels and consonants is deftly patterned: 'stirred bitter instant in a rinsed out cup'.

There are places where Lochhead distances herself from her habitual positions to voice critiques of them. 'Overheard by a Young Waitress' (p. 140) has 'Three thirty-fivish women' considering 'the grounds/ for divorce', not portrayed as victims but merely as ageing individuals who have somehow missed the point about love. 'A Giveaway' (p. 42) talks at one and the same time about a poem's stages of becoming and the phases in a relationship, without allowing either to gain the upper hand. Its assertion that 'Poets don't bare their souls, they bare their skill' is promising, yet the conclusion ('the whole bloody stanza was wonky from the word go') sends the reader back to the emotional entanglement, tending to collapse the distinction between actual experience and the making of poetry which has been established.

'A Gift' (p. 39) offers another kind of doubling. Here a man has usurped the speaker's role, bringing her 'a cargo of poems & photographs' and, along with these, 'the problem of acceptance'. The speaker is led to reconsider her own position, to undo, at least temporarily, the bonds between loving, suffering and writing, to confront the 'gifthorses of nightmare &/ selfhatred' she herself has brought to each of her involvements. The implication needs to be teased out, but it is an interesting one. Could it be that behind the feminist, behind the adoptive Glaswegian, behind the woman writer asserting her right to a place and a voice, there lies a moralist of a very traditional kind? That what is voiced throughout Lochhead's poetry is horror at the confusions of modernity, at abortion, the trade in cosmetics, the obsolescence of the family as traditionally conceived, serial monogamy and the generalised instability of human relationships? 'For my Grandmother Knitting' (p. 137) recalls, with muted respect, the values of another age, as the speaker contemplates what were

> once the hands of the bride
> with the hand-span waist
> once the hands of the miner's wife
> who scrubbed his back
> in a tin bath by the coal fire

once the hands of the mother
of six who made do and mended
scraped and slaved slapped sometimes
when necessary

The ostensible purport of the poem is that there is no sense in the grandmother's continuing to use those hands to knit clothes for grandchildren
who already have more than they can wear. It is as if she were clinging
pointlessly to values that can have no meaning in what the world has
come to be. But the pondered repetition of 'There is no need they say',
'they say there is no need', 'they say there is no need' raises a doubt in
the reader's mind, opening up a space beyond what the poem appears
to be declaring. Could it be that the grandmother was right, and that
the values which kept her at her work still have a relevance to the
contemporary world?

The fact that it comes so naturally to refer to Iain Crichton Smith's
work when discussing Liz Lochhead's indicates a degree of influence of
the older poet on the younger. Or is it merely a case of two roughly
contemporary writers responding to similar stimuli? These are difficult
questions to answer. The links between the two certainly suggest that
concepts such as 'women's poetry' or 'men's poetry' have a limited
usefulness. The fluidity he shows in dealing with concepts of gender and
gendering is one of the most refreshing and reassuring aspects of
Crichton Smith's work.[4]
   He was a bilingual writer in a more acute sense than contemporary
or slightly earlier poets writing in both English and Scots. Gaelic and
English come from different linguistic families, and the English critical
tradition furnishes few tools for dealing with a phenomenon of this
kind, a man who spreads his output across two languages, neither of
which can be assigned a definitive ascendancy over the other. What is
the appropriate audience for such a writer? Does it have to be made up
of people with access to both languages? While including his versions of
major eighteenth-century poems by Alasdair Mac Mhaighstir Alasdair
(c. 1695–c. 1770) and Duncan Bàn MacIntyre (1724–1812), Smith's
collected volume excises his Gaelic texts, offering only the author's
prose translations of them, as if a barrier of discrimination existed
which the Gaelic originals had failed to surmount. Does this indicate a
struggle to make him a monolingual poet, of more or less the only kind
the English tradition is willing to contemplate? Even the openness to
literature from the former colonies and to postcolonial studies which

has characterised the academy in recent years tends to draw the line at anything not written in English.

Born in Glasgow on New Year's Day, Crichton Smith (1928–98) was brought up with his brother in the same Lewis village as Derick Thomson. His mother returned there after the death of her husband. Poverty, ill health and the ever present menace of tuberculosis coloured his childhood. He had no real grasp of English until formal schooling began at the age of five. The lyrical force of Smith's poetry in English derives from its not being his mother tongue but another language he discovered when already a fully conscious and sentient being. Rather than an imposition, this turned out to be an opportunity. Throughout his long period of productivity, Smith retained the attitude to language of a child admitted to a wondrous toyshop, filled with marvellous gadgets, colours and devices which were not his, in whose creation he had taken no part. Individual words never lost their quality of legendary, unpredictable instruments. His linguistic background set in motion a permanent defamiliarisation which means that, more than any other English language poet in this book, his work has a quality of pure melodic untranslatability or, more exactly, resistance to paraphrase. Again and again one is struck by the difficulty of identifying his poetry with its semantic content, with what the words refer to or appear to say. As much is clear in a poem like 'Children, Follow the Dwarfs' (in *From Bourgeois Land* (1969)), with its 'terrible granny' who 'perches and sings to herself/ past the tumultuous seasons high on her shelf'. The poem is a somewhat demented blend of decalogue and commonplaces from children's story books, pervaded by an unhinged, anarchic spirit which is genuinely unsettling. Smith's consistent interest in technique, in rhymes and half-rhymes and varying stanza patterns, is not, as with MacCaig, a touchstone of intellectual discipline and a means of establishing the conscious craftsman's distance from, even superiority to, the reader. It has its source in the fact that, for Smith, English never quite manages to bcome an ordinary language, tarnished and devalued in everyday use. Words persist in offering themselves to him as things, as objects in their own right, rather than as cyphers or as pointers. They never cease to be as real as the concepts or the objects which they stand for.

The experience of radical Calvinism, a potent influence in Gaelic-speaking Scotland since the Disruption and the evangelical revivals of the nineteenth century, was fundamental to Smith's upbringing. That he and Thomson should have grown up in the same village, at more or less the same time, with such contrasting experiences of religion is a warning to us not to conceive of Calvinism as a unitary phenomenon, consistent to itself. Thomson's joke, in *An Rathad Cian*, about playing football with a prophet (poem 11), or his almost rueful acknowledgement of radical Calvinism as an inspirational force in 'Am Bodach-Ròcais' from the same sequence (poem 18 'The Scarecrow'), are made possible by his detached, agnostic stance. He has no overwhelming investment, favourable or unfavourable, in what he is presenting and can therefore adjudge it with relative impartiality, viewing both defects and strengths. Smith's revulsion is consistent and passionate. Something of what he was reacting against can be seen in this extract from the introduction to Alexander Carmichael's *Carmina Gadelica*, in which the collector is dialoguing with one of his informants, a woman from the Long Isle, one name for the Outer Hebrides. The events she is describing date back to the middle of the nineteenth century and would therefore still be a vivid memory in Smith's mother's time, and even when he was himself a child:

'A blessed change came over the place and the people,' the woman replied in earnestness, 'and the good men and the good ministers who arose did away with the songs and the stories, the music and the dancing, the sports and the games, that were perverting the minds and ruining the souls of the people, leading them to folly and stumbling.' 'But how did the people themselves come to discard their sports and pastimes?' 'Oh, the good ministers and the good elders preached against them and went among the people, and besought them to forsake their follies and to return to wisdom. They made the people break and burn their pipes and fiddles. If there was a foolish man here and there who demurred, the good ministers and the good elders themselves broke and burnt their instruments . . .' 'And what have you now instead of the racing, the stone-throwing, and the caber-tossing, the song, the pipe, and the dance?' 'Oh, we have the blessed Bible preached and explained to us faithfully and earnestly, if we sinful people would only walk in the right path and use our opportunities.'[5]

In poem 14 of the Gaelic sequence 'An Cànan' ('The Language'), the humour in dealing with the question, and the whimsical transference of an American movie setting, cannot entirely conceal the virulence of the anger Crichton Smith continued to feel:

Anns an taigh-dhealbh bha Errol Flynn is glainnichean dubha
air a' teàrnadh sìos air na Japs.

'Wake Island' ann am fairge a bha fad às, blàth.
Nuair a thàinig mi mach do dheàrrsadh na grèine bha mi
coltach ri John Wayne a' sgiùrsadh nam ministearan às mo
rathad.[6]

In the cinema Errol Flynn, wearing dark glasses,
was coming down on the Japs.
'Wake Island' was a distant, warm horizon.
When I came out into the sunshine I was like
John Wayne scourging the ministers from
my path.

Emerging from a cinema in Stornoway, perhaps twirling the guns at his hips in his imagination like the John Wayne he has been watching, the boy Smith's enemies are not a rival band of cowboys but representatives of the Church.

In this respect, Crichton Smith can usefully be contrasted with George Mackay Brown. After each of his brief forays southwards, Mackay Brown returned home to Orkney and, with the passage of time, forged for himself a solid and coherent identification with the islands. One can speak, in his case, of a flight from modernity into ideology, into the rigid dogma of Catholic orthodoxy, which was reworked into Mackay Brown's own idiosyncratic, heterodox formulation. For Smith, Lewis is 'the anvil where was made/ the puritanical heart', a place whose 'meagre furniture appals me' with its 'props of rock, of heather, and of sea,/ the constancy/ of ruined walls and nettles', all it had to offer 'Life without art, the minimum . . . a sermon tolling . . . hypothesis of hell, a judging face/ looming from storm,' a world 'where poppies are superfluous, and the rose.'[7] Escape to the mainland, when he left to study at university in Aberdeen, incidentally beholding a train for the first time, was an escape into life. Smith never felt the need to sever himself, with all the reluctant ambivalence of a Derick Thomson rowing in the opposite direction to the one he is looking in, from the world where he had grown up. A passionate relief at that liberation accompanied him throughout his life, bringing with it a thoroughgoing and heartfelt suspicion and rejection of all ideologies.

'Lenin', from *The Law and the Grace* (1965), should be read against the background of the engagement of a series of twentieth-century Scottish poets, among them MacLean and most especially MacDiarmid, with communist ideology and with the cultural and political inheritance of the Bolshevik revolution. In a four-line lyric on the leader's tomb in Red Square, MacDiarmid had spoken of 'The eternal lightning of

Lenin's bones'.[8] Smith's 'image of Lenin' is chill and seated in an iron chair. The poet is unable to join the chorus of praise:

> No, I can
> romanticise no more that 'head of iron'
> 'the thought and will unalterably one'
> 'the world-doer', 'thunderer', 'the stone
>
> rolling through clouds' . . .

He is aware of the extent to which this goes beyond a merely personal statement, derived from his own biography, to articulate his stance with respect to a national and cultural tradition. He finds it all too 'Simple to condemn/ the unsymmetrical, simple to condone/ that which oneself is not.' The poem grows admittedly weaker when attempting to define where Smith's real allegiance lies, with 'the endlessly various, real, human,/ world which is no new era'. A decided rejection of orthodoxy is nonetheless clear.

Smith's sonnet on 'John Knox' from *Thistles and Roses* (1961) introduces a gendered dimension into this rejection. More than three decades had passed since the indiscriminate, at times slightly hysterical rejection of Calvinism by the Scottish Renaissance Movement in its early stages, determined to lay the blame for the nation's perceived failure in self-realisation firmly in that quarter. Radical Calvinism had played such a crucial role in Smith's formation, in bodying forth his world view, that disavowal could never be a wholly or even principally intellectual matter. This is why language of the body, and of the female body in particular, is so crucial to the sonnet. An instance of what Smith is reacting against can be found in Soutar's four jaunty stanzas under the same title.[9] In praising Knox, Soutar again shows his distance from the initial phase of the cultural renaissance. Knox, though so instrumental in having English rather than Scots as the language of worship for Scottish congregations, is celebrated because 'aften frae the poopit/ His mither-tongue he'd speak.' Despite his limited stature, he can terrify both men and animals, and brings back from servitude in the galleys 'The snellness o' the sea' to salt his sermons. Soutar sees little to regret in Knox's spirit still being alive in Scotland.

Smith's poem, on the other hand, abounds in images of cutting and wounding. He chooses a technically exacting form, with two rhymes only in the octave and two in the sestet. End-stopped lines skilfully mimic the lopping and truncation portrayed in the poem. Initially,

Knox's activity is a scythe cutting the corn. In the second quatrain it becomes an undisguised aggression on the body of the queen:

> He pulls the clouds like bandages awry.
> See how the harlot bleeds below her crown.
> This lightning stabs her in the heaving thigh –
> such siege is deadly for her dallying gown.

The mention of bandages suggests that the bleeding could be menstrual, only to yield to imagery of direct attack in the following couplet, borne out by the 'shearing naked absolute blade' at the poem's close. What is attacked and defeated is not only feminine but foreign. Here Smith echoes, as it were in negative, the nationalism of the Soutar poem. Queen Mary, the object of Knox's wrath, is clothed in French satin, and the cry she utters on being stabbed is not a native, but a foreign one.

The poem offers no hope for rescue or escape. Use of the present tense implies that the aggression, rather than being relegated to the past, continues to take place. 'The Law and the Grace' shows the speaker similarly trapped, in a reaction against religious orthodoxy which entangles him in it all the more strongly the more he struggles to break free. Smith returns obsessively to two words of vital importance for the religious teaching he is struggling with: 'grace' and 'works'. The Catholic Church includes in its New Testament the Epistle of St James, which preaches the importance of good works for salvation. Such a doctrine goes against the Calvinist teaching that who will and will not be saved is God's decision alone, one it would be presumptuous for any human being to think of influencing by good actions. Though good works may be pleasing in God's eyes, they are not a means of earning Heaven. Salvation is effected through the operation of grace, a gift of God that can be neither earned nor merited. Within the world of Smith's poem both terms are richly ambiguous. His fundamental concern is the relationship between creative activity and religious orthodoxy. What place is there for the artist in a community whose specific allegiance is to a form of Calvinism? What importance can be attached to aesthetic values? 'Grace' therefore comes to mean, not just God's prerogative, but also what is 'gracious', humanly beautiful, pleasing to perception, and 'works' means not only virtuous action in everyday life, but the accumulation of artefacts the artist has managed to bring into being.

At the outset of the poem, 'they' demand, not beauty, but conformity, obedience to their dictates, 'even if/ graceful hypocrisy obscures my face'. Though 'they' deny the existence of angels, the artist claims familiarity with these, refusing to deny them. He finds himself poised between 'bright angels, of spontaneous love' and the 'black devils' of orthodoxy, determined to 'cure life of itself'. Smith is unlikely to have been unaware of the role accorded to angels, where creativity and inspiration are concerned, in the later poems of Rainer Maria Rilke, and these offer an illuminating intertext for 'The Law and the Grace'. If the ministers reject as insignificant his 'works', in the sense of either virtuous actions or created texts, then what he makes can never be good enough for the angels. At the poem's close the speaker turns to the 'patriarchs', begging them to confirm that, abandoning theirs, he has forged for himself another species of law, no less unbending and pitiless.

The implication is that, abjuring the Calvinism of his upbringing and giving his allegiance instead to inspirational and creative values, Smith will nonetheless reproduce the kind of remorseless, judgemental orthodoxy he had been bent on escaping from. One reason for choosing A Life as marking a major turning point in Smith's production is that it shows him finding a way out of this impasse through discovery of, and adherence to, a specifically Postmodernist perspective. It is neither his largest nor his most significant collection, yet in it an oppressive pattern going back at least two decades begins to release its hold. It can therefore be spoken of with justification as a turning point in his work. The relevant items occur in the book's concluding section, which is headed 'Taynuilt 1982–', referring to the village near Oban to which Smith retired with his wife so as to devote his time completely to writing. The solution is a simple one. In the fifth poem of this section, Smith casts God as the author of a book in which we are the characters. If God is Himself an artist, then there can be no sin in the artist's imitating what God does. Indeed, Smith's experience of writing can be an avenue towards understanding what it is like to be God. And that experience is first and foremost one of joy:

> Are you happy with us, supreme author,
> as other authors are in the evening
> who scrupulously dine with their imaginings?

> Such joy, such joy! Do not recall us to You.
> Let us go on our way rejoicing
> down all the possible avenues we can take.

As the artist does not exert conscious control over all the aspects of what he is creating, so too are limits set for God's omnipotence and omniscience. It was necessary for Him to allow the Devil 'his own perfect will'. Religion and art, rather than caught in eternal hostility, offer insights into one another, each providing valuable guidance to the nature of the other.

The sixth poem places more restrictions on God's role, and on the author's, with its insistence that 'The author is not important, the author dies./ The tale lives on.' The seventh takes implications of liberation and playfulness further still, with one of the most striking openings in all Smith's work: 'I think you will die easily./ You have been a book reader all your life.' The rationale for such a statement is not hard to find. If life is itself a kind of text or a book, then reading books is an effective means of studying life and preparing for death. Learning how books end helps us imagine how life will end. Aesthetic teaching is therefore a kind of spiritual teaching, too, and the tensions between the black devils of the religious establishment and the angels of aesthetic activity can be resolved fruitfully. Playfulness is evident in the reference to the long Victorian novels of authors such as Dickens and Thackeray which place both deaths and marriages at the end, as a means of resolving the plot. This is why 'your death will be like a marriage . . . You will die in a cloud of roses,/ the pages quietly finished . . .' Judgement and the possibility of justification are not what matters. Instead a pattern must be completed, 'the marriages and deaths blossoming/ from the final arranged words'. Aesthetics, it would appear, are not irrelevant to morality, but have their own morality, and artistic activity is a means of bodying forth the good, if one that must always leave room for play and for the unpredictable.

In portraying the victims of the pitiless orthodoxy he so long struggled against, Smith is drawn repeatedly towards female figures. If there can be little doubt how important the poet's own mother was as a model for the old women that recur in a variety of guises throughout his work, nonetheless a strong element of self-projection can be detected in his treatment of women who have sacrificed the possibility of genuine love and physical fulfilment in order to survive within the confines of a society riddled by life-hating orthodoxy. 'The Widow' is a harrowing monologue addressed to an invalid husband, a schoolteacher disabled by a stroke, who is no longer around to listen or reply. The woman who was married to him asks where her jealousy should be directed: towards his books, 'his harem on the shelves', or else the pupils towards whom he trudged each morning, bent as he was on 'leading to stricter joys/ their halting minds'. The marriage has been a childless one. The first night of love with an ageing husband who, like Smith, put off marrying again and again in order to care for his mother, was a travesty of happiness:

> The light burned late, the bare electric light
> mocked my new body. You're an ageing girl.
> The two rooms shook loudly in the night.
> It wasn't right. No, though you're sitting there
> it wasn't right, I tell you.

The speaker is a very different person from the husband she mourns. Filled with anger, she perceives the injustice in their marriage, and will accept no religious consolation for everything it failed to provide: 'Am I God/ so to forgive you or to leave the Why/ nailed to my cross?' He could never forgive himself and she, too, finds it impossible to forgive. The poem closes with the haunting of a martyrdom, a self-mutilation which persists even after he is dead and in spite of all her pleading with him to call a halt:

> Your chair is rocking, rocking,
> as if with grief. I see you with a rod
> whipping your bony body. Stop, I say.
> Stop, child, you mustn't. You were all I had.

Another extended monologue (and Browning's example would have been well known to Smith), presents an analogous female figure. 'She Teaches *Lear*' is composed of thirteen six-line stanzas rhyming consistently *abccab*, with additional, generous use of half-rhyme and assonance. This dauntingly complex poem operates on a number of different levels. One concerns Shakespeare's *King Lear*, given that we are in a secondary school classroom with a mixture of boys and girls ranged along the benches. Another level involves the lesson itself, with observations from the students and comments in response from the teacher. The third level is the teacher's tormented family life. Childless and a spinster, she devotes her evenings to the care of an ageing father, who is disabled and resentful. The speaker consequently looks on herself as Cordelia to her father's Lear. Her students' observations are also judgements about the life choices she has made and her responses to these judgements are not limited to the text being discussed. She attempts to frame some kind of self-defence. It is as if she were offering her own life to them for perusal and evaluation, as much as the play:

> And to read *Lear* to these condemning ones
> in their striped scarves and ties but in the heart,
> tall, cool and definite. Naval, in this art.

They resemble the crew of a ship, vaguely menacing in their uniforms, rather than a class she is in charge of. The speaker sees her students as Regans and Gonerils, 'absolute hunters . . . beautiful too with their own spare beauty', needing no further justification for their barbaric behaviour than the unadulterated nature of the passions which impel them. Only in 'young pale Jean' with her 'library-white face,/ thin-boned and spectacled, speechlessly unhappy/ and ready for all art, especially poetry' can the possibility of a more tender, or self-damaging choice be detected, of the kind the teacher herself has made. Jean is revealed as 'the true Cordelia', as the dichotomy between the hunters, ruthless, uncaring and Philistine yet favoured by brute existence, and the losers, victims whose selflessness opens them up to both art and exploitation, becomes explicit. The poem, however, closes with a warning:

> Admire such ones but know in your own mind
> how they would bring upon us innocent carnage,
> the end of Lear, and *Lear*, their own worse will.

Though it comes from Smith's earlier, trapped world, the poem insists on linking, not merely aesthetic and religious values, but both of these with politics and society in general. For the teacher, her adolescent pupils embody an unthinking, unacknowledged Fascism which if left unchecked would mean the end of culture, and against which culture itself is the only reliable antidote.

Smith was a prolific author, embracing not just two languages but drama and prose fiction as well as poetry, in an extensive output. While teaching in Clydebank, he was in the habit of sending recent work to Derick Thomson for evaluation. Thomson was horrified to discover that poems to which he had an unfavourable reaction were unceremoniously jettisoned. Such spendthrift ways are only thinkable for someone endowed with Smith's untiring capacity to produce. Five more books of poetry appeared after his *Collected Poems*. They include an extended political and philosophical meditation on *The Human Face*, written in the Burns stanza but constantly threatening to strain the form to bursting point. As if the use of English here were not sufficiently jarring, Smith again and again runs the sense on from one stanza to the next, belying and subverting the potential pithy quality of its alternation of long and short lines. Like so much of Smith's poetry, the surface of this book has barely been scratched by critics. And all the present study can do in the face of such an extended and complex body of work is hint at recurrent motifs and try to indicate one possible watershed. It is unlikely that any poet coming after will feel the need for an engagement with established religion as passionate and condemnatory as Smith's. Though church attendance throughout Scotland declined rapidly as the century drew to its close, and despite the waning influence of Christian teaching on social life in the country, Smith's poetry looks set to lose none of its plangently obsessive lyrical force.

Notes

1. Poems are quoted from *Elegies* (London, Faber and Faber 1985) and from *New Selected Poems 1964–2000* (London, Faber and Faber 2003). Robert Crawford and David Kinloch eds *Reading Douglas Dunn* (Edinburgh, Edinburgh University Press 1992) contains, along with essays by several hands, a bibliography of secondary literature on pp. 277–85. See further Cairns Craig 'From the Lost Ground: Liz Lochhead, Douglas Dunn and Contemporary Scottish Poetry' in James Acheson and Romana Huk eds *Contemporary British Poetry* (Albany, New York 1996) pp. 343–72, Marco Fazzini *Crossings: Essays on Contemporary Scottish Poetry and Hybridity* (Venice, Supernova 2000) pp. 121–44, David Kennedy 'What does the Fairy DO? The Staging of Antithetical Masculine Styles in the Poetry of Tony Harrison and Douglas Dunn' in *Textual Practice* 14 (1) (2000) pp. 115–36, J. M. Lyon 'The Art of Grief: Douglas Dunn's *Elegies*' in *English* 40 (166) (Spring 1991) pp. 47–67, Sean O'Brian 'Douglas Dunn: Ideology and Pastoral' in his *The Deregulated Muse* (Newcastle upon Tyne, Bloodaxe 1998) pp. 65–80, Linden Peach 'A Politics of Being: the Poetry of Douglas Dunn' in his *Ancestral Lines* (Bridgend, Mid Glamorgan 1992) pp. 134–53 and Rebecca Smalley 'The Englishman's Scottishman, or radical Scotsman? Rereading Douglas Dunn in the Light of Recent Reappraisal of Philip Larkin' in *Scottish Literary Journal* 22 (1) (May 1995) pp. 74–83.

2. Poems are quoted from *The Bird Path: Collected Longer Poems* (Edinburgh, Mainstream 1989: page numbers only) and *Handbook for the Diamond Country* (Edinburgh, Mainstream 1990: pages numbers preceded by *Handbook*). White's new retrospective volume *Open World: Collected Poems 1960–2000* (Edinburgh, Polygon 2003) appeared when work on this chapter had been completed. See further Gavin Bowd '*Outsiders': Alexander Trocchi and Kenneth White: an Essay* (Kirkcaldy, Akros 1988), 'On the Borders: Geopoetics, Geopolitics' in *Edinburgh Review* 92 (Summer 1994) pp. 131–40 and 'Poetry after God: the Reinvention of the Sacred in the Work of Eugène Guillevic and Kenneth White' in *Dalhousie French Studies* 39–40 (Summer-Fall 1997) pp. 159–80, Michèle Duclos 'Kenneth White et la France' in *La Nouvelle Alliance: Influences francophones sur la littérature écossaise moderne* sous la direction de David Kinloch et Richard Price (Grenoble, Université Stendhal 2000) pp. 115–45, Marco Fazzini *Crossings: Essays on Contemporary Scottish Poetry and Hybridity* (Venice, Supernova 2000) pp. 93–119, Tony McManus 'From the Centred Complex: an Interview with Kenneth White, July 1993' in *Edinburgh Review* 92 (Summer 1994) pp. 122–30 and 'Dwelling in the North' in *Edinburgh Review* 98 (Autumn 1997) pp. 65–72, Graham Dunstan Martin 'A Pict in Roman Gaul: Kenneth White and France' in *Chapman* 59 (January 1990) pp. 8–17, Edwin Morgan 'Kenneth

White: a Scottish transnationalist' in *Books in Scotland* 31 (Summer 1989) pp. 1–2 and Roderick Watson 'Visions of Alba: the Constructions of Celtic Roots in Modern Scottish Literature' *Études Écossaises* 1 (1992) pp. 253–64.

3. Poems are quoted from Liz Lochhead *Dreaming Frankenstein* (Edinburgh, Polygon 1984), which includes the collections *Memo for Spring* (1972), *Islands* (1978) and *Grimm Sisters* (1981). The earliest poems in the volume date from 1967. Lochhead has further published *True Confessions* (Edinburgh, Polygon 1984), *Bagpipe Muzak* (London, Penguin 1991) and *The Colour of Black and White* (Edinburgh, Polygon 2003). See also Robert Crawford and Anne Varty eds *Liz Lochhead's Voices* (Edinburgh, Edinburgh University Press 1993), 'Liz Lochhead Interviewed by Emily B. Todd' in Robert Crawford, Henry Hart, David Kinloch, Richard Price eds *Talking Verse* (St Andrews and Williamsburg, Verse 1995) pp. 115–27, Aileen Christianson 'Liz Lochhead's Poetry and Drama: Forging Ironies' in Aileen Christianson and Alison Lumsden eds *Contemporary Scottish Women Writers* (Edinburgh, Edinburgh University Press 2000) pp. 41–52, Cairns Craig 'From the Lost Ground: Liz Lochhead, Douglas Dunn and Contemporary Scottish Poetry' in James Acheson and Romana Huk eds *Contemporary British Poetry* (Albany, New York 1996) pp. 343–72, and Anne Varty 'The Mirror and the Vamp: Liz Lochhead' in Douglas Gifford and Dorothy McMillan eds *A History of Scottish Women's Writing* (Edinburgh, Edinburgh University Press 1997) pp. 641–58.

4. Throughout this chapter, Crichton Smith's poems are quoted from *Collected Poems* (Manchester, Carcanet 1992), which were followed by *Ends and Beginnings* (1994), *The Human Face* (1996), *The Leaf and the Marble* (1998), and two posthumous collections, *A Country for Old Men* and *My Canadian Uncle* (2000), all published by Carcanet. See also the prose pieces collected in *Towards the Human* (Loanhead, Macdonald 1986), the essay 'Structure in My Poetry' in C. B. McCully ed. *The Poet's Voice and Craft* (Manchester, Carcanet 1994) pp. 104–22, and further Carol Gow 'An Interview with Iain Crichton Smith' in *Scottish Literary Journal* 17 (2) (Nov. 1990) and *Mirror and Marble: the Poetry of Ian Crichton Smith* (Edinburgh, Saltire Society 1992), Colin Nicholson ed. *Iain Crichton Smith: Critical Essays* (Edinburgh, Edinburgh University Press 1992), Mario Relich 'To Hold the Darkness at Bay: a Conversation with Iain Crichton Smith' in *Edinburgh Review* 99 (Spring 1998) pp. 108–21 and Grant F. Wilson *A Bibliography of Iain Crichton Smith* (Aberdeen, Aberdeen University Press 1990) which of course requires updating. Articles include Douglas Gifford 'The True Dialectic: the Development of the Fiction and Poetry of Iain Crichton Smith' in *Chapman* 34 (1983) pp. 39–46 and 'Deer on the High Hills: the Elusiveness of Language in the Poetry of Iain Crichton Smith' in Derick Thomson ed. *Gaelic and Scots in Harmony* (Glasgow, Department of Celtic 1988) pp. 149–62, Michelle MacLeod 'Language and Bilingualism in the Gaelic Poetry of Iain Crichton Smith' in *Scottish Studies Review* 2 (2) (Autumn 2001) pp. 105–13, Donald Meek 'Songs and Tales for a New Ceilidh: the Gaelic Writings of Iain Crichton Smith' in *Aberdeen University Review* LIX (2) 206 (Autumn 2001) pp. 145–53, Colin Milton 'Half of my Seeing: the English Poetry of Iain Crichton Smith' in Gary Day and Brian Docherty eds *British Poetry from the 1950s to the 1990s: Politics and Art* (Basingstoke, Macmillan 1997) pp. 193–220, Stan Smith 'A Double Man in a Double Place: Scotland Between the Symbolic and the Imaginary in the Poetry of Iain Crichton Smith' in *Scottish Literary Journal* 20 (2) (November 1993) pp. 63–74 and

George Watson 'Double Man at a Culloden of the Spirit: Reflections on the Poetry of Iain Crichton Smith' in *Verse* 7 (2) (Summer 1990) pp. 73–82.

5. Alexander Carmichael *Carmina Gadelica: Hymns and Incantations* vol. 1, 2nd edn (Edinburgh and London, Scottish Academic Press 1928) p. xxxvi.

6. Iain Mac a' Ghobhainn *An t-Eilean agus an Cànan* (Oilthigh Ghlaschu, Roinn na Cànan Ceilteach 1978) p. 20 (translation CW).

7. From *A Life* (1986), now *Collected Poems* pp. 245–7.

8. 'The Skeleton of the Future: at Lenin's Tomb', *Complete Poems* I, p. 386.

9. *Poems of William Soutar: a New Selection*, ed. W. R. Aitken (Edinburgh, Scottish Academic Press 1988) p. 253.

9

The 1990s
(Robert Crawford, Kathleen Jamie, Carol Ann Duffy, Aonghas MacNeacail)

A perfectly valid, and often very fruitful way of approaching the work of an individual poet is to read it as if it were a novel, to pick up a collected volume, or a generous selection, and work right through from the beginning to the end as one might do with a prose narrative. Similar stages can be detected in the reading experience. At the beginning it is hard to decide precisely which elements may prove to be significant as the story continues. By the time you reach the central section and all the crucial cards are on the table, everything is more or less at stake, you are both pleased to discern a pattern and surprised at how your expectations have been similarly eluded and fulfilled. You inevitably make conjectures as to how it will all be resolved, what the concluding pattern will look like, and are aware of an increase in speed as the end approaches, of greater selectivity and complexity. Not infrequently a surprise or maverick factor will appear at the last moment, referring back to the opening, before any further movement becomes impossible, and the whole affair is wound up.

Reading in this fashion is not an alternative with poets who have still to reach fifty. Writing about them is a perilous enterprise, one no critic should embark upon without a degree of circumspection. This is not only because it resembles assessing a novel which is only half completed, but because poetry needs time to sediment. It is as if the possibilities for valid criticism were a line leaving the earth at an acute angle, and the further away you move from the present moment, the greater the available space for manoeuvre. The choice of collections and poets to be dealt with throughout this book has been open to discussion, but nowhere is it likely to be more controversial than when dealing with the final decade of the century. No one can truly predict whose work will best stand the test of time or whose reputation is most likely to survive. Nor are these questions of primary importance in the present moment. The wisest course would seem to be to seek out representative figures, those who can manage to give a flavour of what was happening and being written in the 1990s, and consideration of whose output can hopefully raise issues which are also relevant to their contemporaries, any one of whom may well be destined to outshine them in the course of time. Here the metaphor of gradually moving away from a position in the landscape and gaining a better overall view of it is appropriate.

Nevertheless a few general points may be hazarded. At last it is possible to give equal coverage to women poets. If Liz Lochhead's work was far too often promoted thanks to a rather suspect tokenism, this can no longer be the case in the new decade, given the range of female voices and the impossibility of categorising them under any facile headings. Scots and Gaelic have clearly moved into the background, whether definitively or not remains to be seen. The Scots items in Crawford's work all too often have the quality of museum exhibits, accompanied by an exhaustive and exhausting glossary and sometimes by an English version. There is no sense of a connection with living and experienced rhythms of speech, of these breaking through onto the page and enacting a disruption of accepted patterns of spelling, grammar and lexis. Jamie's efforts in this direction are more natural and convincing, though they still retain a cautious, experimental air, as if they were as yet an adjunct to the main body of her writing, a demonstration that something continues to be possible rather than an irresistible necessity. While it is satisfying to round off this book as it began, with a poet who uses Gaelic, one, moreover, who makes no secret of his perceived debt to Sorley MacLean, MacNeacail has moved beyond both MacLean's adumbration of an intact Gaelic world (however deceptive that may have been) and Thomson's chastening insistence that it was not, and could never be, a reality. MacNeacail's experience of socialisation in his first language did not go much beyond early childhood and the start of schooling. At times the parameters within which he moves as a poet writing in Gaelic seem perilously dependent on the perceptions and expectations of an audience with no direct access to the language. He started his career with an English collection and has returned regularly to that language, while experimenting more recently with Scots. This, together with the considerable status he himself accords his more or less ubiquitous facing English translations, implies a conditionality in the use of Gaelic which is certainly new, when not quite simply worrying.

One further element discernible in the poetry of the 1990s is a paradoxical resuscitation of Britishness, with interesting consequences for Scottishness as flagged, for example, in the work of Crawford and Jamie. With the exception of MacNeacail, the poets dealt with in this chapter, like Morgan, Dunn and Crichton Smith, publish in England. If as late as the 1970s to flag Scottishness meant choosing inevitable marginalisation, this is emphatically no longer the case. By the turn of the century, within the context of public promotion of poetry including the entire United Kingdom in its remit, it could be a positive asset. Whether the context meant that 'Scottishness' was itself differently structured is too complex a question to be entered upon here, though it would merit detailed consideration. Since the present approach remains firmly agnostic, 'Scottishness' here refers to a literary strategy, often the result of more or less conscious choice, rather than a quality whose genuineness can be independently verified. There can be no arguing, however, about one significant difference with respect to previous generations. For MacDiarmid, for Goodsir Smith and even for Garioch, the choice of Scottishness involved a profound osmosis with the work of poets writing in different languages or in a different age. This does not hold for any of the poets dealt with in this chapter. Their poetic practice can be satisfactorily accounted for without moving beyond contemporary poetic production in the English language world. Even with MacNeacail, the Black Mountain poets and English language concrete poetry are no less important than the work of Sorley MacLean. And is it not necessary to speak of two distinct MacLeans, with an intimate but by no means straightforward relationship to one another, one available to the English language reader, the other in Gaelic?

Two final points can be added. All four poets (and in this respect they may well be symptomatic of an entire generation) are significantly implicated with the university as an academic institution. The mushrooming of creative writing as a craft to be taught and its integration within universities have meant that the discussion of recently produced work, their own, their contemporaries' and their pupils', plays a considerable role in these writers' professional existence. Even the most outstandingly successful poetry, as is well known, will not keep the economic wolf from anybody's door for long. At the most basic level, the security, however intermittently available, of academic appointments and the ensuing salaries offers a welcome haven from the insecurities of living as a poet. Dunn and Lochhead have had similar involvements, as had MacCaig and MacLean, though for the latter two this occurred at a significantly later stage in their careers. Whether or not this is connected to a diminished interest in closed forms, in poetic technique as traditionally conceived, is a moot point. Could it be possible that a 'you can do it too' syndrome, needing to be maintained if the creative writing industry is to go on developing, lies behind this? The implication that free verse requires less technical ability than closed forms is, of course, deceptive. If anything, the reverse is true, and the practice of free verse, in English at least, now has a considerable and august pedigree, even if the associated technical issues continue to be under-researched. A possible exception here would be Duffy, as eloquently testified by the profoundly moving sonnet entitled 'Prayer' which closes *Mean Time*, and the reaching out for new forms, a new 'formfulness' even, discernible in her most recent collection *Feminine Gospels*.

What makes Crawford's poetry representative is first and foremost its wholehearted identification with the nationalist cause, specifically with the campaign for the reintroduction of a Scottish parliament.[1] This is symptomatic of the transitory but intense love affair which took place between writers and intellectuals and the nationalist movement, reaching its peak at the beginning of the 1990s. More than a decade had gone by since in 1979 a referendum, its terms weighted in favour of the *status quo*, failed to provide Scotland with a parliament of its own on the eve of the Thatcherist years.

Crawford's first solo collection came out in 1990 (a joint volume entitled *Sharawaggi* consisting mainly of experiments in forms of Scots appeared the same year) with the title *A Scottish Assembly*. On the one hand it refers to the poem of the same name. But there is an underlying implication, especially if one is willing to interpret 'assembly' as 'assemblage' or 'collection', that the book itself must be regarded as equivalent to, as an acceptable substitute for, the political institution: an implication that Crawford (1959–) can deliver this to his readers, encapsulating it between two covers, before it has become a reality. Does it have an analogous power to legislate? What limitations might be placed on it?

The poem in question expresses Crawford's longing 'Always to come home to roost// In this unkempt country', though he declines to explain

> why I came back here to choose my union
> On the side of the ayes, remaining a part
>
> Of this diverse assembly – Benbecula, Glasgow, Bow of Fife –
> Voting with my feet, and this hand.

The speaker was faced with a choice. He had alternatives and could have gone, or stayed, elsewhere. Exemplary status is conferred on his decision. Indeed, there are reasons for concluding that the life glimpsed here, and in Crawford's subsequent volumes, is offered as exemplary in its turn. Whether this quality can help to explain the peculiar lack of interiority in Crawford's poetry is a point we will return to. In 'A Scottish Poet', from his most recent collection *The Tip of My Tongue* (2003), he appears to us working 'outdoors' at a 'cubbyholed desk':

> My job description just one long
> Sabbatical from real life.
>
> Always good, though, work after work,
> Commuting to my second, third, and fifth homes
>
> In Glasgow, Hoy, or smeeky Kirkcaldy,
> Feet up on every computer in Scotland . . .

However briefly, Crawford manages to occupy the space in front of each computer screen in his country, all those spaces in which writing is being done. One is reminded of the techniques of self-presentation deployed by Burns in his verse epistles, and there is a sense in which Crawford makes an unequivocal bid to be the Burns of his day, the representative bard of a nation ripe for reorganisation and redefinition.

Precisely what kind of Scotland is celebrated in these poems? One that combines erudition, technology in both its industrial and post-industrial manifestations, and the Scottish obscurely local. The poems are filled with capital letters, with proper names, historical references and citations, with facts picked up who knows where and designed to surprise, delight and presumably to instil confidence. Interestingly, the heroic age Crawford harks back to is that of triumphant Unionism, the period stretching from his country's relatively early industrialisation through to the technical inventions and the intellectual giants of the Victorian period. This may be the effect of Crawford's own geographical origin within the central belt, in Lanarkshire but on the periphery of Glasgow, in that part of Scotland which, more than any other, continues to bear the signs of imperial greatness and decay. Though Crawford's intention is to celebrate potential separateness, this heroism was in fact a very British one. If at times one cannot help being reminded of those dishcloths parading the contributions to science and progress of a range of Scottish notables, this is an inevitable consequence of the kind of nationalist discourse he employs.

'The Dalswinton Enlightenment' (from *A Scottish Assembly*) is typical in this respect. It features a painter who is also an engineer, along with a poet who sings the achievements of the industrial age, bringing both into contact with the Scottish obscurely local:

> The painter will later invent
> The compression rivet, and work out the axial arrangement
> Between propeller and engine. The poet will write about
>   the light
> Of science dawning over Europe . . .

The title's reference to the eighteenth-century Enlightenment draws on a further strand of Scottish cultural nationalism, one which sets itself at something of a tangent to the postwar world, in its refusal to take account of the deconstruction of that very phenomenon of Enlightenment, undertaken by French poststructuralists in particular. Three poems centred on Helensburgh follow 'The Dalswinton Enlightenment', making one wonder if Crawford has or had a specific connection to the town. The celebrities parading through them include Watt, inventor of the steam engine, Frazer, a founder of modern anthropology, the forebears of the novelist Robert Louis Stevenson, celebrated as pioneer lighthouse builders, the philanthropist Andrew Carnegie, the dictionary maker James Murray and John Logie Baird, the inventor of television: an overwhelmingly male inventory. That they function as models for Crawford's own praxis is suggested by the close of another poem in a similar vein, 'Sir David Brewster Invents the Kaleidoscope', whose hero 'Went back to being local, became fact'.

What kind of a relationship do these poems, one possible interpretation of the poetry of facts preached by MacDiarmid, establish with the reader? Displays of humbling yet obscure and even idiosyncratic erudition, they do not spur us on to dialogue, seeking either confirmation or refutation. Nor do they have any clear emotional colouring. The contemporary painter Stephen Conroy is 'potent/ As basic integers' ('Man of Vision'), while a recent love poem to Crawford's wife diffuses its emotion through facts about the natural world: 'As a candle-flame believes in the speed of light . . . As the shoelace of glass believes in the full grown eel' ('Credo' from *The Tip of My Tongue*). Forms of address devoid of emotion are generally preferred. The extended poem 'A Life-Exam' from *Spirit Machines* (1999), dealing with a period of hospitalisation, takes the form of a series of questions from an examination paper. One might have expected the choice of this form to imply protest, a rebellion against the implied situation of fledgling knowledge being put to the test by a larger, more qualified intelligence. Despite the vulnerability and uncertainty of his position, however, Crawford appears to find this kind of discourse appropriate and even comforting. 'Inner Glasgow' (from *A Scottish Assembly*) describes utterance in terms of a mechanism, of functioning or malfunctioning parts: 'When words cut out their starter motor'.

Nationalist discourse creeps into, infiltrates the love poems. When Crawford's wife rolls over towards him in bed, 'in a country that hasn't existed/ For centuries', she whispers, not some inviting tenderness, but 'I've become a nationalist' ('Pimpernel'). 'Photonics' has the lovers 'meet as clearly as two beams in a saltire/ Bonded at the centre', while at the close of 'Credo' the poet makes his wife a 'declaration of dependence'.

Crawford's Scotland is subject to an edict of modernity. The most celebrated item in *A Scottish Assembly*, 'Scotland', is a eulogy to his 'Semiconductor country', his 'micro-nation', this 'chip of a nation'. The choice of words is both specialist and hip, producing felicitous phrases like 'an asylum for anemometers,/ A discotheque of waters' to describe the Inner Hebridean island Coll ('Coll'). At other times, the contemporaneity can be forced and mannered, as when Crawford ('Robert Crawford') predicts the invention of

a noun for the sensation

Of hearing Philip Glass while being driven in a Citroën
Or of sitting down to eat a bag of chips

With two historians of mesmerism near Inverkeithing.

The combination of the local, the demotic and the obscurely erudite in these lines is characteristic. The paradox, however, is that Crawford's celebrations of Scotland, despite their exultation, their deployment of a mint-fresh vocabulary in which the bard can sing his country (following what is after all a thoroughly traditional model) leave a residual taste of insecurity and fragility. Scottishness is never questioned, tested or problematised in Crawford's work. Yet there is something brittle and insubstantial, something resolutely surface to it nonetheless.

In gender terms, he is not a radical. The opening item of *A Scottish Assembly*, 'Opera', moves beyond the 'men make art, women make babies' cliché to redefine this suspiciously foreign form, by means of a witty pun on the manufacturer's name, as the clothes the poet's mother ran up for him on her sewing machine:

It was a powerful instrument. I stared
Hard at its brilliant needle's eye that purred
And shone at night; and then each morning after
I went to work at school, wearing her songs.

The sequence 'Masculinity', from the volume with the same name (Crawford's third, published in 1996) fails to engage with the crucial issue about gender, namely the attribution of social, economic and discursive power on the basis of perceived biological sex, and the cultural encrustations which accrue to this. An individual protestation of harmlessness carries little weight when confronting a mechanism which operates on a collective, effectively a faceless, basis. The degree of self-revelation here and elsewhere in Crawford's work, is disarming and, in its way, humbling. He does not run away from topics like infertility or adoption: a poem from *Spirit Machines* describes the family's elation when suspicion of a cancerous tumour proves unfounded ('The Result'), though again the way the poem's subtitle (*1707–1997: for Alice*) assimilates this new lease of life to the reopening of the nation's parliament jars. In their peculiar way, these too are poems of fact. One's instinctive reading of them (and there is every reason to take this as the poet's intention) is as referring to real events concerning the man whose name is on the spine of the book. This gives a quite specific colouring to their reception. If we understood that Crawford were dramatising situations conjured up from his imagination, we might very well demand a greater degree of interiority, a broadening of the emotional range.

Such a broadening may well not be feasible because of the exemplary quality with which he endows his family in his depictions of them. Father, mother, partner, child rarely move beyond these categories to emerge as individuals engaging, even struggling with the roles in which they find themselves. One has little inkling of the fatedness which inevitably accompanies the collision between an actual personality and any of these roles. In 'Fiat Lux' (from *The Tip of My Tongue*) Crawford borrows the voice of his creator to will his family into being in the context of a wide range of phenomena, natural, scientific and man-made (significantly including 'new parliaments') as if any set of individuals known to one could ever achieve this primordial, God-ordained status:

Let there be lasers, Fabergé crystal eggs,
Hens' squelchy yolks, birch-bark's thin,

> Diaphanous scratchiness, let there be you,
> Me, son and daughter, let the Rhine
>
> Flow through Cologne and Basle . . .

Family values as traditionally understood have an unequivocal place at the core of this universe. The promotion of his own existence, along with that of the people closest to him, to exemplary status goes some way towards explaining the infinitely restrained sensuality of Crawford's poetry, a restraint which can, at times, look like an absence of sensuality. In '*Seuils*', intercourse becomes a kind of reading, with 'Couples/ who last night opened themselves like books', while at the close of 'The Tip of My Tongue' (a poem which gives its title to that volume), though an erection may be hinted at in 'waking at a lover's angle', the last phrase is tinglingly clinical: 'With you on the tip of my tongue'. In this respect, at least, Burns could hardly be at a greater distance.

A poem entitled 'Mr and Mrs Scotland are dead' from Kathleen Jamie's fifth book, *The Queen of Sheba*, provides the title for a retrospective volume issued in 2002 and drawing on all her previous collections, with the exception of the most recent, *Jizzen* (1999).[2] One could be forgiven for assuming, on the basis of its title, that in this particular poem the whole issue of seeking out a Scottish identity and defining Scottishness would be cast aside. A rather different approach is, however, taken. On a dump at the very edge of town, scattered, insignificant objects offer eloquent, but never intimate, testimony to the lives of a long dead Scottish couple, from the kind of lower middle-class background familiar to us in Jamie's poetry. The reliability of the testimony is not questioned. This is what it was really like. The question is how we ought to treat these relics:

> Do we take them? Before the bulldozer comes
> to make more room, to shove aside
> his shaving brush, her button tin.
> Do we save this toolbox, these old-fashioned views
> addressed, after all, to Mr and Mrs Scotland?

The answer is to envision a kind of sedimenting. Before too long, the speaker and those she is addressing will be in a similar position, deceased, well nigh forgotten, persisting only in such casual remains, which will in turn pose the same question to the 'person' who 'enters/ our silent house . . .'

The poem has an elegiac tone. But what strikes one, along with its undisguised piety, is the fundamental stability of its vision of continuity within change, of fidelity, even, to a previous generation or generations seen as solidly and irrevocably connected to us, in the last analysis as our progenitors. A similar investigation is carried out in more combative fashion in 'Forget It' from *Jizzen*. Here a more savage process, 'the great clearance', has led to a not dissimilar exposure:

> turning tenements outside-in,
> exposing gas pipes, hearths
> in damaged gables, wallpaper
> hanging limp and stained
> in the shaming rain.

Movement from what had become slums to the yearned-for scheme and a house with its own 'glass/ front door' is only part of the history the eager schoolgirl in the poem seeks to reconstruct. Emigration with the consequent scattering of siblings is another element, and the possibility of remembering events occurring beyond the confines of one's own life is mooted. The links being uncovered need not be limited to what one person can experience, or what reluctant parents bent on suppression can be forced to reveal. The justification is that 'stories are balm,/ ease their own pain . . .' Jamie's preoccupations here are akin to those of Aonghas MacNeacail in 'Oideachadh Ceart' ('A Proper Schooling').[3] Yet her approach is more determined and energetic. The kind of language barrier that has intervened between MacNeacail and his forebears is unknown to her. The presence and accessibility of parents, however bent on putting the past behind them, makes her task a less formidable one.

The sense of being part of a mesh of connecting and cohering stories gives an assertive, even a serene undertow to Jamie's poetry. It means that at times she feels able to speak for a generation. 'Crossing the Loch', the poem which opens *Jizzen*, recalls 'The way we live', which had given its title to her second collection twelve years before. The earlier poem, as one would expect, is the less confident of the two. It has all youth's clamorous, yet insecure determination to set a trend, to embody a style. Its powerful linking of disparate realities is just a little redolent of an earlier age of nonconformism, the 1960s, though the changes brought about by Thatcherism make the context grimmer:

to launderettes, anecdotes, passions and exhaustion,
Final Demands and dead men, the skeletal grip
of government. To misery and elation; mixed,
the sod and caprice of landlords.

The exhortations to 'pass the tambourine' framing the poem are too artificial. How likely are the kind of people Jamie (1962–) is both describing and addressing to have a tambourine to hand? And yet the poem echoes in the mind, and repays repeated visits. 'Crossing the Loch' looks backward, as if the short journey described could stand for the journey from first youth to maturity and parenthood, the speaker contemplating the achievement of both with the same puzzlement and reverence. It has not always been an easy passage: 'Out in the race I was scared:/ the cold shawl of breeze,/ and hunched hills . . .' A marvellous detail such as 'the glimmering anklets/ we wore in the shallows/ as we shipped oars and jumped' roots the poem in the scenery depicted while at the same time intimating transcendence. The fourth stanza hauntingly evokes the crucial characters who had yet to come onstage, the unknown men and women who would become the fathers and mothers of children unthought of when the incident occurred.

In the third stanza, Jamie compares the craft and its occupants to 'a twittering nest/ washed from the rushes, an astonished/ small boat of saints . . .' and her choice of images prompts a reflection on the undoubted engagement with the Celtic Twilight which is increasingly notable in her two most recent collections. It is a perilous tactic, yet she manages to bring it off. One's thoughts turn briefly to Crawford and the use he makes of Gaelic Scotland in poems like 'Bhidhio' from *A Scottish Assembly*, 'Barra' from *Talkies* or 'Amazing Grace' from the sequence 'Highland Poems' in *Spirit Machines*. For Crawford it represents a reassuring nugget of difference, one he feels no need to investigate or render any less alien, so that at times he iterates familiar stereotypes. His most recent volume includes an imitation from the Gaelic of Mary MacLeod, Màiri Nighean Alasdair Ruaidh, while Jamie closes *Jizzen* with a poem about the tradition according to which 'certain of the Gaelic women poets were buried face down'. The Celtic Twilight as a movement belongs to the end of the nineteenth century and the beginning of the twentieth, and depended for its peculiar projection of doom-laden uncertainty and vagueness on the existence of a solid language barrier impeding general access to the realities of Gaelic language poetry and culture. There is nothing so exploitative or crass in the way Jamie increasingly evokes another world behind the present day, a world of ritual and of traditional power principally associated with female figures.

'The Barrel Annunciation' by its very title evokes a more than human significance for this particular impregnation, as well as suggesting a transcendence of the mundane. Some kind of supernatural intervention was needed for this child to take root. The speaker blames the gestures with which 'seven/ or nine times' she emptied the pail containing the overspill from a blocked pipe into the barrel for setting in motion 'some arcane craft laid/ like a tripwire or a snare', even though she herself would have previously dismissed such 'lore' as just 'a crone's trick'. In the third of a sequence of poems to her infant son Duncan, she recalls feeling compelled, on getting home from the hospital,

> to walk to the top of the garden,
> to touch, in a complicit
> homage of equals, the spiral
> trunks of our plum trees, the moss,
> the robin's roost in the holly.

It is as if these ritual gestures had to be completed for the homecoming, and the birth that preceded it, to take on their full meaning, also in order to protect both occurrences. 'St Bride's', a poem for Jamie's daughter, is undisguisedly Celtic in its titular saint, its evocation of 'a selkie-/ skin' and the concluding comparison of placenta to 'a fist of purple kelp'. 'The Well at the Broch of Gurness' invokes the girl who, at a time of Viking raids, while the others took refuge in their fort, hid down by 'the sunken well' where it was possible to 'step down out of the world'. The well is still accessible today, 'we can follow her' and 'seek/ the same replenishing water'.

Jamie's attraction for the magical, her evocation of dimly perceived female figures from other worlds and other dimensions, and the landscapes which accompany them, can remind one of Marion Angus, though it may be inappropriate to posit a direct influence. What prevents Jamie's work from becoming fey or mannered is the very real importance and effectiveness attributed to these presences in the modern everyday. This is no fading otherworld, but a repertory of potential power to be uncovered and put to use.

'Wee Wifey', from *The Queen of Sheba*, describes a personal demon, the reverse, if you like, of a guardian angel, from whom the speaker is unwillingly and morosely separated. Its companion piece, 'Wee Baby', deals with the 'kingdom' of the child yet to be conceived, a baby girl who 'turns little fishy tricks/ in your wine glass', who 'is tucked up in the in-tray' and 'cradled in the sieve of all potential'. For all its magical qualities, the poem concerns the very real dilemma of the more or less successful professional woman, constantly aware of the tormenting and tantalising option of a pregnancy to which she cannot yet, and may never, commit herself.

There is a sense in which Jamie is engaged in a reCatholicisation of Scottish imagery. The notion might embarrass her, and embarrassment can be detected in the throwaway close of 'A Miracle' (from *Jizzen*), which has the triumphant local girl who saw wonders as a child return home from none other than Hollywood to 'buy Holyrood Palace'. The treatment of John Knox's statue as a miraculous Catholic madonna is, however, unequivocal. The little girl had seen it 'shoogle on its pedestal' while 'milk/ tears start[ed] in his stony eyes', so that admiring pilgrims left 'gobs of tallow' from their votive candles sticking 'to the plinth', and 'babies' booties dangled/ from that upflung arm'.

Celtic strands and the other world come together in the motif of the visitor present in so many of Jamie's poems. 'A Dream of the Dalai Lama on Skye' sets an exotic figure with cultic associations against a Highland landscape. The motif may be inherited from Jamie's own expeditions to the East, which bore fruit in the *Karakoram Highway* sequence from *The Way We Live* and in *The Autonomous Region* (1993), an entire volume dedicated to a journey made at the time of the Tiananmen Square massacre, when the poet was denied entry to Tibet. But it is most powerful when less explicitly presented, in poems like 'Flashing Green Man' or 'Sad Bird'. The briefly illuminated figure telling pedestrians they can cross is himself a kind of visitor, 'refuged in cities', and the description of the city the speaker is currently 'one of' makes it into a place of exile and of longing. The visitors who matter here are a skein of migrant geese heading for the Sidlaw Hills. Jamie's characteristic interest in and compassion for other women, often isolated or depressed, is evident in the 'pale-faced woman peeling potatoes/ as her husband climbed the long stairs' who

> cupped her hands round her eyes
> to acknowledge a sign
> truer than the flashing green man . . .

The geese come from elsewhere and are bound elsewhere, yet they are not merely visitors. The pattern of their flight is a sign demanding interpretation, their 'beating wings' compared to those of angels in an explicit attribution to them of the role of messengers, since that is precisely what an angel is. In 'Sad Bird', a 'grey/ pigeon or kind of dove' presides over the transformation of a derelict house into 'a home now painted cream, pink' while the couple standing watching it struggle to interpret its mood and are perhaps mistaken. Two nights later the bird disappears as inexplicably as it had come, a visitor and also, possibly, a messenger, though its message has proved impossible to decipher. In 'One of Us' the speakers sound like Celtic saints bent on evangelising a distant land, bearing 'the/ golden horn of righteousness,/ the justice harp; what folks expect'. One is reminded of the Children of Lir, transformed into birds in Irish lore, but here the band reach Edinburgh and camouflage themselves as 'normal' people, waiting disquietingly and in disguise for the unfolding of a larger plan whose executors they are. Straddling the gap between the human and the creatural is typical for this aspect of Jamie's poetry. Celebrating the female art of childbirth in 'St Bride's' she had cited the mother hare, 'her leverets' ears/ flat as the mizzen of a ship/ entering a bottle'.

One might expect a conflict between these more magical aspects in her writing and the grittier, realistic exploration of other women's lives which runs through Jamie's collections. 'A shoe' offers a kind of archaeology not too far from that of 'Mr and Mrs Scotland are Dead' as it traces 'a huge platform sole', washed up on Cramond beach, back to the young woman it once belonged to and her leap to a suicidal death. 'Hand Relief' contemplates with alarm, and not without a shade of Puritanical consternation, a former schoolmate who now earns her living giving 'hand relief' to her clients, incidentally discovering 'what the businessmen of Edinburgh/ wear beneath their suits'. 'Child with Pillar Box and Bin Bags' is a bemused reflection on the young mother who chooses the shadowy side of the street to photograph her baby in his pram, nearly letting him run into the passing traffic in the process. But then, choosing or thinking 'it possible to choose' might be alien to this woman's world, though they are evidently not to the speaker's. 'School Reunion', technically experimental in its irregular disposition of lines across the page, is a Maenadic narrative of female socialising. Girls turned into women reminisce, swap notes on what has become of their contemporaries, think of other roles they could have chosen, and look forward to the time 'When we're older than a mattress' and 'again we'll enter The Kestrel Hotel's/ dim loud dance hall'.

'The Queen of Sheba', perhaps Jamie's most outspoken and celebrated poem, marries the otherworldly and the mundane in its triumphant procession. The Queen of Sheba is on a visit to suburban central Scotland, an exotic alien with vague religious associations who jolts 'Presbyterian living rooms' and, like a female Dionysus, brings festive havoc to 'the Curriehill Road',

more audacious even than Currie Liz
who led the gala floats
through the Wimpey scheme
in a ruby-red Lotus Elan
before the Boys' Brigade band
and the Brownies' borrowed coal-truck . . .

There is nothing vague or Celtic about this figure, emerging from the Bible to take revenge on the Bible, demanding that a Scottish Solomon be found to match her learning. What she brings with her is rebellion and, rather than following her lead, the crowds of hitherto quite ordinary and remissive Scottish women forming her entourage identify with her. They have all become Queens of Sheba.

It is possible to speak of a coalescence in Jamie's two most recent volumes, a harmonious coming together of different elements which also involves a reconciliation with tradition, with traditionally feminine areas of activity and kinds of power. Rather than colliding with the roles of wife, mother, homemaker, the speaker merges with them, entering magically into them, informing them with a sense of power which also impresses one as a recovery of what had always lain there, latent, hidden. Scottishness in Jamie's poetry is not a problem. She does not hunt for or struggle to define her identity, more concerned instead to transcend the often mundane realities surrounding her by establishing connections with another plane of being, capable of galvanising and eventually transforming them.

Carol Ann Duffy's Scottishness remains problematic, though receipt of a Scottish Arts Council Book Award and her inclusion in both editions of Donny O'Rourke's *Dream State* anthology for Polygon, as well as in Dorothy Macmillan and Michel Byrne's *Twentieth-Century Scottish Women's Poetry* for Canongate, indicate a willingness to be labelled as a Scottish writer.[4] If her poetry breathes any landscape, it is that of Midlands England, and her origins within the Catholic Irish immigration suggest that, even if her family had not moved south when she was nine, questions might still be raised in certain quarters about her belonging to Scotland in terms of both race and religion. Rather than moving towards harmonisation and reconciliation as Jamie's does, Duffy's poetry pushes further and further away from charted territories, most strikingly and even alarmingly in *Feminine Gospels*, her latest collection. Where Jamie's work is celebratory, Duffy's is resolutely, even fatedly exploratory. Celebration may in the end be the more demanding task, more tricky to succeed at. But exploration has an allure which it is difficult to match.

One reason for this exploratory quality is the need to body forth lesbian contents. Male lovers are explicitly mentioned in Duffy's poetry. But an ungendered presence is more common, or two ungendered presences, with a language of the body which employs lesbian tropes while retaining a sense of hiddenness, of the unspoken and unidentified. Morgan's love poetry could at times sound sufficiently like the traditional male address to a woman for it to be misread, or only partially read, across more than two decades. Gender polarity is at the core of Lochhead's love poetry and, if she does assert a feminine voice, there is never any doubt about the fact and the centrality of the male presence. In 'Sleeping' (from *Mean Time*) a sultry vagueness predominates, with touches of the uncanny, because the landscape of this love defies identification and, in any case, the poem takes place at a different level from daytime consciousness. It is a kind of drowning or submersion beneath 'the dark warm waters of sleep' and, if the name on the spine of the book still simplistically prompts us to assume a woman is speaking, a clear assignation of active and passive roles is impossible. The trope of 'hot fruit' for the lover's mouth is hardly masculine. The preceding mention of hands which 'part me' implies a receptive orifice, so that oral to genital contact may well be the substance of this dream. Speaking is assimilated to penetration in the third section, and where the lover is described as 'in now, hard,/ demanding' it is possible to speculate that a tongue may have replaced the phallus as penetrative instrument. Despite this aggression, it is the lover who panics at the end, who 'hold[s] on tight, frantic,/ as if we were drowning', with an implicit demand for rescue by the speaker.

This is not an instance of self-censorship. The uncanny quality of Duffy's erotic writing destroys any potential for coyness. There is no artful concealment, no hint of 'now I say it, now I don't'. What matters is an absence, of the male, of the familiar speaking position, of the phallus, with a simultaneous presence of what at once demands and defies articulation. The edict of silence weighing for so long on female to female erotic experience has of course been infinitely heavier than that on male to male. In 'Crush' (from *Mean Time*) only the title identifies an emotion, and a compulsion, whose very poignancy consists in its avoidance of anything explicit:

> Imagine a girl
> turning to see
> love stand by a window, taller,
> clever, anointed with sudden light.

The object of desire becomes the embodiment of an abstract 'love', almost a sexless, or doubly sexed angel caught up in a sacrament of unction. As with Morgan, more direct and explicit items interspersed among these poems act as levers, helping us to hoist Duffy's texts into the light and try to see what lies beneath them. 'Before You Were Mine' (from *Mean Time*), which pictures the beloved as a 'bold girl winking in Portobello, somewhere/ in Scotland before I was born' is one of these. 'Warming Her Pearls' (from *Standing Female Nude*), with its reminiscence of Genet's *Les bonnes*, as the maid lies awake, knowing the pearls she has worn against her own skin 'are cooling even now/ in the room where my mistress sleeps', is another. 'Oppenheim's Cup and Saucer' (from *Standing Female Nude*) with its graphic evocation of a lesbian seduction and citing of the mirror trope, is another still.

For certain lesbian writers, treating the love of gay men has often represented a kind of last ditch stance before complete openness. With Duffy (1955–), the feeling of kinship is there in 'Café Royal' (from *Mean Time*), as a young gay man thinks himself back longingly into the years of Oscar Wilde. As has been said, vagueness in Duffy's poetry is much more than concealment or reticence. It is a potent enabler in its own right, as can be seen in her elegy for a friend succumbing (or succumbed) to AIDS, 'Dream of a Lost Friend' (from *The Other Country*). As with 'Sleeping', dreaming, and the awareness that one is dreaming, generate a productive chaos. Chronology is reversed, or turned backwards, or set leapfrogging over itself, and the resultant uncertainty gives an appropriately nightmarish quality to the poem. The encounter between the sick friend and the healthy takes place in a hospital which the speaker has never visited. Dreaming competes with conscious relegation, 'this is a dream' with 'that must have been a dream'. Probably the friend is dead, and the speaker dreams he is still alive. Within the dream, she insists his illness is only a dream. Like many of 'the healthy', she looks forward to a time when these stressful moments will become a matter for dreaming. The dream becomes a posthumous meeting where she is able to confess to having missed the funeral. At one point the virus itself comes alive and dreams its victims:

> Some of our best friends nurture a virus, an idle,
> charmed, purposeful enemy, and it dreams
> they are dead already.

However uncanny, even Gothic, the mechanics of the poem may be, it evokes more effectively than a more prosaic account could do the experience of watching a friend succumb to that illness – a sense of being trapped, relentless uncertainty, impotence and fatedness, denial, and a longing for it all to be over that cannot help resembling a betrayal.

A similarly suffused quality lends 'Where We Came In' (from *Standing Female Nude*) its unsettling air of conviction. The poem begins and ends in mid-sentence, with a clear reference in the title to older practice which allowed one to enter the cinema at any point during a film, and leave when that scene came round again. Two former lovers face each other across a restaurant table, each accompanied by a new partner. Though Duffy does not push the issue, it works much better if all four participants are women. The poem is neither detached nor satirical, but rather a brooding, deeply felt, ultimately sceptical meditation on serial monogamy and the lies, or at least hypocrisies, it entails:

> Our new loves sit beside us guardedly,
> outside the private jokes. I think
> of all the tediousness of loss but, yes,
> I'm happy now. Yes. Happy. Now.

That fourth line is meant not to convince. In defiance of the socially acceptable, even obligatory script, there can be no neat endings and beginnings. The most substantial intimacy is still between the two who have parted, and the seemingly infinite mirroring of gestures (considerably more powerful if no men are present) conveys hauntingly the difficulty, if not the impossibility, of ever truly letting go:

> I see our gestures endlessly repeated as
> you turn to yours the way you used
> to turn to me. I turn to mine. And

Persistent references to the ceremony of the Catholic Mass (passing the bread, the candles, the illusion of endless repetition which is also a gesture towards the infinite) confer a sacramental air upon the meal. We are encouraged to invest it with richer and more universal meanings.

Duffy does not, like Jamie, seek and to a certain extent establish a secure link with previous and present generations, nor does she, like Lochhead, intone a barely veiled diatribe against a new, alienating fluidity of roles and expectations. This fluidity allows Duffy to exist. She subsists within it and creates herself with its assistance. The speakers in her poems resonate with what they encounter at a level almost below speech, at times suffering notable levels of pain, but never protesting or lapsing into self-pity. 'Prayer', which closes *Mean Time*, can be read as closing a sequence of four poems about the break-up of a relationship and the consequent separation. Duffy's persistent awareness of form rarely leads her to coincide with or enter into the traditionally accepted, and yet it is peculiarly moving to notice how this poem falls with perfect naturalness, yet without conceding any of its uncomfortable modernity, into the mould of a sonnet. Remembered Catholicism impregnates the poem, in the repetitions of 'pray' and 'prayer', in the confession that faith is lost, in references to music as a potential other language and to the far off 'Latin chanting' of childhood, now impersonated by a train. Latin is an other language used for speaking to God, and at the poem's close four placenames from the shipping forecast, from a radio left switched on by one whose loneliness knows no other balm, become that language, articulating consolation and transcendence. It is no accident that the poem's final word signifies the ending of land, transition to another element, another plane. At the poem's start, the prayer had spoken itself, while here it is a machine which becomes the speaker's proxy, uttering the prayer she is unable to say. It is as if the other language will seize on whatever opaque words are to hand so as to render itself present and perceptible, if never fully comprehensible.

If a poem such as 'Standing Female Nude' shows a clear debt to feminist discourse, Duffy has no time for simplistic dogma. The free availability of abortion is undoubtedly a civic victory. Things, however, can never be straightforward for the women directly involved. The title 'Free Will' (from *Standing Female Nude*) raises a question not so much about choice as about the consequences of choice, that which choice can neither contain nor control. The poem is not indignant or angry, not loud in any way. It displays a sustained, unfussy compassion, honest and profoundly real. As elsewhere in Duffy's work, absolute endings, definite truncation, are the stuff of illusion:

> What she parted would not die despite
> the cut, remained inside her all her life.

The least surprising poem in Duffy's latest volume *Feminine Gospels* is a love poem celebrating 'the soft hours of our married years'. Only the foolish would interpret that last word but one as implying a male addressee. The poem turns on the paradoxes of saying and not saying, of writing while at the same time erasing, defying the edict of silence which is perhaps the ultimate enemy and nemesis of Duffy's poetry by both negotiating and incorporating it. Vows, prayers, laws, rules and news are in turn negated. Indeed, the relationship Duffy would appear to be celebrating is denied any legal or institutional substance, condemned by the politics of family and sex to an invisibility that never quite succeeds in making it disappear. The last negation is of poems, yet here we have a poem in a book of poems, paradoxically and defiantly present, before us in black and white despite the title's advertising of 'White Writing'.

Predominantly, though, the collection marks a resolute departure into the uncanny, the Gothic, the fantastic. It is as if Duffy has managed to ditch a whole assemblage of rules and expectations in order to sally forth, to set sail without yet reaching the new shore. An anorexic girl dwindles in size until she is gulped down by a fat woman and imprisoned in her stomach ('The Diet'). Another woman grows into a giant whose stature projects her beyond the larger planets and is nevertheless able to stoop and catch the souls of the falling victims of the September 11th terrorist attacks ('Tall'). At the heart of the poem is an epic and at the same time novelistic narration in forty-seven thirteen-line stanzas, using a long, flexible line hovering between pentameter and heptameter without ever settling for either. 'The Laughter of Stafford Girls' High' (not, incidentally, Duffy's own school) is everything except funny. Though it is about laughter, it prompts no laughter on its own account. The word disquieting comes to mind, though the poem is utopistic. Laughter is a corrosive and uncontrollable demon which ultimately dissolves the all-female institution, releasing certain of its inmates into lives that might otherwise never have been possible.

It is tempting to speak of a chilling in this latest collection, but that is not quite accurate. There had always been a coolness in Duffy's poetry, a detached contemplation which refused to be taken in or convinced. Reading through *Feminine Gospels* one experiences few of the more 'normal' human emotions, rather a mixture of alienation and wonderment, a constant urge to speculate over what is going to happen in a miraculous world where the rules we know are void. It would be wrong, too, to speak of Duffy as a formalist. Yet as she broadens her range and experiments with unprecedented subject matter, she is constantly attentive to the forms that are associated with that subject matter, enabling it in their turn. It is perfectly possible that, for the poet, these forms were what she set out in search of, and the subject matter a means of reaching out for them. The book certainly feels like an investigation. Whether the dissolution it achieves will eventually coalesce into new, more recognisable forms, and the tone which will accompany these, are questions only Duffy's continuing explorations can resolve.

It would be unfair to imply that Aonghas MacNeacail's verse, placed at the conclusion of this study, should somehow balance Sorley MacLean's, placed at the start, in spite of their sharing a language. To do so would be to place too great a strain on the younger poet's work. It lacks the dazzling breadth of reference that characterised MacLean's writing as the Second World War broke out, his capacity again and again to confront us with grim realities beyond poetry without ultimately devaluing the practice of that art. If MacLean, Campbell Hay and Thomson straddled different cultures, seeking to fuse and conciliate them in their poetry, this is true to a much lesser extent of MacNeacail (1942–). The older poets were profoundly eclectic in their approach. Nothing could have been further from their minds than to mime a Gaelic 'otherness' for the wider audience in Scotland and beyond, a risk discernible here and there in MacNeacail's work. They combine elements from the tradition of their chosen language with different elements culled elsewhere. What makes their work constantly fascinating is its effect of surprise, a constant putting into question and redefinition of what it can mean to write in Gaelic.

With four Gaelic and two English collections to his credit, MacNeacail is truly a bilingual poet.[5] He does not appear to privilege one strand in his production above the others. The relationship is not, of course, balanced, in that almost without exception he offers a facing English translation for his Gaelic work, but not the other way round. His poetry in Gaelic and English has, then, a doubleness which his poetry in English only lacks. The relation of translation to original is far from being a servile one. Whereas it might be an exaggeration to say he attributes an equal value to both, the English does serve to destabilise and energise the Gaelic, as notably in the title of a poem towards the end of *A Proper Schooling / Oideachadh Ceart* where 'seunaidhean', which would conventionally be glossed as 'charms' or 'enchantment', is rendered 'telepathies'. Readers who have both languages are being encouraged to redefine, to re-experience the Gaelic text in terms of its English double, as if the facing versions constituted an overarching whole, more complete than either of its components could ever hope to be. MacNeacail's Gaelic texts, then, have a subtly but profoundly different status from those of his predecessors. One could justifiably ask if this reveals a weakening of the Celtic language, a perceived need to help it along, to offer it completion. MacNeacail's poetic bilingualism is without doubt a peculiar and specific phenomenon demanding close investigation.

His first publication was a pamphlet in English, *Imaginary Wounds*, with a cover illustration by Alasdair Gray. MacNeacail and Gray, like Lochhead and Leonard, benefited from the nurturing influence of Philip Hobsbaum in informal writing workshops held in Glasgow in the 1960s. Though originally from Skye, and a Gaelic monoglot until he started school, MacNeacail's coming of age as a writer took place in a Lowland, urban context and in an overwhelmingly English-speaking environment, in one, moreover, with a clear link to universities.

His next two publications were sustained long poems in parallel versions, brought out in an artbook format with illustrations by Simon Fraser. Throughout *An Cathadh Mór* (*The Great Snowbattle*) the Gaelic and the English texts, in sections of varying length, dance unpredictably down and across the page, so that each double spread offers a new relationship between these, the empty spaces, and the accompanying illustrations. It had already been obvious, in *Imaginary Wounds*, that visual presentation plays an important role in MacNeacail's verse. He was to stick to the policies adopted here when repossessing Gaelic as a language for his poetry. Punctuation is absent, with even the first person pronoun appearing in small case, though apostrophes are admitted. Within a line, a space of greater than usual length between two words indicates a pause. These spaces, along with line breaks (not necessarily corresponding to a pause as, in the English, they can intervene between a pronoun and its verb, or between a verb and its pronoun object) are fundamental rhythmic elements in MacNeacail's verse, dictating its scansion.

The effect is a staccato one, rather like a phrase of music where each note is detached from the next. MacNeacail's discourse is broken up into segments, some longer, some shorter. One is reminded of Tom Leonard citing William Carlos Williams, for what happens is that bits of language, a word or a group of words, are held up for estranged contemplation. If conventional metre encourages us to hurry on, to build up a certain momentum, MacNeacail's encourages us constantly to stop. The same technique does not mean the same thing, however, when applied to two different languages. Almost all readers of this poetry will be more literate in English than in Gaelic. One could argue that Gaelic, in its printed form, especially when accompanied by an English double, is already objectified and defamiliarised. Given that most of MacNeacail's readers hear and use English (in one of its multiple forms) every day, to be asked to inspect isolated fragments of that language, like stones chipped out of a larger block, could have a powerful effect. Gaelic subsists under different conditions, tending already to have the status of an exception, one MacNeacail's practice exasperates rather than dissolving.

In this respect, his work certainly can be spoken of as straddling or constructing a bridge between two cultures. Much of his aesthetic was formed in that first blossoming period in Glasgow, in an environment where the influence of North American literature was powerfully felt.

This helps to explain distinctly New Age qualities in MacNeacail's work – a preference for natural imagery, a faith in 'natural', instinctive pulsions and processes, suspicion of the intellectual or cerebral, and an implicit and pervasive pleading for free emotional and sexual expression, opposed to forms of Puritanism ('ach dèan dannsa dèan dannsa/ 's e obair th' ann a bhith dannsa') ('but be dancing be dancing/ it is work to be dancing') (*An Seachnadh*, pp. 98–9). The role MacNeacail arrogates to himself at the start of *An Seachnadh* combines the bard and the holy fool with more than a hint of the hippy:

> a charaid, is mise
> an t-amadan naomh
> am bàrd
> amhairc is èisd rium
>
> *friend, i am*
> *the holy fool*
> *the bard*
> *observe and listen.*

Using 'natural' imagery can get round Gaelic's lack of contemporary vocabulary. The danger, however, is of strengthening 'ecological' projections onto Gaelic, as nearer to the earth and the elements, older, wiser, closer to our origins (and therefore more 'feminine', with shades of Renan and Malcolm Arnold) than English. A language fighting for its survival would do well to be wary of reification of this sort.

Where MacNeacail gets beyond a staccato and builds up a more sustained pace, this is generally achieved by means of parallelism. 'chùm mi seachad' ('i kept on past') from *Oideachadh Ceart* works like this. Repetitions of a single line produce an incantatory quality rather like the chanting of a slogan, whose rhythm can in fact distract one from the meaning of the words. The poem's vitalism is true to an insistent, unmotivated optimism underpinning MacNeacail's work. It reads as a heroic narrative, an excerpt from one of the heroic tales collected in the Hebrides, transcribed and published during the last two centuries. 'beul beag' ('little mouth'), surely one of the most enchanting poems ever dedicated by a father to an infant child, makes similar use of parallelism, the title's repetitions in the vocative case giving rhythmic energy and urgency to the poem's development. MacNeacail's poem about the bomb, 'uiseag uiseag' ('skylark skylark') comes close to rap in the persistency of its repetitions, rather like the warning taps of an approaching drum. After all, this is a poem against the military:

uiseag uiseag anns na speuran
seachain duslach dubh an dadaim
na àite fhéin chan eil droch ghnè ann
neo-bhuairte rèidh chan eil e riasladh
uiseag uiseag anns na speuran

skylark skylark soaring high
beware the atomic dust
in its place it is no menace
undisturbed it's no destroyer
skylark skylark soaring high.

In 'marilyn monroe' the one word 'òr' ('gold') is obsessively repeated. Marilyn is first and foremost the victim of those who exploited and manipulated her:

òr, o
bhàrr calgach do chlaiginn gu
buinn rùisgte do chas
òr, òr, òr,
beò no marbh

gold, from the maned top of your skull
to the bare soles of your feet
gold, gold, gold,
alive or dead.

The English translation of that line about the skylark is symptomatic of MacNeacail's attitude to these matters, cavalier and creative at one and the same time. Where the Gaelic simply has 'in the skies', the English 'soaring high' adds a different and potentially valuable element. Another instance comes at the end of section 1 of *An Cathadh Mór*. The Gaelic 'siosarnaich shocair aig lòineag air bradhadair' translates literally as 'gentle hissing of a snowflake on firewood', while the accompanying English reads 'somewhere sibilant crystals turn steam on the fireglow'. The English is richer and more evocative than the Gaelic, positioning the speaker with 'somewhere' and emphasising the coming together of contrasting elements with 'steam' and 'fireglow'. Nor are we aware of the fire's luminosity in the Gaelic. Rather than the English offering a version of the Gaelic which is the 'original', both realisations of the poem need to be taken into account if we are to experience its full effect.

'An Cathadh Mór' is reprinted in its entirety, but without the illustrations, in *An Seachnadh*. Divided into four sections and fourteen
subsections, with major line beginnings uniform on the left side of the
page, rather than dancing across it as they had done previously, this
somewhat different poem is nonetheless MacNeacail's most ambitious
and sustained achievement. The opening evocation of a landscape under
snow recalls the stupendous beginning of Joseph Brodsky's elegy on
John Donne,[6] with the addition here of a wanderer somewhere out
there, longing for home ('h-uile siubhlaiche deònachadh dachaigh').
The world is addressed as a woman, clothed in a whiteness which is
also her skin. A litany to snow follows, before the speaker evokes a
memory of sexual initiation with a girl whose parents were engaged in
religious worship only yards away:

> chuibhl gaothan ar deòin sinn
> tro shailm gheal an eòlais
> is dhùisg sinn
> 's cha do sheas an latha
>
> *the gusts of our desire spiralled us*
> *through white psalms of knowing*
> *we awoke*
> *but the day did not endure.*

The whiteness is a carver with a scalpel, then a woman spreading her
cloak over the world, before shepherds and fishermen are evoked with
their differing experiences of the blizzard. The first section culminates
in a birth of Venus, indicating the new paganism which animates
MacNeacail's treatment of nature. In the second section blizzard and
love affair are assimilated to one another, in an atmosphere of considerable ambiguity. The prevailing whiteness is at once protective and
chilling and includes sharp knives of ice among its manifestations:

> gur e mùirean cho teann ris an deigh ud a
> ghlas sinn a-staigh leis
> a' ghilead a thog sinn son gaol
> cha d'fhairich sinn aiteamh a' tighinn
>
> *it was walls encaging as ice*
> *locked us in with*
> *the whiteness that we took for love*
> *we didn't feel thaw come.*

In the third section, the predominantly negative associations of whiteness become explicit. There is a diatribe against the three-faced goddess, protector and divider, blanket and barrier, responsible for the destruction of love. MacNeacail plays sensitively with the phonetic similarity of 'cidhis' ('mask'), and 'cidheachan' ('snowdrift'). Nature may have an alluring, serene beauty, but it is also the scenario against which a 'snow-white owl' hunts 'jenny wren', where a 'cat's footprint' can be seen beside the blood of a thrush and one single feather. Thaw begins in the fourth section, a series of haikus where the ground peeps out from beneath melting drifts as promises once made get broken. The image of peeing on the snow revives ambiguity about the whiteness and its destruction.

Traces of a renewed paganism, a religiosity which sets no bounds between the human and the creatural, occur throughout *A Proper Schooling / Oideachadh Ceart*. 'bha 'n oidhch' ud nuair a dh'fhàg an cat' ('there was that night the cat left') follows the disappearance and return of a pet, unpredictable, mysterious, yet following its own idiosyncratic pattern. In 'do choin' ('your dogs') the lover envisages himself as his beloved's dog, in a variety of different disguises. The collection closes with 'salm an fhearainn' ('psalm of the land'), an ecological sermon, a ciphered history of the Gael taking no account of Christianity in its Catholic or its Protestant forms, and focusing instead on the injustice of landlords and the trauma of eviction and emigration. Unusually for MacNeacail, the poem is in regular metre, quatrains alternating lines of three and two stresses. A chanting quality can be discerned. But the flowing onward movement of this verse contrasts with the staccato energy that pervades elsewhere in MacNeacail's work. The end brings decided rejection of city life in favour of the countryside. We are warned that human beings must share the earth with other species. The closing prescription is Biblical in flavour, even though this is a religion of nature:

> tha 'n ainm ro dhìomhair dhan an treubh
> san duilleag is sa chlach
> 's i 'n àile fhéin tha tàirneanadh
> a neart do bhiast is lus

> tri ràithean dhut is ràith an tàimh
> ràith cur is fàs is buain
> bi cùramach mun talamh chrìon
> tha aighear anns an fhàs

the name too secret for the tribe
inhabits leaf and stone
the air itself in thunder gives
its strength to beast and herb

three active seasons one of rest
you sow you grow and reap
be careful of the fragile earth
for there is joy in growth.

More than a decade older than any of the other poets in this chapter, MacNeacail's position is both more multifaceted and more awkward than theirs, and not just in linguistic terms. The pastoralism of 'salm an fhearainn' may hark back to the time of the Scottish Renaissance Movement and, indeed, Jamie's treatment of city life is hardly sympathetic. Yet it would be mistaken to see this as a throwback. Rather it is a case of issues representing themselves after a space of time and demanding renewed responses in a changed context. When compared to their predecessors of the interwar years, each of the poets dealt with in this chapter has been forced to find strategies for coping with the relentless and unpitying glare of publicity. MacNeacail's engagement with 'ecological' perceptions of the Gaelic language is another instance of this, of the extent to which image threatens to become essence. The contemporary poet has to renegotiate the relationship of private to public space, of that which is on the surface to that which is not. And these four are still young enough for any certainty as to their final answer to be impossible.

Notes

1. Unless otherwise indicated, poems are quoted from *A Scottish Assembly* (London, Chatto and Windus 1990), since which Crawford has published *Talkies* (London, Chatto and Windus 1992), *Masculinities* (London, Jonathan Cape 1996), *Spirit Machines* (London, Jonathan Cape 1999) and *The Tip of My Tongue* (London, Jonathan Cape 2003). He is also the author of *Devolving English Literature* (Oxford, Oxford University Press 1992) and *Identifying Poets: Self and Territory in Twentieth-Century Poetry* (Edinburgh, Edinburgh University Press 1993). See further David Kennedy *New Relations: the Refashioning of British Poetry 1980–1994* (Bridgend, Seren 1996) pp. 176–9 and Sean O'Brien 'Don Paterson, Robert Crawford, Kathleen Jamie, W. N. Herbert: Scotland! Scotland! Actual/Virtual' in his *The Deregulated Muse* (Newcastle upon Tyne, Bloodaxe Books 1998) pp. 261–9.

2. Poems are quoted from *Jizzen* (London, Picador 1999) or from *Mrs and Mrs Scotland are Dead: Poems 1980–1994* selected by Lilias Fraser (Tarset,

Northumberland, Bloodaxe 2002). The latter draws on *Black Spiders* (Edinburgh, Salamander Press 1982), *A Flame in Your Heart* (1986, joint with Andrew Greig), *The Way We Live* (1987), *The Autonomous Region* (1993) and *The Queen of Sheba* (1994) (all Newcastle upon Tyne, Bloodaxe Books). See also Caroline Blyth 'Autonomies and Regions: an Interview with Kathleen Jamie' in *Oxford Poetry* VII (Summer 1993) pp. 57–63, Helen Boden 'Kathleen Jamie's Semiotic of Scotlands' in Aileen Christianson and Alison Lumsden eds *Contemporary Scottish Women Writers* (Edinburgh, Edinburgh University Press 2000) pp. 27–40, Raymond Friel 'Women Beware Gravity' in *Southfields: Criticism and Celebration* 1 pp. 29–47, 'Kathleen Jamie interviewed by Lilias Fraser' in *Scottish Studies Review* 2 (1) (Spring 2001) pp. 15–32, Kaye Kossick 'Roaring Girls, Bogie Wives, and the Queen of Sheba: Dissidence, Desire and Dreamwork in the Poetry of Kathleen Jamie' in *Studies in Scottish Literature* XXXII (2001) pp. 195–212, Dorothy McMillan 'Here and There: the Poetry of Kathleen Jamie' in *Études Écossaises* 4 (1997) pp. 123–34 and 'Twentieth-Century Poetry II: the Last Twenty-Five Years' in Douglas Gifford and Dorothy McMillan eds *A History of Scottish Women's Writing* (Edinburgh, Edinburgh University Press 1997), pp. 549–78, Andrew Monnickendam 'Changing Places with What Goes Before: the Poetry of Kathleen Jamie' in *Revista Canaria de Estudios Ingleses* 41 (November 2000) pp. 77–86 and Joanne Winning 'Curious Rarities? The work of Kathleen Jamie and Jackie Kay' in Alison Mark and Deryn Rees-Jones eds *Contemporary Women's Poetry* (Basingstoke and New York 2000) pp. 226–46.

3. Aonghas MacNeacail *A Proper Schooling and Other Poems / Oideachadh Ceart agus dàin eile* (Edinburgh, Polygon 1996) pp. 12–17.

4. Poems are quoted here from *Standing Female Nude* (1985), *Selling Manhattan* (1987), *The Other Country* (1990), *Mean Time* (1993) (all London, Anvil Press) and *Feminine Gospels* (London, Picador 2002). See further Vicci Bentley 'Interview with Carol Ann Duffy' in *Magma* 3 (Winter 1994) pp. 17–24, Simon Brittan 'Language and Structure in the Poetry of Carol Ann Duffy' in *Thumbscrew* 1 (Winter 1994–5) pp. 58–64, 'Carol Ann Duffy Interviewed by Jane Stabler' in *Verse* 8 (2) (Summer 1991) pp. 124–8, David Kennedy *New Relations: the Refashioning of British Poetry 1980–1994* (Bridgend, Seren 1996) pp. 227–30, Linda Kinnahan '"Look for the Doing Words": Carol Ann Duffy and Questions of Convention' in James Acheson and Romana Huk eds *Contemporary British Poetry: Essays in Theory and Criticism* (New York, State University of New York Press, 1996), '"Now I am Alien": Immigration and the Discourse of Nation in the Poetry of Carol Ann Duffy' in Alison Mark and Deryn Rees-Jones eds *Contemporary Women's Poetry* (Basingstoke and New York 2000) pp. 208–25, Andrew McAllister 'Interview with Carol Ann Duffy' in *Bête Noire* 6 (Winter 1988) pp. 69–77, Dorothy McMillan 'Twentieth-Century Poetry II: the Last Twenty-Five Years' in Douglas Gifford and Dorothy McMillan eds *A History of Scottish Women's Writing* (Edinburgh, Edinburgh University Press 1997), pp. 550–4, Susannah Radstone 'Remember Medea: the Uses of Nostalgia' in *Critical Quarterly* 35 (3) (Autumn 1993) pp. 54–63, Deryn Rees Jones *Carol Ann Duffy* (Plymouth, Northcote House 2002, 2nd edn), Anthony Rowland 'Love and Masculinity in the Poetry of Carol Ann Duffy' *English* 50 (198) (Autumn 2001) pp. 199–218 and Jane E. Thomas '"The Intolerable Wrestle with Words": the Poetry of Carol Ann Duffy' *Bête Noire* 6 (Winter 1988) pp. 78–88.

5. *Imaginary Wounds* (Glasgow, Print Studio Press 1980) is included in *Rock and*

Water (Edinburgh, Polygon 1990) while *An Cathadh Mór / The Great Snowbattle* (originally Nairn, Balnain Books 1984, with illustrations by Simon Fraser) is included in *an seachnadh agus dàin eile / The Avoiding and Other Poems* (Edinburgh, Macdonald 1986). Further collections are *Sireadh Bradan Sicir / Seeking Wise Salmon* (Nairn, Balnain Books 1983, again with illustrations by Simon Fraser) and *A Proper Schooling and Other Poems / Oideachadh Ceart agus dàin eile* (Edinburgh, Polygon 1996). See also 'Poetry in Translation' in Murdo Macdonald ed. *Nothing is Altogether Trivial: an Anthology of Writing from the Edinburgh Review* (Edinburgh, Edinburgh University Press 1995) pp. 65–79, 'Being Gaelic, and Otherwise' in *Chapman* 89–90 (1998) pp. 151–7, 'Il ritorno dell'esule' [interview with Carla Sassi] in *Diverse Lingue* 12 (1993) pp. 87–96 and Máire ni Annracháin 'The Force of Tradition in the Poetry of Aonghas MacNeacail' in Colm Ó Baoill and Nancy R. McGuire eds *Rannsachadh na Gàidhlig 2000* (Aberdeen, An Clò Gaidhealach 2002) pp. 117–26.

6. See Joseph Brodsky *Elegy to John Donne and Other Poems* selected, translated and with an introduction by Nicholas Bethell (London, Longman 1967) p. 63ff.

Conclusion

Were the approach taken in this book more conventional, indeed predictable, then it would be possible to predict the appropriate words of conclusion. The state of the nation, and the state of its poetry at the beginning of the new century would be assessed, not without a touch of deserved celebration. Predictions for the years to come would follow. The poets from the 1940s, still to a certain extent pertaining to the heroic period in which an independent Scottish literature was relaunched, would be set against those from the 1990s, to find out how each had managed to fulfil the allotted role, to offer that which the nation has a right to expect. It would be crucial to decide how far poets had succeeded in bodying forth a pre-existing narrative, reconstituting and projecting into the future a Scottishness whose essence would never be questioned.

Instead this book has aimed to open up both poems and the discourse about them. It assumes that criticism of Scottish literature, in particular of modern Scottish literature, can now abandon militancy for something more complex and more tolerant, at once more honest and more uncertain. The 'question about Scottishness' will never really be negotiable. Along with other extraneous agendas, it needs setting aside, so that we can concentrate on the agenda that matters most and provokes most anxiety, the literary one. Scottish writing no longer demands or requires special pleading. The time for excuses is long past, even for the excuse that a country where Calvinism once played a significant role may not be ready to make space for purely aesthetic considerations, to give due reverence and consideration to the beautiful.

A writer exiled to New York, a fugitive from the communist dictatorships which were the bitter legacy of Russian pseudo-liberation to such great areas of the continent, comments wrily in his diaries on a visit his adoptive son made to the barber. Jani resented being dealt with by a bald man because such a barber could only feel hostility and envy towards his clients. My feelings were much the same, the writer concludes, when reading critics of my work.[1]

What is the critic left with at the end of a book like this one? Scattered hair cuttings to be swept up from the floor? In the last analysis all critical readings need to be situated within a circular process, one which starts with the text and returns to the text. The purpose of criticism is to enrich the experience of reading, to send us continually back to the text and underline its inexhaustibility, the impossibility of giving a complete account of it. It is the very opposite of squeezing oranges, where the peel and pulp can be discarded because the juice has been successfully extracted and can now be drunk. If the critic has done his or her work well, then the oranges will still be there when his task is over, intact and more inviting than ever.

Barcelona / Edinburgh / Budapest
November 2000–October 2003

Note

1. Sándor Márai *Geist im Exil: Tagebücher 1945–1957* trans. Tibor and Monika Podmaniczky (Hamburg, Broschek 1959) p. 349.

Translation of Epigraphs

p. i   Sándor Márai: 'I could do with a cup of hot coffee as strong as poison in this cold weather. But all they have on offer here is *café national*. What *national* really means is that one gets a substitute. Wherever one goes these days, the description "national" means something is not all right, is no longer what it ought to be.' *translation CW*

p. 5   Marcel Proust: 'No right-minded person would dispute that, by de-nationalizing a work, one deprives it of its universal value . . . But isn't it a truth of the same order to say that one takes away a work's universal and even its national value by seeking to nationalize it?' *translation Kilmartin*

         Hofmannsthal: 'everyone thinks he knows the last word about the nation, as he thinks he knows the last word about himself. But were one to ask him what it is, his answer would be the same as Augustine's when asked about the essence of time: "If nobody asks me, I know what it is; but if they ask me, then I don't know."' *translation CW from his* Buch der Freunde

p. 18   Montale: 'All we can tell you today/ is what we are *not*, what we do *not* want' *translation CW from the first poem in his 'Ossi di sepia' sequence*

p. 34   Hofmannsthal: 'National mystique is a mirroring of the self turned into a totem.' *translation CW from his* Buch der Freunde

Index